TI-Nspire™ Strategies

Algebra

Author

Pamela H. Dase, M.A.Ed.
Recipient of PAESMEM
and
Certified National T³ Instructor

SHELL EDUCATION

Credits

Editor
Sara Johnson

Associate Editor
Torrey Maloof

Editorial Assistant
Kathryn Kiley

Editorial Consultant
Sharon Ice

Editorial Director
Emily Smith, M.A.Ed.

Editor-in-Chief
Sharon Coan, M.S.Ed.

Editorial Manager
Gisela Lee, M.A.

Creative Director/Cover Design
Lee Aucoin

Print Production Manager
Don Tran

Interior Layout Designer
Robin Erickson

Print Production
Juan Chavolla
Phil Garcia

Publisher
Corinne Burton, M.A.Ed.

Mathematics Consultants

Rebecca B. Caison
Ruth Casey
Certified National T3 Instructor

Aimee Evans, M.A.
Barbara Post, M.A.
Carlene L. Wymer, M.A.

Shell Education

5301 Oceanus Drive
Huntington Beach, CA 92649-1030
http://www.shelleducation.com
ISBN 978-1-4258-0308-7

© *2009 Shell Education*

Table of Contents

Table of Contents *(cont.)*

Table of Contents (cont.)

Introduction

Research Base

Teachers of mathematics have the dual challenge of managing the varying dynamics of their diverse classrooms as well as increasing student achievement across a wide range of mathematical concepts and skills. In the various mathematical subject areas, the TI-Nspire can be an important tool that teachers introduce to their students in order to meet these challenges. With proper use, handhelds can meet the needs of all students by promoting higher levels of thinking, increasing student performance in mathematics, and allowing access to mathematical exploration, experimentation, and enhancement of mathematical concepts (Waits and Pomerantz 1997). Graphing calculators were first introduced in 1986 by Casio and started a dynamic change in the way that mathematics was taught and learned (Waits and Demana 1998). As these tools improved and as researchers studied their effectiveness in mathematical instruction, well-known mathematical organizations, such as the National Council of Teachers of Mathematics (NCTM), have recommended that appropriate types of calculators be used in mathematics instruction from kindergarten through college (NCTM 2000).

The TI-Nspire is the next step in handheld technology. It dynamically links spreadsheets, graphing environments, geometry settings, and symbolic expressions, allowing students to take meaningful actions on mathematical objects and immediately see the consequences of those actions (Burrill 2008). Students can study the relationships between the graph of a function, the equation of the function, and a table of values interactively on the same screen. They can also manipulate circles, triangles, and quadrilaterals, automatically transfer measurements to a coordinate grid and a spreadsheet, and then investigate the geometric properties algebraically. The handheld includes many features that allow students to learn and use accurate mathematical expressions. TI-Nspire technology allows more effective linking of key mathematical expressions, allowing students to grasp mathematical concepts more readily with deeper understanding (SRI International 2006).

However, this tool will not achieve the lofty goals that educators have for student success all by itself. It is not enough to simply provide students with technology. Teachers need access to research-based effective strategies that they can employ for comprehensive mathematics instruction using the technology (NCTM 2003).

TI-Nspire Strategies: Algebra offers the necessary foundation for teachers to translate the use of the TI-Nspire into actual student comprehension of mathematical concepts, as well as the ability to perform mathematical skills. With the lessons provided in this book, teachers are given valuable techniques for integrating the TI-Nspire into their instruction. *TI-Nspire Strategies: Algebra* directs teacher instruction in maximizing student use of the handhelds while processing and learning geometrical concepts.

The lessons in this book are designed to give new and veteran teachers the best strategies to employ. How well students understand mathematics, their abilities to use it to work out problems, and their confidence and positive attitudes toward mathematics are all shaped by the quality of the teaching they encounter in school (NCTM 2005). Teachers no longer

Research Base (cont.)

have to construct well-planned handheld lessons unaided. Besides lesson descriptions and materials lists, this book offers step-by-step instructions for four key instructional phases: Starting the Lesson, Explaining the Concept, Applying the Concept, and Extending the Concept. Each element has an easily-identified title heading.

TI-Nspire Strategies: Algebra lessons move students from the concrete understanding of mathematical concepts through the abstract comprehension level, to real-life application, while at the same time allowing students to develop skill in the use of the handheld. For teaching to be effective in a mathematics classroom, it is necessary to provide focused instruction that moves the student from the concrete, to the abstract, to the application of the concept (Marzano 2003). The TI-Nspire technology can build on conceptual understanding by allowing students to dynamically interact with numerous representations of concepts and experiences in a way that is not possible with paper and pencil alone. As a result of this technology, teachers are able to engage students more effectively by addressing different learning styles and developing understanding that leads to higher-level thinking.

In the Starting the Lesson section, students are reminded of important button-pushing sequences on the handheld that they will use throughout the lessons. In the Explaining the Concept activities, students move toward abstract understanding. The lessons offer guidance in directing the students to practice using handhelds and improving their skill levels. The Applying the Concept and Extending the Concept sections bring the students to real-life applications and further practice. As students move through each phase of learning, they are exposed to a concept or skill numerous times.

Per research, students should have multiple experiences with topics, allowing them to integrate the topics into their knowledge base (Marzano 2003). Overall, the challenging and interesting tasks found in application problems help teachers engage students in learning as they actively apply their knowledge (Seely 2004). As a result, students take ownership of new strategies and gain greater understanding of the ideas and concepts. Through the lesson extension ideas and the activity sheets, the students gain ample opportunities to practice. This is important because students need to have extra time to process concepts and look at problems in different ways (Sutton and Krueger 2002).

Many teachers dread handheld use because of the classroom management issue; however, with proper use, handhelds allow teachers to spend more time developing mathematical understanding, reasoning, number sense, and application (Waits and Pomerantz 1997). Therefore, these lessons help teachers respond to that concern by including an introduction with easy-to-follow tips for differentiating the lessons, grouping students, managing the handhelds in the classroom, planning the integration of these lessons with standards-based curriculum, and using the handhelds in activity centers. The skills reinforced throughout *TI-Nspire Strategies: Algebra* teach multiple representations of mathematical concepts so that students thrive in the mathematics classroom.

Correlation to Standards

The No Child Left Behind (NCLB) legislation mandates that all states adopt academic standards that identify the skills students will learn in kindergarten through grade 12. While many states had already adopted academic standards prior to NCLB, the legislation set requirements to ensure that the standards were detailed and comprehensive.

Standards are designed to focus instruction and guide adoption of curricula. Standards are statements that describe the criteria necessary for students to meet specific academic goals. They define the knowledge, skills, and content students should acquire at each level. Standards are also used to develop standardized tests to evaluate students' academic progress.

In many states today, teachers are required to demonstrate how their lessons meet state standards. State standards are used in the development of Shell Education products, so educators can be assured that they meet the academic requirements of each state.

How to Find Your State Correlations

Shell Education is committed to producing educational materials that are research and standards based. In this effort, all products are correlated to the academic standards of all 50 states, the District of Columbia, and the Department of Defense Dependent Schools. A correlation report customized for your state can be printed directly from the following website: **http://www.shelleducation.com**. If you require assistance in printing correlation reports, please contact Customer Service at 1-800-877-3450.

McREL Compendium

Shell Education uses the Mid-continent Research for Education and Learning (McREL) Compendium to create standards correlations. Each year, McREL analyzes state standards and revises the compendium. By following this procedure, they are able to produce a general compilation of national standards.

Each handheld strategy used in this book is based on one or more of the McREL content standards. The chart on the following pages shows the McREL standards that correlate to each lesson used in the book. To see a state-specific correlation, visit the Shell Education website at **http://www.shelleducation.com**.

Correlation to Standards *(cont.)*

NCTM Standard—Grades 6–8	Lesson Title and Page Number
Students will understand and use ratios and proportions to represent quantitative relationships.	Direct Variation (p. 41)
Students will understand and use the inverse relationships of addition and subtraction, multiplication and division, and squaring and finding square roots to simplify computations and solve problems.	Coefficients and Exponents (p. 101)
Students will develop, analyze, and explain methods for solving problems involving proportions, such as scaling and finding equivalent ratios.	Direct Variation (p. 41)
Students will represent, analyze, and generalize a variety of patterns with tables, graphs, words, and, when possible, symbolic rules.	Exploring Equations of Lines (p. 55); Forms of Equations of Lines (p. 71)
Students will relate and compare different forms of representation for a relationship.	Forms of Equations of Lines (p. 71)
Students will identify functions as linear or nonlinear and contrast their properties from tables, graphs, or equations.	Exploring Equations of Lines (p. 55); Forms of Equations of Lines (p. 71)
Students will develop an initial conceptual understanding of different uses of variables.	Direct Variation (p. 41); Exploring Equations of Lines (p. 55); Forms of Equations of Lines (p. 71)
Students will explore relationships between symbolic expressions and graphs of lines, paying particular attention to the meaning of intercept and slope.	Direct Variation (p. 41); Exploring Equations of Lines (p. 55); Forms of Equations of Lines (p. 71)
Students will use symbolic algebra to represent situations and to solve problems, especially those that involve linear relationships.	Direct Variation (p. 41); Exploring Equations of Lines (p. 55); Forms of Equations of Lines (p. 71)
Students will model and solve contextualized problems using various representations, such as graphs, tables, and equations.	Direct Variation (p. 41); Exploring Equations of Lines (p. 55); Forms of Equations of Lines (p. 71)

Correlation to Standards (cont.)

NCTM Standard—Grades 6–8	Lesson Title and Page Number
Students will use graphs to analyze the nature of changes in quantities in linear relationships.	Direct Variation (p. 41); Exploring Equations of Lines (p. 55); Forms of Equations of Lines (p. 71)
Students will create and critique inductive and deductive arguments concerning geometric ideas and relationships, such as congruence, similarity, and the Pythagorean relationship.	Pythagorean Theorem (p. 112)
Students will use two-dimensional representations of three-dimensional objects to visualize and solve problems such as those involving surface area and volume.	Coefficients and Exponents (p. 101)
Students will use geometric models to represent and explain numerical and algebraic relationships.	Coefficients and Exponents (p. 101)
Students will solve problems involving scale factors, using ratio and proportion.	Direct Variation (p. 41)
Students will solve simple problems involving rates and derived measurements for such attributes as velocity and density.	Direct Variation (p. 41)
Students will select, create, and use appropriate graphical representations of data, including histograms, box plots, and scatterplots.	One-Variable Statistics (p. 32)
Students will find, use, and interpret measures of center and spread, including mean and interquartile range.	One-Variable Statistics (p. 32)
Students will discuss and understand the correspondence between data sets and their graphical representations, especially histograms, stem-and-leaf plots, box plots, and scatterplots.	One-Variable Statistics (p. 32)
Students will use observations about differences between two or more samples to make conjectures about the populations from which the samples were taken.	One-Variable Statistics (p. 32)

Correlation to Standards (cont.)

NCTM Standard—Grades 9–12	Lesson Title and Page Number
Students will compare and contrast the properties of numbers and number systems, including the rational and real numbers, and understand complex numbers as solutions to quadratic equations that do not have real solutions.	Completing the Square/Quadratic Formula (p. 182)
Students will understand vectors and matrices as systems that have some of the properties of the real-number system.	Systems of Linear Equations (p. 86)
Students will judge the effects of such operations as multiplication, division, and computing powers and roots on the magnitudes of quantities.	Coefficients and Exponents (p. 101)
Students will develop an understanding of properties of, and representations for, the addition and multiplication of vectors and matrices.	Systems of Linear Equations (p. 86)
Students will generalize patterns using explicitly defined and recursively defined functions.	Direct Variation (p. 41); Exploring Equations of Lines (p. 55)
Students will understand relations and functions and select, convert flexibly among, and use various representations for them.	Forms of Equations of Lines (p. 71)
Students will analyze functions of one variable by investigating rates of change, intercepts, zeros, asymptotes, and local and global behavior.	Factors, Zeros, and Roots (p. 172)
Students will understand and perform transformations such as arithmetically combining, composing, and inverting commonly used functions, using technology to perform such operations on more-complicated symbolic expressions.	Systems of Linear Equations (p. 86); Factors, Zeros, and Roots (p. 172)
Students will understand and compare the properties of classes of functions, including exponential, polynomial, rational, logarithmic, and periodic functions.	Coefficients and Exponents (p. 101); Exponential Growth (p. 193)

Correlation to Standards (cont.)

NCTM Standard—Grades 9–12	Lesson Title and Page Number
Students will understand the meaning of equivalent forms of expressions, equations, inequalities, and relations.	Forms of Equations of Lines (p. 71); Generating Parabolas (p. 122)
Students will write equivalent forms of equations, inequalities, and systems of equations and solve them with fluency—mentally or with paper and pencil in simple cases and using technology in all cases.	Forms of Equations of Lines (p. 71); Generating Parabolas (p. 122); One-Variable Inequalities (p. 135); Two-Variable Linear Inequalities (p. 147)
Students will use symbolic algebra to represent and explain mathematical relationships.	Forms of Equations of Lines (p. 71); Generating Parabolas (p. 122); One-Variable Inequalities (p. 135); Two-Variable Linear Inequalities (p. 147); Exponential Growth (p. 193); Exponential Decay (p. 206)
Students will approximate and interpret rates of change from graphical and numerical data.	Direct Variation (p. 41); Exploring Equations of Lines (p. 55); Forms of Equations of Lines (p. 71); Absolute Value (p. 160);
Students will understand and represent translations, reflections, rotations, and dilations of objects in the plane by using sketches, coordinates, vectors, function notation, and matrices.	Pythagorean Theorem (p. 112); Completing the Square/Quadratic Formula (p. 182); Exponential Decay (p. 206)
Students will understand and use formulas for the area, surface area, and volume of geometric figures, including cones, spheres, and cylinders.	Coefficients and Exponents (p. 101) Generating Parabolas (p. 122)
Students will understand histograms, parallel box plots, and scatterplots, and use them to display data.	One-Variable Statistics (p. 32)
Students will, for univariate measurement data, be able to display the distribution, describe its shape, and select and calculate summary statistics.	One-Variable Statistics (p. 32)

How to Use This Book

TI-Nspire Strategies: Algebra was created to provide teachers with strategies for integrating TI-Nspire technology into their instruction for common algebraic concepts. The lessons are designed to move students from the concrete, through the abstract, to real-life application, while developing students' TI-Nspire skills and promoting their understanding of mathematical concepts.

The table below outlines the major components and purposes for each lesson.

Lesson Components	
Mathematics Objectives • Includes the mathematical concepts students will learn **Applications and Skills** • TI-Nspire applications, skills, and menus used **Materials** • Lists the activity sheets included with each lesson • Lists the TI-Nspire (TNS) file needed for each lesson • Lists any additional resources needed for each lesson **Starting the Lesson** • Instructions for beginning the activity	
Explaining the Concept • Instructions for explaining the concepts of the lesson **Applying the Concept** • Instructions for applying the concepts in the lesson **Differentiation** • Additional ideas for differentiation strategies within the application problem **Extending the Concept** • Additional ideas for practicing concepts and skills • Can be used to review, extend, and challenge student thinking	
Activity Sheets • Student reproducibles outlining each step in using the handheld • Provides places for student response to the problem	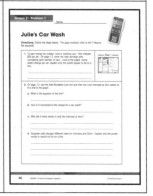

How to Use This Book (cont.)

Teacher Resource CD

The CD provided with this book has copies of all the student activity sheets. The CD also contains TNS lesson and solution files, as well as teacher resource materials. In addition, the TI-Nspire font has been included along with detailed directions on how to properly install the font on your computer. (See pages 263–264 for detailed information on the CD.)

Integrating This Resource into Your Mathematics Curriculum

When planning instruction with this resource, it is important to look ahead at your instructional time line and daily lesson plans to see where *TI-Nspire Strategies: Algebra* can best be integrated into your curriculum. As with most lessons, the majority of the planning takes place before the students arrive.

The title of each lesson describes the concept taught with the handheld strategies. Preview the lesson titles to find a lesson that correlates with the objective listed in your time line. The *Instructional Time Line* template (page 15) is provided to help integrate this resource into long-range planning.

Implementing the Lessons

After integrating this resource into your instructional time line, use the steps below to help you implement the lessons. The *Instructional Plan* template (page 16) is provided to help determine the resources and lessons to be used for the instructional phases: Explaining the Concept, Applying the Concept, Differentiation, and Extending the Concept.

1. Familiarize yourself with the lesson plan. Make sure you have all the materials needed for the lesson.

2. Determine how you want to pace the selected lesson. Each of the lesson parts or instructional phases are mini-lessons that can be taught independently or together, depending on the amount of instructional time and the students' needs.

   - For example, you may choose to use the Explaining the Concept section in place of the lesson taught in the textbook, or use the Applying the Concept and Extending the Concept sections to supplement the textbook.

   - The lesson parts can be taught each day for two or three days, or the lesson can be modified and all three parts can be taught in the course of a 50- to 90-minute instructional block.

3. Solve the problems before class to become familiar with the features on the TI-Nspire as well as with the mathematical concepts presented.

4. Because space is limited in lesson plan books, use a three-ring binder or a folder to keep detailed plans and activities for a specific concept together.

How to Use This Book (cont.)

Directions: In the first column, record the date or the days. In the second column, record the standards and/or objectives to be taught that day. In the third and fourth columns, write the lesson resources to be used to teach that standard and the specific page numbers. In the fifth column, include any adaptations or notes regarding the lesson resources.

Instructional Time Line				
Date	Standards/ Objectives	Lesson Resources (e.g., *TI-Nspire Strategies*, textbook)	Pages	Adaptations or Notes

How to Use This Book (cont.)

Directions: Write the date(s) of the lesson in the first column. Write the standards and/or objectives to be taught in the second column. In the remaining columns, write the lesson resources and page numbers to be used for each phase of instruction, as well as any notes and plans for modifying the lessons or differentiating instruction.

Instructional Plan

Lesson Resources Per Instructional Phase

Date	Standards/ Objectives	Explaining the Concept	Applying the Concept	Extending the Concept	Assessments	Adaptations/ Differentiation
		pgs.	pgs.	pgs.	pgs.	
		pgs.	pgs.	pgs.	pgs.	
		pgs.	pgs.	pgs.	pgs.	
		pgs.	pgs.	pgs.	pgs.	
		pgs.	pgs.	pgs.	pgs.	

How to Use This Book *(cont.)*

Differentiating Instruction

Students in today's classrooms have a diverse range of ability levels and needs. A teacher is expected to plan and implement instruction to accommodate English language learners (ELL), gifted students, on-level, below-level, and above-level students. The lessons in this resource can be differentiated by their content (what is taught), process (how it is taught), and product (what is created). Below are some strategies that can be used to adapt the lessons in this resource to meet most students' needs. This is not an all-inclusive list, and many of the strategies are interchangeable. It is important to implement strategies based on students' learning styles, readiness, and interests.

ELL/Below Level	On Level	Above Level/Gifted
• Reduce the number of problems in a set. • Write hints or strategies by specific problems. • Simplify the text on activity sheets. • Create *PowerPoint*™ presentations of lessons and have students use them as a review or reference. • Have students take notes. • Use visual aids and actions to represent concepts and steps of a process. • Act out problems. • Model skills and problems in a step-by-step manner. • Use manipulatives to explain concepts, and allow students to use them to complete assignments. • Have students work in homogeneous or heterogeneous groups. • Have students draw pictures of how they solved the problems.	• Have students take notes. • Use activities centered on students' interests. • Have students generate data. Engage students using *PowerPoint*™, games, and applets. • Have students work in homogeneous or heterogeneous groups. • Have students write explanations for how they solved the problems. • Use the Extending the Concept section to review concepts or skills.	• Have students create how-to guides for functions on the handheld. • Have students use multimedia, such as TI-Nspire computer software or *PowerPoint*™ to present how they solved the problems and/or used the handheld. • Have students work in homogeneous groups. • In addition to or in place of an activity sheet, assign the Extending the Concept sections. • Have students take on the role of teacher or mentor. • Have students create games for practicing concepts and skills.

How to Use This Book *(cont.)*

Grouping Students

Recommendations for cooperative groups and independent work are given throughout the lessons in this resource. The table below lists the different types of groups, a description of each, and management tips for working with each.

Group Type	Description of Group	Management Tips
Heterogeneous Cooperative Groups	Three to six students with varied ability levels	Give each student a role that suits his or her strengths. Give each group a sheet with directions for the task and a description of each role in completing that task.
Homogeneous Cooperative Groups	Three to six students with similar ability levels	Give each student an equal role in the task by having each student take the lead in a different part or problem of each assignment.
Paired Learning	Two students with similar abilities or mixed abilities	When completing assignments, have students sit side by side and give students opportunities to manipulate the materials.
Independent Work	Students work individually	Closely monitor students' work to correct any misconceptions; this will help students retain the information and develop confidence in their abilities. This is also a good time to work one-on-one with struggling students or gifted students.

Overview of TI-Nspire

The TI-Nspire consists of a set of mathematical tools for algebra, geometry, number sense, statistics, and data collection. These tools can be used interactively with each other in the TI-Nspire document.

The TI-Nspire document allows the teacher to offer students many different kinds of learning experiences. Teachers can link prepared documents to students. These documents may contain text in addition to graphs, geometry, lists, spreadsheets, calculations, statistics, and data. The text can include directions, information, and instructions, or provide question/answer formats. Students can also prepare their own documents. The rest of this section provides hints that should help a beginner use the TI-Nspire with the lessons.

Each document is composed of one or more problems, and each problem is composed of pages. A problem may include pages containing any or all of the applications. In each problem, the pages can share data and work interactively. Changes in the data on a page are reflected on other pages in that problem. The problems in each document are independent of one another.

The home screen of the handheld is accessed by pressing the (Home) key. The first five icons provide access to the five applications available on the handheld. Choosing any of these will insert a new page with that application into the document that is currently open. If you do not wish to include the new page in the current document, choose **New Document**. At the prompt, either choose **Yes** to save your work, or use the NavPad to move to **No** and press (Enter). Choose the desired application at the prompt.

Each application features menus that are accessible by pressing (Menu). The Calculator, Graphs & Geometry, and Lists & Spreadsheet menus each contain Actions. Although the Actions submenus are different for each of the applications, they allow the user to access features specific to that application.

In the Calculator Application, the items in the Actions menu control the use of variables. In the Graphs & Geometry Application, they allow the user to perform operations on the graph screen using the pointer, adding text, locating points and equations, and collecting data. In List & Spreadsheet, the Actions menu controls the behavior of the spreadsheet. Each of the other menus is specific to the application. The ✒ (Tools) menu, accessed by pressing (ctrl)(⌂), contains commands similar to familiar computer menus.

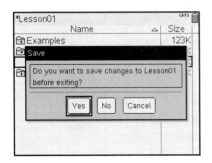 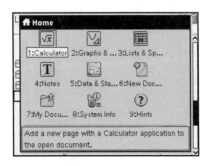 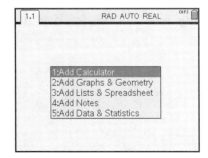

Overview of TI-Nspire (cont.)

Texas Instruments periodically releases updates of the handheld operating system. Routinely check the website **http://www.education.ti.com** to download these updates and instructions for updating the TI-Nspire handheld using TI-Nspire Computer Link. You may also sign up to receive email from Texas Instruments when updates are available.

Using the TI-Nspire Computer Software

The TI-Nspire Teacher Pack includes TI-Nspire computer software. The software is not an emulator, but is stand-alone software that includes the functionality of the handheld. Most of the handheld operations have analogous operations in the computer software. These applications are accessed by clicking **Insert** on the menu bar across the top of the screen. The icons immediately above the document page access the same items as the Menu key on the handheld.

Using the TI-Nspire with the Lessons

All lessons are accompanied by a TNS file (e.g., *lesson01.tns*) that must be loaded on to each student's TI-Nspire handheld device before the lesson begins. (Note: Lessons 12 and 14 do not include TNS files. This is because the students will create their own TNS files for these two lessons.) Each lesson provides instructions for using the file and directs the students' mathematical exploration. The solutions to the problems in the TNS files (e.g., *solution01.tns*) are included as well. Step-by-step directions for performing different processes on the handheld are included in Appendix B. By using these directions with the lesson, students will be able to accurately complete the steps on the handheld device in order to deepen their understanding of the mathematical content.

TI-Nspire Computer Link software is required to transfer the TNS file from the Teacher Resource CD to a TI-Nspire handheld device. This software is available at no charge from the Texas Instrument educational website, **http://www.education.ti.com**.

After the file is loaded to a TI-Nspire handheld, the file can be linked to additional TI-Nspire handhelds. (See page 226 for detailed directions on transferring TNS files.) It is also possible to connect to as many as 14 handhelds at a time using the *Connect-to Class* kits. In this system, the handhelds are linked to the teacher computer using USB hubs. For more information on purchasing *Connect-to Class* kits, visit **http://www.education.ti.com**.

Utilizing and Managing TI-Nspire Handhelds

Methods for Teaching TI-Nspire Skills

Unlike a regular graphing calculator, the TI-Nspire has five applications that can be used to complete the activities in this resource. To help students feel comfortable using the TI-Nspire, follow the steps below before starting a lesson.

1. Before beginning the lesson, demonstrate the handheld skills that students must know to be successful in the lesson.

2. To teach a skill, have students locate the keys and functions on the handhelds, and familiarize students with the menus and screens these keys and functions access.

3. If multiple steps are needed to complete the activity, list the steps on the board or on the overhead for the students to use as a reference while working. Or, use a projector to display the corresponding pages from the *How-to Manual*, which can be found on pages 223–246 or printed from the Teacher Resource CD.

4. Ask students who are familiar with and comfortable using the TI-Nspire to assist others. Let the other students know who those TI-Nspire mentors are.

5. Allow time to address any questions that the students may have after each step or before continuing on to the next part of the lesson.

Utilizing and Managing TI-Nspire Handhelds (cont.)

Storing and Assigning Handhelds

It is important to establish a management system that works best for you and your students. Here are a few suggestions:

- Before using the handhelds with students, number each handheld with a permanent marker or label.

- Assign each student or pair of students a handheld number. Since each student will be using the same handheld every time they are distributed, it will help keep track of any handhelds that may be damaged or lost.

- Store the handhelds in a plastic shoebox or an over-the-door shoe rack. Number the pockets on the shoe rack with the same numbers as the handhelds.

Distributing Handhelds

To distribute the handhelds, consider at which point during the class period the students will need to use them.

- If the students will need the handhelds at the beginning of the class period, write on the board or overhead *Get your handhelds*.

- If the handhelds are stored in the plastic container, make sure they are in numerical order. This will help students find their handhelds faster.

- If the handhelds are stored in an over-the-door shoe rack, a note to take a handheld can be placed on the door. This way, the students can grab their handhelds as they walk into the classroom.

- If the handhelds will not be used until later in the class period, have the students retrieve their handhelds by rows.

- Once the students have their handhelds, use the *Check-Off List* (page 24) to keep track of which handhelds have been used during that day or class period.

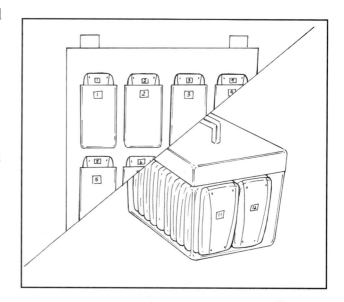

Utilizing and Managing TI-Nspire Handhelds *(cont.)*

Checking for Damage and Returning Handhelds

After distributing the handhelds, have students check their handhelds for any damage.

- If a handheld is damaged, complete the *Damage Report* (page 25). You can then refer back to the *Check-Off List* (page 24) to see which students last used the handheld.

- Have students return their handhelds by rows.

- If the handhelds are stored in a plastic shoebox, have them put the handhelds back in numerical order.

- If the handhelds are stored in an over-the-door shoe rack, have the students place them in the correct pockets.

- DO NOT forget to count the handhelds before students leave.

Utilizing and Managing TI-Nspire Handhelds (cont.)

Check-Off List							
		DATE					
Student Name	Handheld Number						

Utilizing and Managing TI-Nspire Handhelds (cont.)

Damage Report				
Date	Handheld Number	Class Period	Damage	Reported By

Utilizing and Managing TI-Nspire Handhelds *(cont.)*

Facilitating a Handheld Center

If only a few handhelds are available, create a handheld center in the back of the classroom. One suggested classroom layout is shown below. To prevent students from being distracted and to allow the teacher to work with small groups in the center while monitoring the other groups, have students sit in the handheld center with their backs to the other groups. Use the Handheld Center Rotation Schedule below to keep track of which students have been to the center. While working with the students in the center, provide the other students with independent work. Use the *Check-Off List* (page 24) to keep track of which students used the handhelds.

Classroom Layout

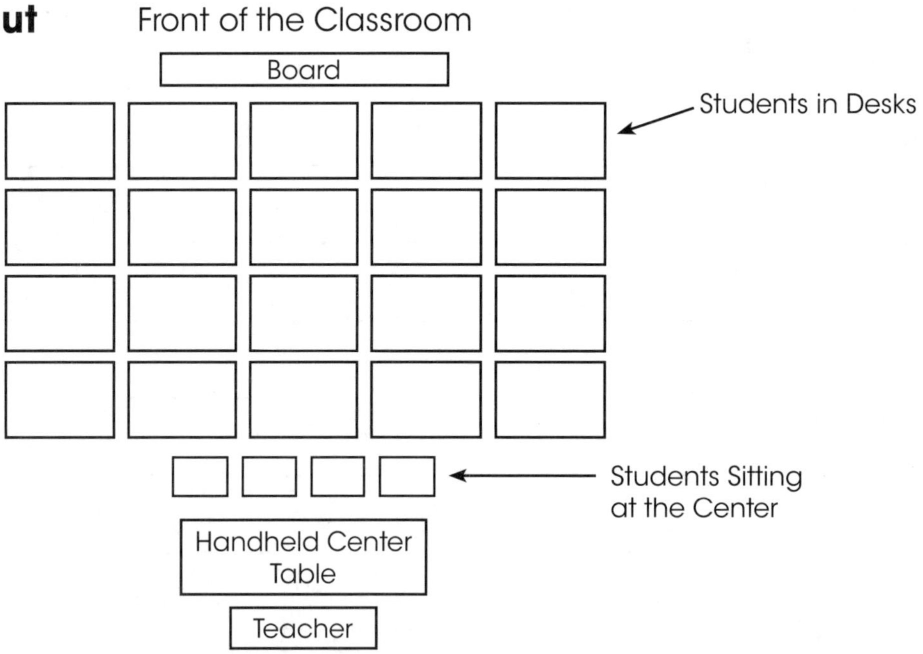

Front of the Classroom

Board

Students in Desks

Students Sitting at the Center

Handheld Center Table

Teacher

Handheld Center Rotation Schedule

Days of the Week & Date	Monday	Tuesday	Wednesday	Thursday	Friday
Group Names					
Students					

Assessment

For each lesson, activity sheets are provided that can be used to assess the students' knowledge of the concept. These activities could be considered practice, in which students' progress and understanding of the concept is monitored through in-class assignments or homework. The activity sheets used in the Applying the Concept section of each lesson could also be assigned as a formal assessment.

Completion Grades

To give a completion grade for an activity, have students exchange papers. Review the problems together. Model problems on the overhead, or have students model the problems. Have students count the number of problems completed. Then use the *Completion Grades* template (page 28) to record students' scores.

Write students' names above each column on the *Completion Grades* template. Write the assignment title in the first column. Record students' scores as a fraction of the number of problems completed over the number of problems assigned. At the end of the grading period, add the number of problems completed for each student to the number of problems assigned. Divide the fraction to calculate a numerical grade.

Using a Point System for Formal Grades

When grading activities that serve as assessments, it is best to grade them yourself. This provides you with an opportunity to analyze students' performances, evaluate students' errors, and reflect on how instruction may have influenced their performances. It also prevents student error in grading. Depending on a school's grading procedures, assessments can be graded with fractions similar to completion grades. Determine the number of points that each problem is worth. You may want to assign two or more points for each problem if students are expected to show work or explain how they solved a problem. One point is awarded for the correct answer; the other points are for the students' work and/or written explanations. Write a fraction of the number of points a student earned out of the total number of points possible. Record these grades as fractions or convert them to percentages. Then, enter them into your grade book or an online grading system.

Grading with a Rubric

A rubric is an alternative way to grade activities or problems that involve multiple steps or tasks. It allows both the student and teacher to analyze a student's performance for the objectives of the task or assignment by giving the student a categorical score for each component. For example, if the students had the task of solving a problem and explaining how they solved it, a rubric would allow the teacher to identify in which subtasks students excelled or could improve. The problem may be correct, but the explanation may be missing steps needed to solve the problem. The *General Rubric* (page 29) and the *Create Your Own Rubric* (page 30) can be adapted for various types of activities. By using an all-purpose rubric, students can also be individually assessed on specific skills and objectives.

Assessment *(cont.)*

Completion Grades Template

Student Names										
Total Points Earned										
Total Points Possible										

Practice Activities

Key

Record Fractions for:
Number of Problems Completed
Number of Possible Problems

Assessment (cont.)

Directions: This rubric includes general criteria for grading multistep assignments that involve written explanations to questions. In each of the Level columns, specify each criterion by explaining how it relates to the activity and the levels of performance that can be achieved. Give the rubric to students for self-evaluation and peer evaluation. To evaluate an activity, circle a level of performance for each criterion and assign a number of points. Total the points and record them in one of the last three columns.

General Rubric

Criteria	Level I (0–4 points)	Level II (5–8 points)	Level III (9–10 points)	Self-Score	Peer Score	Teacher Score
Steps in the activity have been completed. Question(s) have been answered.						
Calculations are shown and/or explained.						
Responses relate to the questions being asked.						
Ideas are supported with logical reasoning and/or evidence.						

Assessment *(cont.)*

Directions: Write the criteria for the assignment in the first column. Then for each criterion, fill in the level of performance students may achieve. Give the rubric to the students for self-evaluation and peer evaluation. To evaluate an activity, circle a level of achievement for each criterion and then assign a number of points. Total the points and record them in one of the last three columns.

Create Your Own Rubric

Criteria	Level I (0–4 points)	Level II (5–8 points)	Level III (9–10 points)	Self-Score	Peer Score	Teacher Score

Notes

One-Variable Statistics

Mathematics Objectives

- Students will use box plots to analyze data and compare data sets.

- Students will investigate measures of central tendencies and their uses.

Applications and Skills

Lists and Spreadsheets
Using formulas to define lists

Data and Statistics
Box Plots
Dot Plots
Adjusting Window Settings

Calculator
Finding mean, median, minimum, and maximum of a list

Materials

- Heights of class members measured in feet and inches (See note below.)

- TI-Nspire handhelds

- TNS file: lesson01.tns

- *Measuring Up*
  (page 37; page037.pdf)

- *Gigantic!*
  (pages 38–39; page038.pdf)

- *That's Tall*
  (page 40; page040.pdf)

Note: The students' heights can be measured manually or with the CBR2 and a TI-84 using the Easy Data APP with events with entry. If the CBR2 is used, the lists can then be copied and pasted into the Lesson 1 TNS file.

Starting the Lesson

After loading the TNS file (lesson01.tns) on each handheld, begin the exercise by instructing students to do the following:

1. Turn on the TI-Nspire by pressing (on).

2. Press (⌂) and choose **My Documents**.

3. In the folder *Algebra TCM*, choose *lesson01*.

4. Remind students how to navigate through the TNS file. To move forward through the pages, press (ctrl) ▶. To move backward through the pages, press (ctrl) ◀. To choose a particular page, press (ctrl) ▲, position the cursor on the desired page and press (enter). To undo previous steps, press (ctrl) (Z) or (ctrl) (esc). Show students that any time they are using a menu that they wish to exit, they should press (esc).

Note: Page numbers refer to the TI-Nspire file lesson01.

Explaining the Concept

Problem 1—Measuring Up

Step 1   Distribute copies of *Measuring Up* (page 37) to students so they can record their findings as appropriate during the instructional steps of this problem.

Step 2   If you did not enter the heights into the TNS file, show students how to enter the data into each cell on page 1.2 by clicking in it, typing in the numbers, and pressing (enter) or (⊙). Students can also move from cell to cell by using the arrows on the NavPad.

Step 3   Discuss changing feet and inches into a measurement using only inches. Have students write the formula for the conversion. Show them column C on page 1.2 by using the NavPad to move to it until it is highlighted. Then press (enter) or (⊙). To enter the formula, highlight the box beneath the list name (*htin*) and press (enter) or (⊙). Type in the formula. Press (enter) when done to populate the data. The variable in the formula must be the name of a previous name list. It can be typed in or recalled by pressing the (sto var) key.

Step 4   In question 2a, the students will need to split page 1.3. Before doing this, students can change the window settings in the dot plot by pressing (menu), choosing **Window/Zoom**, and then **Window Settings**. To split the page, press (ctrl) (⌂). Choose **Page Layout**, **Select Layout**, and then **Layout 3**. The top part is a dot plot of the list *htin*. Move to the bottom part of the page by pressing (ctrl) (tab). Press (menu) and choose **Add Calculator**.

Step 5   Using the handheld, show students how to find the mean by typing *mean(htin)* on the bottom of the page and pressing (enter). Point out that they can also type *mean(* and press (sto var), choose *htin* from the list, type the closing parenthesis, and then press (enter). Similarly, find the median by typing *median(htin)*, the maximum by typing *max(htin)*, and the minimum by typing *min(htin)*. Point out that these commands are also available by pressing (menu) and choosing **Statistics** and then **List Math**.

Step 6   Discuss that mean, median, and mode are three different measures of central tendency.

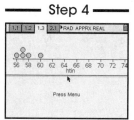
Step 4

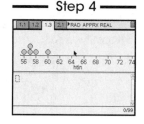
Step 4

Step 5

Step 5

Note: Page numbers refer to the TI-Nspire file lesson01.

Explaining the Concept *(cont.)*

Problem 1—Measuring Up *(cont.)*

Step 7   Change the dot plot to a box plot. To move back to the top of the page, press ⌃ctrl⌄ ⌃tab⌄. Press ⌃menu⌄ and choose **Plot Type** and then **Box Plot**. Looking at the box plot helps to determine which measure of central tendency is the best representative of the data as a whole. If the data is fairly evenly distributed on either side, the median may be the best. If the extremes are not too far from the median, the mean may be the best. The mode is useful mainly when some kind of preference or vote is being observed. Ask the students which one they think best describes their class.

Step 8   For question 3a, change the graph to include or exclude the outliers by pressing ⌃menu⌄ and choosing **Plot Properties**. The choices of **Show Box Plot Outliers** and **Extend Box Plot Whiskers** switch back and forth, depending on the status of the current graph. Your class data may or may not have outliers. One will be added in the next problem. Have students use the NavPad to trace the graph.

Step 9   If the students have difficulty visualizing the meaning of the box plot, line them up and create a human box plot. This might also help them decide which measure of central tendency best describes the class.

Problem 2—Gigantic!

Step 1   Distribute copies of *Gigantic!* (pages 38–39) to students so they can record their findings as appropriate during the instructional steps of this problem.

Step 2   In question 2, students create their own pages. Instruct them to press ⌃ctrl⌄ ▲ to access the page sorter. Next, move to page 1.2 in the page sorter and press ⌃ctrl⌄ ⓒ to copy the page. Then, have students move to page 2.1 in the sorter and paste in their copies of page 1.2 by pressing ⌃ctrl⌄ ⓥ.

Step 3   They can now remove the blank page in problem 2. Use the NavPad to move to the blank page and press ⌃clear⌄ to remove it. Then, press ⓒ to open the new page 2.1.

—— Step 7 ——

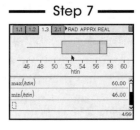

—— Step 7 ——

—— Step 2 ——

—— Step 2 ——

—— Step 3 ——

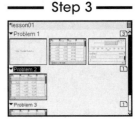

Note: Page numbers refer to the TI-Nspire file lesson01.

Explaining the Concept (cont.)

Problem 2—Gigantic! (cont.)

Step 4 To enter the new height for questions 2 and 3 into the lists, use the NavPad to move to the first empty cell at the bottom of the *ft* list. Type *15* and then press (enter). An error message will occur. Click **OK**. Move to the cell next to the 15 and type *0*. Press (enter). The error will automatically be corrected. The new height in inches will appear in row C.

Step 4
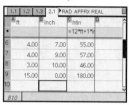

Step 5 Insert a new page by pressing (ctrl) (I). Choose **Add Data & Statistics**. Use the NavPad to move the cursor to the bottom of the page. Click on the *x*-axis to add *htin* as the variable. Be sure to show students how to adjust the window settings so that all the data is visible. To do this, press (menu), choose **Window/Zoom**, and adjust the window settings to the appropriate dimensions.

Step 5

Step 6 For question 5, discuss the difference between an object being the middle measurement, the median, and the average measurement or the mean. (See Steps 4 and 5 on page 33 for more detailed instructions.)

Step 5
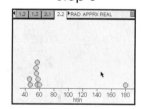

Step 7 For question 6, change the graph to a box plot. Remind students how to use the Expand Box Plot Whiskers option. (See Steps 7 and 8 on page 34 for more detailed instructions.)

Step 8 In question 7, emphasize the concept of outliers by inventing a situation where the income of 30 mechanics and one big-name movie star or athlete is analyzed. Think about the mean and the median of this group. Look at a box plot with and without the box plot whiskers extended.

Step 7
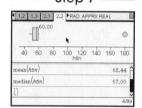

Applying the Concept

Problem 3—That's Tall

Step 1 Distribute copies of *That's Tall* (page 40) to students so they can record their findings.

Step 7
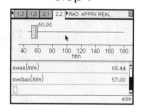

Note: Page numbers refer to the TI-Nspire file lesson01.

Applying the Concept *(cont.)*

Problem 3—That's Tall *(cont.)*

Step 2   The data is included on page 3.1. These were the actual heights from the preseason rosters of the Cleveland Cavaliers (cc) and the Los Angeles Lakers (la) in 2007.

Step 3   For question 2, have students insert a new Data and Statistics page by pressing (ctrl) (I). Click on the *x*-axis to add *cc* as the variable. Now have students split the screen by pressing (ctrl) (⌂). Choose **Page Layout** then **Select Layout**. To split the page horizontally, choose **Layout 3**. Remind students to press (ctrl) (tab) to move back to the new section. Press (menu) and choose **Data & Statistics**. This time have students add the variable *la*.

Step 4   To switch the dot plots to box plots for question 3, have students press (menu) and choose **Plot Type** and then **Box Plot**.

Differentiation

- **Below Grade Level**—Work through question 1 on *That's Tall* (page 40) with students. Once the chart has been successfully completed, have students work in pairs to complete the remaining questions.

- **Above Grade Level**—Have students complete *That's Tall* (page 40) independently. Then have students pair up. Instruct students to study the sports section of the local newspaper or to find statistics of local sports teams using the Internet. Have the pairs create a dot plot or a box plot using the statistics for one of the local sports teams. Have each pair share their plot and explain the reasoning behind it with another pair of students.

Extending the Concept

- Have students analyze box plots they find in the media.

- Have students find and discuss misleading graphs in the media.

- Ask students to identify outliers in day-to-day statistics.

Name _____

Measuring Up

Directions: Follow the steps below. The page numbers refer to the TI-Nspire document *lesson01*.

---

1. If your teacher has given you the heights of the members of your class, enter them into lists *ft* and *inch* on page 1.2. If the data was already included, proceed to question 1a.

   a. Write a formula using the variables *inch* and *ft* that would describe each student's height (*htin*) expressed in inches (*inch*). Enter this formula into the *htin* list.

   _____

——— Step 1 ———

ft	inch	htin	
		htin:=	
4.00	9.00		
4.00	10.00		
4.00	8.00		
3.00	11.00		
5.00	0.00		

htin:=

---

2. On page 1.3, split the page horizontally.

   a. Use the Calculator application to find the mean, median, maximum, and minimum of *htin*. Are the mean and median values nearly the same?

   _____

   b. Look at the graph to identify the mode and the extreme values of your data.

   _____

——— Step 2 ———

---

3. Return to the top of page 1.3. Make a box plot of the data in *htin*. Use the Extend Box Plot Whiskers option. Use the NavPad to trace your graph to find the extremes, the median, and the Q1 and Q3 scores.

   a. Imagine that you have lined up the class from shortest to tallest. Which class members would be included in the low whisker? Which class members would be included in the high whisker?

   _____

   b. Which class members would be included in the left-hand side of the box? Which class members would be included in the right-hand side of the box?

   _____

Name _____

Gigantic!

Directions: Follow the steps below. The page numbers refer to the TI-Nspire document *lesson01*.

---

1. Copy page 1.2 in the Lesson 1 TNS file. Paste the page at the end of problem 2. Clear the blank page, and the copied page will become page 2.1.

——— Step 1 ———

---

2. Imagine that a giant who is 15 ft. tall was included in your class data. How do you think the measures of central tendency (the mean, median, and mode) would change?

_____

_____

---

3. On page 2.1, enter 15 feet, 0 inches at the bottom of the lists.

---

4. Insert a new page and choose data and statistics. On the *x*-axis, choose *htin* for the variable. Be sure that you can see all of the data. If not, use the Zoom options to change the window settings. How does this dot plot differ from the one in *Measuring Up*?

——— Step 2 ———

_____

_____

---

5. Split the page horizontally and use the Calculator application to find the maximum, minimum, mean, and the median. Are the mean and median nearly the same? Why do you think this happened?

_____

_____

Gigantic! *(cont.)*

Directions: Follow the steps below. The page numbers refer to the TI-Nspire document *lesson01*.

6. Change the graph to a box plot of the data in *htin*. Use the Extend Box Plot Whiskers option. Use the NavPad to trace on your graph to find the extremes, the median, and the Q1 and Q3 scores.

_____

_____

7. An outlier is an observation that is numerically distant from the rest of the data. Change your box plot to the show box plot outliers.

   a. Who is the outlier on your data? Use the NavPad to trace on your graph to find the extremes, the median, and the Q1 and Q3 scores.

   _____

   b. Are the mean and median about the same as in *Measuring Up*?

   _____

   c. Why is the median about the same and the mean significantly different?

   _____

   _____

   d. Which measure of central tendency (mean, median, or mode) do you think best describes the class as a whole when the giant is included?

   _____

   _____

   _____

   _____

   _____

Name _____

That's Tall

Directions: Follow the steps below. The page numbers refer to the TI-Nspire document *lesson01*.

---

1. The heights of two basketball teams, the Cleveland Cavaliers (*cc*) and the Los Angeles Lakers (*la*), are shown in the lists on page 3.1. Insert a new calculator page. This will become page 3.2. Find the mean, median, maximum, and minimum height of each team.

	Mean	Median	Max.	Min.
cc				
la				

   _____

   _____

   _____

   ——— Step 1 ———

---

2. Insert a Data and Statistics page (page 3.3), split it horizontally, and make dot plots for *cc* and *la*. Be sure that you have the same window settings for each graph. (An Xmin of 68.5 and Xmax of 88.5 work well.) Which team do you think is taller? Why?

   _____

   _____

---

3. Switch to box plots. Be sure that you have the same window settings for each graph. Which one would you expect to be a more successful basketball team? Use the box plots to explain your answer.

   _____

   _____

   _____

   _____

Direct Variation

Mathematics Objectives

- Students will assign variables to represent changing quantities.

- Students will use the standard form of a mathematical formula.

- Students will recognize direct variation and apply it to a real-life situation. They will identify k in $y = kx$ as the constant of variation and also as the rate of change and relate it to slope.

Applications and Skills

Graphs and Geometry
    Text Box to Graph Equation
    Movable Point

Data and Statistics
    Data Entry
    Quick Graph
    Add Movable Line
    Lock Intercept at Zero
    Automatic Data Capture

Materials

- TI-Nspire handhelds

- TNS file: lesson02.tns

- *Julie's Car Wash*
  (pages 46–49; page046.pdf)

- *Don't Fence Me In*
  (page 50; page050.pdf)

- *Mr. Diaz Washes His Car*
  (pages 51–54; page051.pdf)

Starting the Lesson

After loading the TNS file (lesson02.tns) on each handheld, begin the exercise by instructing students to do the following:

1. Turn on the TI-Nspire by pressing (on).

2. Press (⌂) and choose **My Documents**.

3. In the folder *Algebra TCM*, choose *lesson02*.

4. Remind students how to navigate through the TNS file. To move forward through the pages, press (ctrl) ▶. To move backward through the pages, press (ctrl) ◀. To choose a particular page, press (ctrl) ▲, position the cursor on the desired page and press (enter). To undo previous steps, press (ctrl) (Z) or (ctrl) (esc). Show students that any time they are using a menu that they wish to exit, they should press (esc).

Note: Page numbers refer to the TI-Nspire file lesson02.

Explaining the Concept

Problem 1—Julie's Car Wash

Step 1   Distribute copies of *Julie's Car Wash* (pages 46–49) to students so they can record their findings as appropriate during the instructional steps of this problem.

Step 2   Point out that the $25 per car is a rate that indicates that the total earned increases by $25 dollars each time the number of cars increases by one.

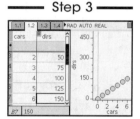

——— Step 3 ———

Step 3   Have students complete page 1.2 for question 1. Show students how to enter their answers into the chart by pressing ▶ to move into the second column. Then, type in each number and press (enter) or (⊙). To move to the graph, press (ctrl) (tab).

Step 4   Discuss that the increase of the same amount for each car causes the points to lie on a line.

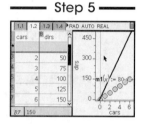

——— Step 5 ———

Step 5   For question 2, have students move to the graph. Show students how to add the movable line by pressing (menu) and choosing **Analyze** and then **Add Movable Line**.

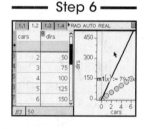

——— Step 6 ———

Step 6   Demonstrate how to lock the intercept at zero by pressing (menu) and choosing **Analyze** and then **Lock Intercept At Zero**.

Step 7   To move the line, select it by using the NavPad to move the cursor to the line. When the cursor changes to (⟨⟩), press (ctrl) (⊙). Use the NavPad to fit the line to the points. To release the line, press (⊙) twice or press (esc). If you need to move the equation, use the NavPad to move the cursor to the equation. When the cursor changes to a hand (☜), grab the equation by pressing (ctrl) (⊙). Now you can drag it. To release the equation, press (⊙) twice or press (esc).

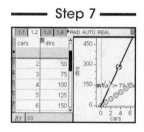

——— Step 7 ———

Step 8   Make sure the students adjust their lines so that the equation is $y = 25x$ ($ml(x) := 25 \cdot x$). Have them test a few ordered pairs from the chart with the equation so that it makes sense to them. Be sure to look at the ordered pair (0, 0). Discuss its meaning in the car-washing problem and its connection to the Lock Intercept at Zero option.

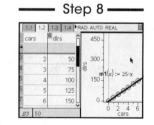

——— Step 8 ———

Note: Page numbers refer to the TI-Nspire file lesson02.

Explaining the Concept *(cont.)*

Problem 1—Julie's Car Wash *(cont.)*

Step 9 For question 3, have students complete page 1.3. Students should realize that the points will not line up with increases of differing amounts.

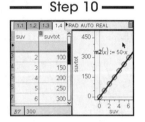
—— Step 9 ——

Step 10 For questions 4, 5, and 6, have students complete pages 1.4 and 1.5. Discuss how Julie's total earnings increase if she washes SUVs or minivans. Relate that to the steepness (slopes) of the graph. Discuss where the earnings are increasing faster and slower.

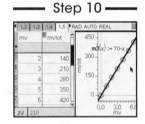
—— Step 10 ——

Step 11 For question 7, have students complete page 1.6. Show the students how to use a text box to graph an equation. Move the cursor to a blank area on the graph. Press (menu). Choose **Actions** and then **Text**. Press (enter) or (☝). When the box opens, type the equation in it and press (enter). If you need to edit the text box, move the cursor over the text until it flashes, then press (☝) twice. To move the equation, move the cursor close to the equation until it turns into a hand. Press (ctrl) (☝) to grab it. Drag it to the *x*-axis until the line appears and then press (enter).

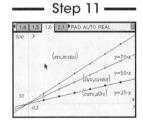
—— Step 10 ——

Step 12 Make sure students see that the standard form $y = kx$ can be applied with any variables chosen for y and x. Identify k as the constant of variation, the rate of change of the total earned with respect to the number of vehicles washed, and as the slope of the line (the rate of change of y with respect to x). When they add the new graphs, help them recognize the effect of changing slope (steepness).

—— Step 11 ——

Problem 2—Don't Fence Me In

Step 1 Distribute copies of *Don't Fence Me In* (page 50) to students so they can record their findings during the instructional steps of this problem.

Step 2 Ask students how you find the area and perimeter of a rectangle. Draw several rectangles of the same length with differing widths and find their areas and perimeters.

Note: Page numbers refer to the TI-Nspire file lesson02.

Explaining the Concept *(cont.)*

Problem 2—Don't Fence Me In *(cont.)*

Step 3   For question 2, have students complete page 2.1. Show them how to drag point F. (See page 224 for detailed instructions on how to drag a point.) Drag it *slowly* towards the barn, watching the values of area and perimeter change. Remind them to move point F to the barn just once. If they move it too many times, the number of points makes the graph difficult to view. If students need to clear the data on page 2.2 and begin again, show them how to move the cursor into the cell that says *capture* and hit ⏎ twice.

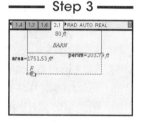

──── Step 3 ────

──── Step 3 ────

Step 4   On page 2.2, have the students move to the first graph by pressing ⌃ tab. They may need to adjust the window settings to see the entire graph. (See page 236 for detailed instructions on adjusting window settings.)

──── Step 4 ────

Step 5   Have students use the Movable Line tool and the Lock Intercept at Zero option. (See pages 241 and 242 for detailed instructions on this tool and option.) Make sure students know how to grab the line near the ends to be able to rotate it freely. If they grab the line in the middle, they will not be able to change the slope. Discuss which graph looks as if it might go through the origin.

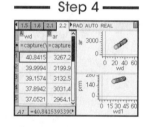

──── Step 5 ────

Step 6   The students should recognize that the graph of *area vs. width* is an example of direct variation because the line goes through the origin, while the graph of *perimeter vs. width* does not.

Step 7   For question 4, remind students how they graphed using the text box in *Julie's Car Wash*. Make sure they understand that when they write the equation in the form $y = kx$, they are putting the relationship into standard form and that y and x are used for ease of communication.

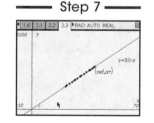

──── Step 7 ────

Applying the Concept

Problem 3—Mr. Diaz Washes His Car

Step 1   Distribute copies of *Mr. Diaz Washes His Car* (pages 51–54) to students so they can record their findings.

Note: Page numbers refer to the TI-Nspire file lesson02.

Applying the Concept (cont.)

Problem 3—Mr. Diaz Washes His Car (cont.)

Step 2   For question 1, have students complete page 3.1. Emphasize the use of negative numbers because Mr. Diaz is removing the money. Students should notice that the line slants down from left to right. Help them realize that this is because the amount in the fund is decreasing.

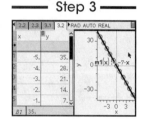
——— Step 2 ———

Step 3   For question 2, have students complete page 3.2. Explain the ordered pairs where *x* is negative and *y* is positive. Return to Mr. Diaz and think about how his fund would have compared at times prior to when we began looking at it (one week before—$25 more; two weeks before—$50 more, etc.).

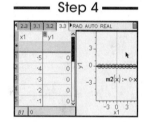
——— Step 3 ———

Step 4   For question 3, have students complete page 3.3. Point out that the equation could be written $y = 0x$ or $y = 0$. In either case, the constant of variation and slope are zero, meaning that the *y*-value does not change.

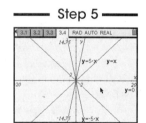
——— Step 4 ———

Step 5   When students complete page 3.4, discuss the slope of each line and its effect on the graph. Be sure to point out that $y = x$ is the same as $y = 1x$ and $y = -x$ is the same as $y = -1x$. (Note: The label for $y = -x$ will not be visible on the screen unless the window settings are adjusted.)

——— Step 5 ———

Differentiation

- **Below Grade Level**—Work through question 1 on *Mr. Diaz Washes His Car* (pages 51–54) as a class, sketching the graph on the board. Have students work in pairs to complete question 2. You may want to supply students with copies of pages 241–242. (These contain detailed instructions on how to add a movable line and how to lock the intercept at zero.) Have students solve question 3 independently. Reconvene as a group to solve question 4.

- **Above Grade Level**—Have students independently solve questions 1–3 on *Mr. Diaz Washes His Car* (pages 51–54). Allow students to pair up to solve question 4.

Extending the Concept

- Have students find examples of direct variation in nature or in science class.

Name _____

Julie's Car Wash

Directions: Follow the steps below. The page numbers refer to the TI-Nspire file *lesson02*.

1. To earn money for college, Julie is washing cars. She charges $25 per car. On page 1.2, enter her total earnings after completing each number of cars. Look at the graph. Using Julie's charge per car, explain why the points appear to lie on a line.

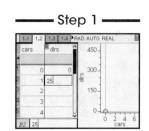
——— Step 1 ———

_____

_____

2. On page 1.2, use the Add Moveable Line tool and then the Lock Intercept at Zero option to fit a line to the graph.

   a. What is the equation of the line?

   _____

   b. How is it connected to the charge for a car wash?

   _____

   c. Why did it make sense to lock the intercept at zero?

   _____

   _____

   d. Suppose Julie charged different rates for minivans and SUVs. Explain why the points would or would not lie on a line.

   _____

   _____

   _____

Julie's Car Wash (cont.)

Directions: Follow the steps below. The page numbers refer to the TI-Nspire file *lesson02*.

---

3. To test your theory, suppose that Julie continues to charge $25 for each car but charges $50 for an SUV and $70 for a minivan. Assume that the first vehicle she washes is a car, the second is an SUV, the third is a car, the fourth and fifth are minivans, and the sixth is a car. On page 1.3, fill in the total money she will have earned after completing each vehicle and look at the graph. How did the different charges affect the graph?

_____

_____

_____

---

4. Suppose Julie specialized in just SUVs at $50 each. Fill in the values on page 1.4 and look at the graph.

a. Write an equation for the total amount earned.

_____

b. Use the Add Moveable Line tool with the Lock Intercept at Zero option to fit a line to the graph. Was your equation correct?

_____

---

5. Suppose Julie specialized in just minivans at $70 each. Fill in the values on page 1.5 and look at the graph.

a. Write an equation for the total amount earned.

_____

b. Use the Add Moveable Line tool with the Lock Intercept at Zero option to fit a line to the graph. Was your equation correct?

_____

Julie's Car Wash (cont.)

Directions: Follow the steps below. The page numbers refer to the TI-Nspire file *lesson02*.

6. The relationship between the number of vehicles and the total earned is called direct variation. This means that you can write a formula in the form $y = kx$. In this case, x is the number of vehicles, y is the total earned, and k is the amount per vehicle. The y and x are variables because their values change. The k in $y = kx$ is a number and is called a constant because its value does not change. This constant, k, is named the constant of variation and represents how much the value of y changes each time x increases by one.

  a. For the SUV, you could write TOTAL = 50 • SUV. For the minivan, you could write TOTAL = 70 • MV. What formula would you write for the cars?

  _____

  b. Identify the variables and the constant value in each equation.

  _____

7. Page 1.6 shows the scatter plots of the cars, SUVs, and minivans. Enter your equation for washing cars in the form $y = kx$ into a text box and drag into the x-axis. Repeat for the SUVs and the minivans.

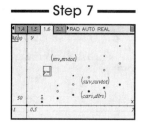
——— Step 7 ———

  a. Which equation produced the steepest line? Why?

  _____

  _____

  b. Write an equation for a line that you think would be steeper than any of the lines on your graph.

  _____

  c. Write an equation for a line that you think would be flatter than any of the lines on your graph.

  _____

  d. Test the equations on your graph. Were you correct?

  _____

Julie's Car Wash (cont.)

Directions: Follow the steps below. The page numbers refer to the TI-Nspire file *lesson02*.

8. The k in the formula $y = kx$ represents the constant of variation. When you filled in the lists, you increased the amount of money by adding k each time the number of vehicles increased by one. This is called the rate of change of y with respect to x. On the graph of a line, this number is called the *slope of the line*.

   a. What were the slopes of the lines on page 1.6?

   b. What were the slopes of the lines you added?

   c. How does the slope of the line affect the steepness of its graph?

Name _____

Don't Fence Me In

Directions: Follow the steps below. The page numbers refer to the TI-Nspire file *lesson02*.

1. Direct variation occurs in many situations. For example, a farmer wishes to build a cattle pen next to the back of his barn. The barn is 80-feet long, but he has not decided upon the width of his enclosure. What is the formula for the area of any rectangular pen he builds?

   _____

2. On page 2.1, move point F slowly toward the barn to change the size of the enclosure. Watch how the area and perimeter change. Then, look at the quick graphs on page 2.2. You may need to adjust your window settings to see the entire graph. Use the Movable Line tool to find the equations of the lines. Try them with and without locking the intercept at zero.

   Sketch the graph here. Be sure to label the axes.

   ——— Step 2 ———

   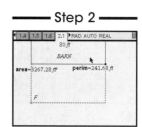

3. Which graph demonstrates direct variation? How can you recognize direct variation from the graph?

   _____

4. Write the formula for the area in the form $y = kx$. Then, on page 2.3, enter it into a text box and drag it to the *x*-axis to check your equation. Was your equation correct?

   _____

Name _____

Mr. Diaz Washes His Car

Directions: Follow the steps below. The page numbers refer to the TI-Nspire file *lesson02*.

1. Suppose Mr. Diaz put money aside for washing his car, and Julie washes it once a week at a charge of $25. Complete the chart on page 3.1 to show the total amount his fund has gone down after each car wash. Because he is removing money from the fund, use negative numbers.

   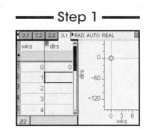
   ——— Step 1 ———

   a. Sketch the graph here. Be sure to label the axes.

   b. How did the graph differ from the ones in *Julie's Car Wash* and *Don't Fence Me In*?

   _____

   _____

   c. What is happening to the amount of money in the car-wash fund?

   _____

   _____

Mr. Diaz Washes His Car (cont.)

Directions: Follow the steps below. The page numbers refer to the TI-Nspire file *lesson02*.

2. Look at the lists and the graph on page 3.2. Use the Add Moveable Line tool with the Lock Intercept at Zero option to find the formula for the data.

------ Step 2 ------

2.2	2.9	3.1	3.2 |RAD AUTO REAL
x	y		
	-5.	35.	
	-4.	28.	
	-3.	21.	
	-2.	14.	
	-1.	7.	
B1	35.		

   a. What equation did you find?

   _____

   b. How is the equation different from the ones in *Julie's Car Wash* and *Don't Fence Me In*?

   _____

   _____

   _____

   c. Why is this equation an example of direct variation?

   _____

   _____

   _____

   d. What is the value of k?

   _____

   e. How does the negative affect each value of *y*?

   _____

   _____

   _____

Mr. Diaz Washes His Car (cont.)

Directions: Follow the steps below. The page numbers refer to the TI-Nspire file *lesson02*.

3. Look at the lists and the graph on page 3.3. Use the Add Moveable Line tool to find the formula for the data. Use the Lock Intercept at Zero option.

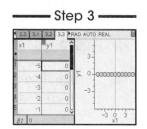

Step 3

   a. Sketch the graph here. Be sure to label the axes.

   b. What are the equation of the line, the constant of variation, and the slope of the line graphed?

   _____

   _____

   _____

Mr. Diaz Washes His Car (cont.)

Directions: Follow the steps below. The page numbers refer to the TI-Nspire file *lesson02*.

4. On page 3.4, graph the lines $y = 5x$, $y = x$, $y = 0$, $y = -x$, and $y = -5x$ by entering each equation into a text box and dragging it to the *x*-axis. For each line, notice the steepness and the direction it tilts.

    a. Sketch the graph here. Be sure to label the axes. Write the equation of each line next to the appropriate line.

    b. Explain how the sign of k in $y = kx$ affects the way the line tilts.

_____

_____

_____

    c. What happens to the line when k is zero?

_____

_____

_____

Mathematics Objectives

- Students will review the coordinate plane.

- Students will learn the relationship of the equation of a line with its slope and y-intercept.

- Students will recognize the relationships between the slopes of parallel and perpendicular lines.

Applications and Skills

Graphs and Geometry

Construct and Label Point
Redefine Point
Movable Point
Measure Distance
Measure Slope
Construct Parallel Lines
Construct Perpendicular Lines
Coordinates and Equations Tool
Calculate Tool

Materials

- TI-Nspire handhelds

- TNS file: lesson03.tns

- *Darting Around*
  (pages 62–63; page062.pdf)

- *Tilt*
  (page 64; page064.pdf)

- *On Target*
  (pages 65–68; page065.pdf)

- *Lines, Man*
  (pages 69–70; page069.pdf)

- graph paper

Starting the Lesson

After loading the TNS file (lesson03.tns) on each handheld, begin the exercise by instructing students to do the following:

1. Turn on the TI-Nspire by pressing (on/off).

2. Press (⌂) and choose **My Documents**.

3. In the folder *Algebra TCM*, choose *lesson03*.

4. Remind students how to navigate through the TNS file. To move forward through the pages, press (ctrl) ▶. To move backward through the pages, press (ctrl) ◀. To choose a particular page, press (ctrl) ▲, position the cursor on the desired page and press (enter). To undo previous steps, press (ctrl) (Z) or (ctrl) (esc). Show students that any time they are using a menu that they wish to exit, they should press (esc).

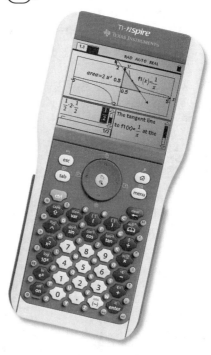

Note: Page numbers refer to the TI-Nspire file lesson03.

Explaining the Concept

Problem 1—Darting Around

Step 1   Distribute copies of *Darting Around* (pages 62–63) to students so they can record their findings as appropriate during the instructional steps of this problem.

Step 2   You may need to discuss the word *respectively* with the students. Many of them do not know that it means *in that order*. Also, remind students that the quadrants are numbered counterclockwise, starting with the top-right quadrant.

Step 3   Note: Steps 3–7 are all needed to complete question 1. To place and label a point on page 1.2, students should press (menu) and choose **Points & Lines** and then **Point**. Show students that they can label a point immediately after placing it by pressing the appropriate letter and then (enter). To use an uppercase letter, press (ctrl) (CAPS) before choosing the letter. Remind students to press (esc) after placing all the points.

——— Step 3 ———

Step 4   To change a letter, move the cursor to the letter. When it becomes a hand, press (enter) twice, clear the old letter, type the new one, and press (enter).

Step 5   If you wish to label the points after placing them, press (menu) and choose **Actions** and then **Text**. Move to the point until it flashes and press (enter). Type in the letter and press (enter) again.

Step 6   Remind the students that they can drag points to new positions by hovering over the point and pressing (ctrl) 🖐 to grab the point. Use the NavPad to drag the point. Press (esc) to release the point.

——— Step 6 ———

Step 7   To show the coordinates of the points, move to the point until it flashes and press (menu). Choose **Actions** and then **Coordinates and Equations**. Move to each point. When the hand appears, you will see a shadow of the ordered pair. Press (enter) twice to display it. You can drag it to a more convenient location if you wish by hovering over the coordinate pair and pressing (ctrl) 🖐 to grab it.

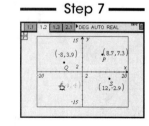

——— Step 7 ———

Note: Page numbers refer to the TI-Nspire file lesson03.

Explaining the Concept (cont.)

Problem 1—Darting Around (cont.)

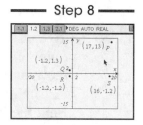

——— Step 8 ———

Step 8 Ask the students what their highest scores were. Ask them how they decided where to look. Insist that they describe the position in terms of the quadrants. Review the answers to question 1c.

Step 9 For question 2, redefine the points by pressing (menu) and choosing **Actions** and then **Redefine**. Click on a point and the axis to which it is being moved. Tell students to be careful not to click on a tick mark. Check the students' answers for question 2d. Have students describe the positions of their darts.

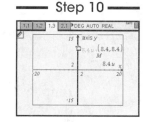

——— Step 9 ———

Step 10 Go over the values of the coordinates in the quadrants and on the axes. Have students use a signal to indicate if a coordinate will have a positive (stand), negative (sit), or zero (raise hand) value. For example, say "the *x*-coordinate in the first quadrant." Students should stand to indicate it will be positive. After saying, "*y*-coordinate when on the *x*-axis," students should raise their hands. Emphasize that points that lie on an axis are not included in any quadrant. Ask the students how to identify the position of the origin.

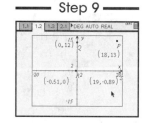

——— Step 10 ———

Step 11 For question 3, students will need to measure the distance from the point to an axis on page 1.3. To do this, press (menu) and choose **Measurement** and then **Length**. Select the point, and then move the cursor to the axis until it flashes. Then press (enter).

——— Step 11 ———

Step 12 Point out that the distance to the axis is equal to the absolute value of the coordinate, because distance is a *scalar* (without direction) quantity. Be certain they understand that the absolute value applies in all cases, but it is not obvious for the positive coordinates. Discuss the possible scores on question 3d.

Problem 2—Tilt!

Step 1 Distribute copies of *Tilt!* (page 64) to students so they can record their findings as appropriate during the instructional steps of this problem.

Note: Page numbers refer to the TI-Nspire file lesson03.

Explaining the Concept (cont.)

Problem 2—Tilt! (cont.)

Step 2   To construct the line on page 2.1, press (menu) and choose **Points & Lines** and then **Line**. Click on P and then Q when they flash. Find the equation. (See page 245 for detailed instructions on using the Coordinate and Equations tool.) Find the slope. (See page 244 for detailed instructions on finding the slope.)

Step 3   Students should recall the slope and the relationship between the tilt and positive and negative slope from Lesson 2. Ask them what is happening to the *y*-value when the line tilts up or down so that they will remember the terms *increasing* and *decreasing*. Make certain that they recognize the connection between the slope and the equation of the line and the *y*-intercept and the equation of the line. Emphasize that this form of the equation of a line is called *slope-intercept form*.

Step 4   Look at several different equations and *y*-intercepts. Substitute the value of the *y*-intercept into the equation and ask them what *x*-value would make the equation true. Emphasize that the *y*-intercept is the *y*-value of the point on the line where the *x*-value is zero and is the point where the graph crosses the *y*-axis. Have them graph some lines through the origin. (See page 243 for detailed instructions on how to use a text box to graph an equation.) Be sure to look at horizontal and vertical lines. Discuss what happens to the slope as the line nears the vertical and horizontal axes.

Step 5   Ask students what the graph would look like if the *y*-intercept were zero. Ask them how this relates to direct variation. Make sure they understand that the graph of direct variation is just a form of $y = mx + b$ where b is 0.

Step 6   Survey the students about Jamal's best scores. Have them describe how to achieve the best scores and how to recognize an equation that would yield them.

—— Step 2 ——

—— Step 3 ——

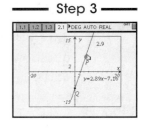

—— Step 4 ——

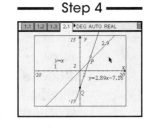

—— Step 4 ——

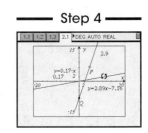

—— Step 4 ——

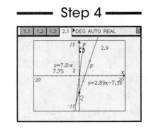

Note: Page numbers refer to the TI-Nspire file lesson03.

Explaining the Concept *(cont.)*

Problem 3—On Target

Step 1 Distribute copies of *On Target* (pages 65–68) to students so they can record their findings as appropriate during the instructional steps of this problem.

Step 2 In question 1, students should recognize the parallel lines on page 3.1. They should understand that the distance between them remains constant. They should notice that the slopes are the same. Help them recognize that the *m* in $y = mx + b$ is the same for parallel lines.

Step 3 Note: Steps 3–5 are all needed to complete question 2. For question 2, ask the students why the 90° is significant on page 3.2. Point out that perpendicular lines need not be vertical and horizontal; it is the 90° angle that makes the lines perpendicular.

Step 4 To find the product of the slopes, create a text box in an empty area on the graph on page 3.3. Type Ⓜ Ⓧ Ⓝ and press ⏎. Press (menu), choose **Actions**, and then **Calculate** to select the Calculate tool. Then, move the cursor until the hand hovers over the *m•n* and flashes. Press ⏎. To identify the variable, move to *slope1* and press ⏎. Then, move to *slope2* and press ⏎. Move the hand into a clear area of the screen and press ⏎ again to paste the product. Students probably understand the product of –1 but may miss the opposite reciprocal relationship when dealing with decimals.

Step 5 On question 2e, to change values for *m3* and *m4* on the upper-left side of the screen on page 3.4, click on the expression twice, edit the number in the text box, and then press ⏎. Although the students enter fractions, the handhelds will change them to decimals. Be sure students choose both whole numbers and fractions to reinforce the opposite reciprocal concept. Make sure they choose very large and small values for the slopes to demonstrate lines that approach horizontal and vertical. Ask the students to speculate on the slopes of horizontal and vertical lines. (Note: Inform students that the Ymin needs to be set at –27 to see point V.)

—— Step 2 ——

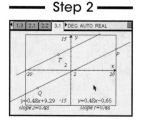

—— Step 3 ——

—— Step 4 ——

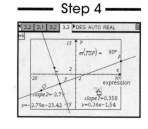

—— Step 4 ——

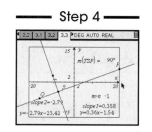

—— Step 5 ——

Exploring Equations of Lines *(cont.)*

Note: Page numbers refer to the TI-Nspire file lesson03.

Explaining the Concept *(cont.)*

Problem 3—On Target *(cont.)*

Step 6 For question 3 on page 3.5, remind students that the equation of a line can be written in the form $y = mx + b$. Ask them to find the y-intercept of $y = 4$ and to find the number for the slope that would yield the equation $y = 4$. Ask them to identify the equation of any horizontal line as having the form $y = b$. Explain that the equation means that the line has the same y-value for any x-value.

Step 7 For question 4 on page 3.6, demonstrate the construction of a perpendicular line by pressing (menu) and choosing **Construction** and then **Perpendicular**. Move the cursor until the x-axis flashes and press (enter). Then, move to the point until it flashes and press (enter) again. Ask the students what kind of line is perpendicular to a horizontal line. Ask why they cannot use the opposite reciprocal of 0 to find the slope. Most sources say that a vertical line has *no slope*, although others describe it as *undefined*.

Step 8 Explain to the students that the formula $y = mx + b$ does not apply to the vertical line because the formula requires that only one y-value can exist for any x-value, and it requires a definite number for m. Explain the formula for a vertical line (the x-value is always the same for any y value).

Applying the Concept

Problem 4—Lines, Man

Step 1 Distribute copies of *Lines, Man* (pages 69–70) to students so they can record their findings.

Step 2 Tell students to pay particular attention to the line labels. It may be helpful to make a transparency of the graph on page 69 and place it on the overhead to make sure students correctly understand which label goes with which line. This can be done by naming the line and then tracing the line with a marker on the overhead.

Note: Students do not need the TI-Nspire to complete the *Lines, Man* activity sheet.

—— Step 7 ——

—— Step 7 ——

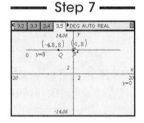

—— Step 7 ——

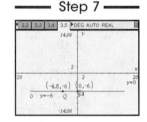

—— Step 8 ——

Exploring Equations of Lines *(cont.)*

Note: Page numbers refer to the TI-Nspire file lesson03.

Applying the Concept *(cont.)*

Problem 4—Lines, Man *(cont.)*

Differentiation Strategies

- **Below Grade Level**—Create an overhead transparency of the *Lines, Man* activity sheets (pages 69–70). Work as a group to answer the questions. Have student volunteers come to the overhead to shade the appropriate portions of the lines.

- **Above Grade Level**—After completing the *Lines, Man* activity sheets (pages 69–70), have students work in small groups to create a series of questions that, when answered, will produce a simple geometric shape on a graph. Students will need graph paper for this part of the activity.

Extending the Concept

- Ask students to find real-world examples of slope. Have them look for graphs in newspapers, magazines, and online that demonstrate positive and negative slopes with varying steepness. Have them discuss the meaning of the slopes on these graphs.

- Have students investigate the difference between velocity and speed and how they relate to the slope of a line.

- Discuss the meaning of infinity in relation to 1/0 or –1/0. Show that as lines approach the vertical, the slope increases (or decreases) without bound. Discuss the word *unique* as used in mathematics and how it relates to $y = mx + b$.

Name _____

Darting Around

Directions: Follow the steps below. The page numbers refer to the TI-Nspire file *lesson03*.

1. Jamal threw darts at a target that looks like the coordinate plane. His first four darts each landed in a different quadrant.

   a. On page 1.2, represent Jamal's darts by placing points P, Q, R, and S in the 1st, 2nd, 3rd, and 4th quadrants respectively. Use the Coordinates and Equations tool to show the coordinates of each point. Record your points below.

   P (,)   Q (,)   R (,)   S (,)

   b. Jamal's score is determined by the sum of the *x*-coordinates plus the sum of his *y*-coordinates. What was Jamal's score?

   _____

   c. Jamal realizes that the fact that the coordinates are positive in some quadrants and negative in others affects his score. Fill in the blanks below with + or – to show the signs of the *x* and *y* coordinates in each quadrant.

   1st (,)   2nd (,)   3rd (,)   4th (,)

   d. On page 1.2, drag each point around its quadrant to see if it is possible to improve Jamal's score and still keep the points in all four quadrants. How should the points be arranged to give him a good score?

   _____

   _____

   _____

   _____

   _____

Darting Around (cont.)

Directions: Follow the steps below. The page numbers refer to the TI-Nspire file *lesson03*.

2. Jamal thinks that his score might be improved if he were able to place points on the axes instead of just in the quadrants.

   a. Use the Redefine tool to place P and R on the *x*-axis and Q and S on the *y*-axis.

   b. What is true about the ordered pairs of all of the points on the *x*-axis?

   c. What is true about the ordered pairs of all of the points on the *y*-axis?

   d. Suppose Jamal must put two darts in different quadrants and a dart on the *x*-axis and a dart on the *y*-axis. In which quadrants and on what part of the axes will he get the highest score?

3. In another game, the score is determined by the total of the *distances* of the *x*-coordinates from the *x*-axis, plus the total of the distances of the *y*-coordinates from the *y*-axis.

   a. On page 1.3, construct a point M anywhere on the coordinate plane. Show its coordinates to two decimal places. Find the distance from M to each axis by measuring the distance. Drag the point around the plane (all four quadrants) and look at the relationship between the ordered pairs and the distances.

   b. How are the distances related to positive coordinates?

   c. How are the distances related to negative coordinates?

   d. If Jamal can position his four darts any place in the coordinate plane, where should he place them to get the highest score?

Name _____

Tilt!

Directions: Follow the steps below. The page numbers refer to the TI-Nspire file *lesson03*.

1. Jamal's algebra teacher invented a new game. The student throws two darts, and the score is determined from the line connecting the points. The score is the product of two important numbers that describe the line: its slope and its *y*-intercept.

   ── Step 1a ──

   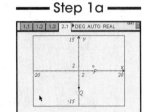

   a. On page 2.1, draw a line through points P and Q. Label the line with its equation and its slope. Grab and drag point P and notice the changes in the equation and the slope.

   b. Describe how the direction of the tilt of the line affects the slope.

   _____

   _____

   c. What does the slope have in common with the equation of the line?

   _____

   d. On page 2.1, show the coordinates of point Q. Drag point Q along the y-axis and watch the equation of the line. What does the *y*-coordinate of point Q have in common with the equation of the line?

   _____

   e. On page 2.2, drag points P and Q to find the equation of the line that will give Jamal the highest score.

   _____

Name _____

On Target

Directions: Follow the steps below. The page numbers refer to the TI-Nspire file *lesson03*.

1. Jamal will get extra points if he can put two pairs of darts on a pair of parallel lines.

   Step 1a

   a. On the page 3.1, drag points P, Q, and T. Watch the relationship of the lines and their slopes.

   b. What is the relationship between the lines?

   _____

   _____

   c. What did you notice about the slopes of the two lines?

   _____

   _____

   d. How can Jamal recognize parallel lines just by looking at them?

   _____

   _____

   e. How can he recognize parallel lines from their equations?

   _____

   _____

   _____

   _____

   _____

   _____

On Target *(cont.)*

Directions: Follow the steps below. The page numbers refer to the TI-Nspire file *lesson03*.

2. Jamal can get even more points from perpendicular lines.

    a. On page 3.2, the angle between the lines is m(TSP). Drag points P and T. Watch the angle and the relationship of the lines. What was the measure of the angle?

    _____

    b. What is the relationship between the lines?

    _____

    c. On page 3.3, create a text box and use the Calculate tool to see what happens when the slopes of the perpendicular lines are multiplied together. Use the variable *m* for slope1 and the variable *n* for slope2. What is the value of *m•n*?

    _____

    d. What is the product of the slopes of perpendicular lines?

    _____

    e. On page 3.4, create perpendicular lines by choosing fractional values for *m3* (the slope of line UT) and for *m4* (the slope of line UV). Watch the values of *m3•m4* and the measure of ∠UTV to check your choices.

    f. Give some examples of pairs of slopes that created perpendicular lines.

    _____

    g. What is the relationship between the numbers?

    _____

    h. How can Jamal pick perpendicular lines by looking at them?

    _____

    i. How can he tell from the equations of the lines?

    _____

—— Step 2a ——

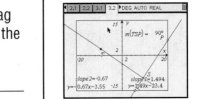

—— Step 2 c ——

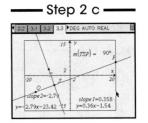

—— Step 2 e ——

On Target (cont.)

Directions: Follow the steps below. The page numbers refer to the TI-Nspire file *lesson03*.

3. Jamal can get the most points by hitting horizontal and vertical lines.

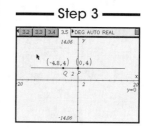

—— Step 3 ——

   a. On page 3.5, use the Coordinates and Equations tool to find the equation of the horizontal line. Use the Measurement tool to find the slope of the line. Slide point P up and down on the *y*-axis.

   b. How can you find the equation of the horizontal line?

   _____

   _____

   c. Move Q right and left on the horizontal line. What is the *y*-coordinate of every point on the line?

   _____

   d. What is the equation of a horizontal line with every *y*-coordinate equal to −3?

   _____

   _____

   e. How could you write the equation in slope-intercept form?

   _____

   f. What is the slope of a horizontal line?

   _____

   g. How can Jamal recognize horizontal lines from their equations?

   _____

   _____

   _____

On Target *(cont.)*

Directions: Follow the steps below. The page numbers refer to the TI-Nspire file *lesson03*.

4. On page 3.6, find the equation of line PQ.

_____

━━━ Step 4 ━━━

a. What is the slope of line PQ?

_____

b. Use the Construction tool to make lines perpendicular to the first line at points P and Q.

c. Use the Coordinates and Equation tool to find the equations of the vertical lines. What are the equations of the vertical lines?

_____

_____

d. Slide point P left and right. What is true about all of the *x*-coordinates of the lines?

_____

_____

_____

e. How can Jamal recognize a vertical line from its equation?

_____

_____

_____

f. Use the Measurement tool to find the slope of each vertical line.

_____

Name _____

Lines, Man

Directions: Use the graph below to answer the following questions.

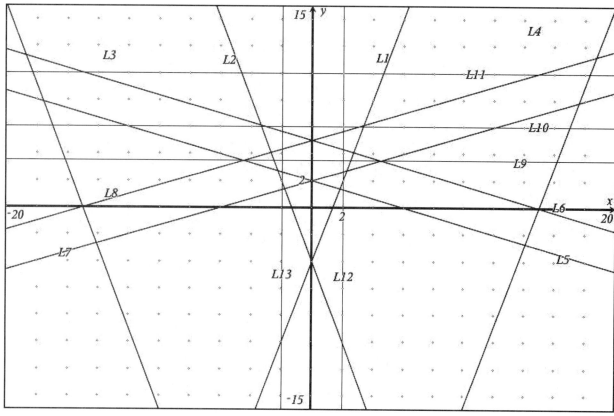

1. The slope of L_1 is –3. What is its equation? Shade the portion of L_1 that is below L_9.

   _____

2. The slope of L_2 is 3. What is its equation? Shade the portion of L_2 that is below L_9.

   _____

3. L_6 is perpendicular to L_2. What is its slope? What is its equation?

   _____

4. L_7 is perpendicular to L_1. What is its slope? What is its equation?

   _____

Lines, Man (cont.)

Directions: Use the graph on the previous page to answer the following questions.

---

5. L_3 is parallel to L_1, and L_4 is parallel to L_2. What are their slopes? Which lines are they perpendicular to?

_____

6. Which lines have a slope of 0? What are their equations?

_____

7. Which lines have no slope? What are their equations?

_____

8. Shade the portion of L_9 that is between L_6 and L_8. Shade the portion of L_8 that is below L_9 and in the second quadrant. Shade the portion of L_6 that is below L_9 and is in the first quadrant.

9. Shade the y-axis above the intersection of L_1 and L_2 and below L_{10}.

10. Shade the portion of L_4 that is between L_8 and L_7, then the portion of L_3 that is between L_6 and L_5.

11. Finally, lightly shade inside the square formed by L_{11}, L_{13}, L_{10}, and L_{12}.

Mathematics Objectives

- Students will use Point-Slope Form of linear equations to write equations.

- Students will use Standard Form of linear equations to represent mixture problems.

- Students will use x- and y-intercepts to graph lines given in the equations in Standard Form.

- Students will express equations in Point-Slope, Standard, and Slope-Intercept Forms.

Applications and Skills

Lists and Spreadsheets
Using the Fill Down Tool

Graphs and Geometry
Function Editor
Scatter Plot
Use of Text Box to Graph
Define and Use Variables
Function Table

Materials

- TI-Nspire handhelds

- TNS file: lesson04.tns

- *Money in the Bank* (pages 79–81; page079.pdf)

- *Walk a Mile?* (pages 82–84; page082.pdf)

- *What's My Line?* (page 85; page085.pdf)

Starting the Lesson

After loading the TNS file (lesson04.tns) on each handheld, begin the exercise by instructing students to do the following:

1. Turn on the TI-Nspire by pressing (off/on).

2. Press (⌂) and choose **My Documents**.

3. In the folder *Algebra TCM*, choose *lesson04*.

4. Remind students how to navigate through the TNS file. To move forward through the pages, press (ctrl) ▶. To move backward through the pages, press (ctrl) ◀. To choose a particular page, press (ctrl) ▲, position the cursor on the desired page and press (enter). To undo previous steps, press (ctrl) (Z) or (ctrl) (esc). Show students that any time they are using a menu that they wish to exit, they should press (esc).

Forms of Equations of Lines *(cont.)*

Note: Page numbers refer to the TI-Nspire file lesson04.

Explaining the Concept

Problem 1—Money in the Bank

Step 1 Distribute copies of *Money in the Bank* (page 79–81) to students so they can record their findings as appropriate during the instructional steps of this problem.

Step 2 Explain that on the day Jung decided to begin to save, his account contained no money. One month from that day, he deposited $25. When students write the equation $y = 25x$, the ordered pair (0, 0) represents the decision day and (1, 25) represents the day of his first deposit.

Step 3 On page 1.2, have students use a text box to graph the equation $y = 25x$. (See page 243 for more detailed directions on using a text box to graph equations.)

Step 4 Point out that the domain and range of the line $y = 25x$ are real numbers. Discuss the domain and range of the problem situation. Have students change the window settings. (See page 236 for detailed instructions on adjusting window settings.) Ask students if it makes sense to have a continuous line for this problem.

Step 5 Note: Steps 5–8 are needed to complete question 1d. In 1d, students should split page 1.2 vertically by pressing (ctrl) (⌂). Choose **PageLayout**, then **Select Layout**, and finally **Layout 2**. Move to the right side of the page by pressing (ctrl) (tab). Now press (menu). Choose **Add Lists & Spreadsheet**.

Step 6 To enter the names into the columns, use the NavPad to move to the top cell in the column. Use the letter buttons to enter *month* in the first column and *dlrj* in the second column.

Step 7 Enter the first two numbers in each column. Drag the cursor (press (CAPS ⇧) and use the NavPad) through the first two cells, press (menu) and choose **Data** and then **Fill Down**. Drag the cursor through the thirteenth cell. Press (≈ enter).

Step 8 Return to the graph side of the screen by pressing (ctrl) (tab). To enter the scatter plot, press (menu) and choose **Graph Type** and then **Scatter Plot**. Press (≈ enter). Choose *month* for the *x*-axis and *dlrj* for the *y*-axis. To move from the *x* drop-down menu to the *y* drop-down menu, press (tab). To exit the drop-down menu, press (esc).

—— Step 3 ——

—— Step 4 ——

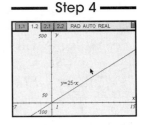

—— Step 5 ——

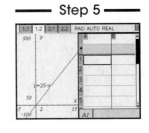

—— Step 7 ——

—— Step 8 ——

Note: Page numbers refer to the TI-Nspire file lesson04.

Explaining the Concept *(cont.)*

Problem 1—Money in the Bank *(cont.)*

Step 9 Point out the difference between continuous and discrete data. Ask the students which kind really illustrates Jung's savings.

Step 10 In 2a, to insert a row above the current data on page 1.2, enter the cursor into the first row in the far right column, and then move to the left until the entire row is highlighted. Then, press ⟨menu⟩ and choose **Insert** and then **Insert Row**. Repeat until five rows have been inserted. In the *month* column, the zeros in the new cells should be replaced with –5, –4, –3, –2, and –1.

—— Step 10 ——

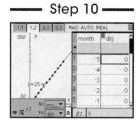

Step 11 In question 2b, students should configure the new scatter plot for Mita in *s2*. When they make the new scatter plot in 2b, it is important to emphasize that the *x*-coordinates for both scatter plots are the same. They should change the window to see all of the points. Ask students how the scatter plot for Jung's money changed. Ask them about the relationship between Mita's scatter plot and the original part of Jung's scatter plot. (Note: Split screens can get crowded quickly. Students may find it helpful to resize the column widths. To do this, move the cursor in a cell in the column you want to adjust. Press ⟨ctrl⟩ ⟨menu⟩. Choose **Resize** and then **Resize Column Width**. You can use the NavPad to adjust the width of the column. Remind students they can also hide the entry line by pressing ⟨ctrl⟩ ⟨G⟩).

—— Step 11 ——

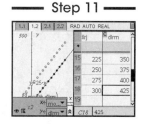

—— Step 11 ——

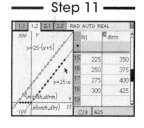

Step 12 In 3a, students can use the Fill Down tool for the zeros.

Step 13 In 3c, because Anya has been saving for three fewer months than Jung, the equation $x - 3$ makes sense. She began with $20, so at *months* = 3, she had $20 and thus, the ordered pair (3, 20). Help the students see that Anya's line is the same as Jung's, but shifted right 3 and up 20. Anya's equation should be $y = 25(x - 3) + 20$.

Step 14 Have the students graph the equation using a text box. (See page 243 for more detailed directions on using a text box to graph an equation.) Help students see that the new line is the same as the old one but shifted three units to the right.

—— Step 14 ——

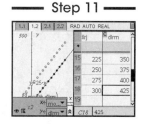

Note: Page numbers refer to the TI-Nspire file lesson04.

Explaining the Concept (cont.)

Problem 1—Money in the Bank (cont.)

Step 15   For question 4, explain to the students that the subscripts in the ordered pair (x_1, y_1) are identification numbers to match the coordinates to a particular point. The x_1 and y_1 are not variables. They represent the numbers in the ordered pair. Point out that the line is parallel to the line through the origin with slope 25 but has moved right 3 and up 20.

Step 16   Open page 1.3. For 4c, help students plot the point by instructing them to press (menu) and choose **Points and Lines** and then **Point**. Place the point in any convenient location and press (enter). Press (menu) and choose **Actions** and then **Coordinates and Equations**. Move to the point until the shadow of the ordered pair appears and then press (enter). Press (esc) and move the cursor to a coordinate in the ordered pair until it flashes and then press (enter) twice. Now you can change the coordinate to the desired value. If students have not previously used a text box to graph, instruct them to press (menu) and choose **Actions** and then **Text**. Press (◉) and type *y = 40x*. Press (enter) to escape from the text box. Press (esc) to exit the Text tool. Drag the equation and press (enter) when the line appears. When the crosshairs (✛) appear, grab the line in the middle and drag it until it goes through the point. It may not be possible to exactly fit the point.

—— Step 16 ——

—— Step 18 ——

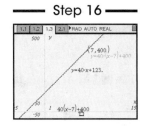

Step 17   In 4d, help the students simplify the equation in 4b to determine what the simplified equation of the line should be.

Step 18   In 4e, to help the students identify possibilities, show them how to add a function table. This can be done by entering the equation into *f1* and then pressing (menu). Choose **View** and then **Add Function Table** or press (ctrl) (T). Have students suggest possibilities and simplify them. Point out that they all simplify to the same equation in slope-intercept form.

Problem 2—Walk a Mile?

Step 1   Distribute copies of *Walk a Mile?* (pages 82–84) to students so they can record their findings as appropriate during the instructional steps of this problem.

Note: Page numbers refer to the TI-Nspire file lesson04.

Explaining the Concept *(cont.)*

Problem 2—Walk a Mile? *(cont.)*

Step 2   Review the formula $d = rt$ with the students. Emphasize that the units must agree. If the speed is expressed in miles per hour, the distance must be in miles and the time must be in hours. Discuss that this is an example of a rate. Look at some other rates, such as pay rate in dollars per hour or dollars per day, apartment rental in dollars per month, or gasoline used in miles per gallon.

Step 3   Help students write expressions for Andre's distances walking and running.

Step 4   On 1a, if students have difficulty writing the equation, help them by writing *Walking + Running = 18*, and then ask them to replace the words with the equivalent expression.

Step 5   In 2b, discuss why this point would be the *x*-intercept. In 2d, discuss why this point would be the *y*-intercept.

Step 6   In 2f, students should realize that two line segments having the same slope means that they lie in a line.

Step 7   In question 3, plot the points on the graph on page 2.1. (See Step 16 on page 74 for detailed instructions.)

Step 8   To draw the line through the points in 3b, press (menu) and choose **Points & Lines** and then **Line**. Move the cursor to one of the points on the far right until it becomes a hand (👆) and press (enter). Move to another point on the far left and press (enter) again.

—— Step 8 ——

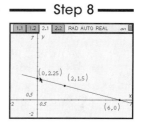

Step 9   In 3c, find the equation of the line by pressing (menu) and choosing **Actions** and then **Coordinates and Equations**. Move the cursor to the line until it becomes a hand and the line flashes. Press (enter) twice. Explain to the students that the handheld rounds the numbers in the equation it displays. If they want to check the actual slope of the line, have them measure the slope. (See page 244 for detailed instructions on measuring slope.)

—— Step 9 ——

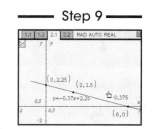

Note: Page numbers refer to the TI-Nspire file lesson04.

Explaining the Concept (cont.)

Problem 2—Walk a Mile? (cont.)

Step 10 In 4a, students are familiar with slope-intercept form for the equation of the line. Discuss its advantages. The slope and the *y*-intercept are visible, and it is easy to find values for *y* given the values of *x*. If you have discussed functions, you can also point out that it can easily be written as $f(x) = mx + b$.

Step 11 Note: Steps 11–13 are needed to complete question 5. In question 5, students will recognize the relationship between the coefficients in standard form and the slope and *y*-intercept. Have them try a few other equations for practice.

Step 12 Change the value of the variable by moving the cursor until the variable flashes. Press ⟨enter⟩ twice.

Step 13 On page 2.2, open a text box by pressing ⟨menu⟩ and choosing **Actions** and then **Text**. Enter the expression $\frac{-a}{b}$. Evaluate the expression using the Calculate tool. To do this, press ⟨menu⟩ and choose **Actions** and then **Calculate**. Move the cursor to the expression until the expression flashes and press ⟨enter⟩. Move the cursor to the first requested variable, press ⟨enter⟩; move to the second requested variable and press ⟨enter⟩ twice. To define the variable *slope*, press ⟨esc⟩ and then hover over the value until it flashes. Press ⟨enter⟩. Press ⟨sto var⟩ and select **Store Var**. Type *slope*. Open another text box and type the expression $\frac{c}{b}$ in that text box. Name this variable *yint*.

Step 14 Note: Steps 14–16 are needed to complete question 6. To move into the Function Editor, press ⟨tab⟩. Enter *slope•x+yint* into *f1(x)*. To enter the variable *slope*, press the ⟨sto var⟩ key and choose *slope* from the drop-down menu. Or you can type the word *slope,* and it will recognize it as the variable that has been defined. Repeat this step to access the variable *yint*.

Step 15 Have students mark the points of intercept. (See page 230 for detailed instructions on finding intersection points.)

Step 16 Use the Coordinates and Equations tool. (See page 245 for detailed instructions on how to use this tool.)

—— Step 14 ——

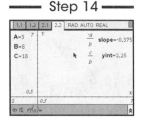

—— Step 15 ——

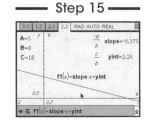

—— Step 16 ——

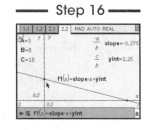

—— Step 17 ——

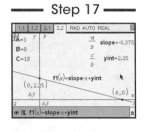

Note: Page numbers refer to the TI-Nspire file lesson04.

Explaining the Concept *(cont.)*

Problem 2—Walk a Mile? *(cont.)*

Step 17 Note: Steps 17–19 are needed to complete question 7. Add a function table. (See page 245 for detailed instructions on how to add a function table.)

—— Step 18 ——

Step 18 In 7a, have students discuss their different ideas about Andre's best strategy. The discussion will emphasize the meaning of the ordered pairs as time walking and time running.

Step 19 In 7b, after students have looked at various options, point out the advantage of standard form in having the rates for walking and running easily inputted and changed.

Applying the Concept

Problem 3—What's My Line?

Step 1 Distribute copies of *What's My Line?* (page 85) to students so they can record their findings.

Step 2 After completing the activity sheet, discuss how they could determine when to use point-slope and when to use standard form of the equation of the line.

Differentiation

- **Below Grade Level**—Write the point-slope form $[y - y_1 = m(x - x_1)]$, slope-intercept form $[y = mx + b]$, and standard form $[Ax + By = C]$ on the board or overhead so students can easily reference them while working on their activity sheets. Work through question 1 on *What's My Line?* (page 85) as a group. For parts a and b, have volunteers write the equations on the board or overhead. Have students work with partners to solve question 2. Check the answers to question 2 as a group.

Note: *Page numbers refer to the TI-Nspire file lesson04.*

Applying the Concept *(cont.)*

Problem 3—What's My Line? *(cont.)*

Differentiation *(cont.)*

- **Above Grade Level**—After completing *What's My Line?* (page 85), have the students exchange their answers with partners to see if their answers match. Once students have correctly solved both questions, have them work in small groups to create their own real-world problems using equations in point-slope, standard, and slope-intercept form. If time permits, the groups can then exchange papers and solve each other's problems.

Extending the Concept

- Create groups of students to work on the handhelds. Simulate making purchases involving mixtures of costs. Add the variables for slope and *y*-intercept to the TNS file before linking it to the students.

- Have students make up additional mixture situations and look at the lines that represent them.

- Discuss that the line in a mixture problem represents all possible solutions. Ask the students to use the graph to identify particular solutions.

- Compare finding the equation of a line using point-slope and substitution into $y = mx + b$. Ask the students when each of them is easier to use.

- Have the students investigate the 2-intercept form of a linear equation ($\frac{x}{a} + \frac{y}{b} = 1$).

Name _____

Money in the Bank

Directions: Follow the steps below. The page numbers refer to the TI-Nspire file *lesson04*.

1. One day, Jung decided to save $25 per month. One month later, he made his first deposit of $25.

   a. Using *y* to represent his savings, write an equation for how much money he will have saved after *x* months.

   _____

   b. Graph the equation on page 1.2. Be sure to choose an appropriate window. Sketch the graph here. Be sure to label the axes.

   c. Choose a window that will show Jung's savings for at least a year. What window did you use?

   _____

   d. Split the page vertically and choose Lists and Spreadsheets for the right-hand side of the page. Use the Fill Down tool to enter months 0 through 12 in a list named *month* and the dollars in Jung's account in a list named *dlrj*. Make a scatter plot using *month* on the *x*-axis and *dlrj* on the *y*-axis. Sketch the scatter plot below.

Money in the Bank (cont.)

Directions: Follow the steps below. The page numbers refer to the TI-Nspire file *lesson04*.

2. Mita also saves $25 each month, but she started five months before Jung. Insert five rows above the current data in the lists on page 1.2.

   a. How can you represent the months before Jung began saving? How much money was in Jung's account at this time? Fill in the blank spaces in *dlrj*. In a new list *dlrm*, use the Fill Down tool to enter Mita's savings each month.

   _____

   b. Make a new scatter plot using *month* on the *x*-axis and *dlrm* on the *y*-axis. Choose a window that will show all of the activity in Mita's account. What window did you choose?

   _____

   c. Because Mita has been saving five months longer than Jung has and she began with no money, the number of months that she has been saving could be represented as $x + 5$. So, we could write the equation of the line passing through the points on her graph as $y = 25(x + 5)$. Graph this equation. Does it pass through the points of the scatter plot of Mita's savings over time? What is the ordered pair that describes the point where Mita decided to begin saving?

   _____

3. Anya found out that Jung and Mita were saving money and decided to save $25 each month as well. She began three months after Jung, but she decided to put her savings in an account that already had $20 in it.

   a. Make a new list named *dlra*. Enter the amount in Anya's account over the time period since Mita began to save and make a scatter plot of Anya's savings over time.

   b. Look at the equation you wrote in 2c. Because Anya was saving for a shorter period of time, what would you write in the parentheses? How would you account for the $20 she began with?

   _____

   c. Write an equation describing Anya's account after she began saving $25 per month in the form you used for Mita's savings. Graph the equation. What is the ordered pair of the point at which Anya decided to begin saving?

   _____

Money in the Bank (cont.)

Directions: Follow the steps below. The page numbers refer to the TI-Nspire file *lesson04*.

4. The way you wrote the equation for Anya's account is called the *Point–Slope form* of a linear equation. It describes how to find the equation of a line if you know its slope and a point on it. Usually m is used for the slope and (x_1, y_1) for a point that the line passes through. Point-Slope form is written $y = m(x - x_1) + y_1$. Notice that the sign in the parentheses is a minus.

a. Ezra joined the savings plan with $40 each month, but he won't tell anyone when he did it or how much he had in his account when he started. He did tell the others that 7 months after Jung began saving, he had $400 in his account. Write an ordered pair that represents his account 7 months after Jung began saving.

_____

b. Use point-slope form to write an equation representing Ezra's account over time.

_____

c. On page 1.3, plot Ezra's point on the graph and graph the equation $y = 40x$ using a text box. Drag it so that it goes through Ezra's point. Enter your equation from 4b in the Function Editor. Are your graphs the same?

_____

━━━ Step 4c ━━━

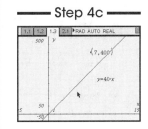

d. Simplify your equation from 4b. Is it the same as the equation from the line that you dragged?

_____

e. When is the earliest time Ezra could have begun saving? What are some other possibilities?

_____

_____

Name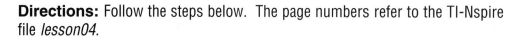

Walk a Mile?

Directions: Follow the steps below. The page numbers refer to the TI-Nspire file *lesson04*.

1. Andre tells his sister Sophie that he thinks he can travel 18 miles on foot in under 3.5 hours.   If he can't, he has promised to take her and her best friend to a movie of their choice. He is not sure if he can do it, and he needs to plan a strategy for walking and running. He walks at 3 mph and runs at 8 mph.

    a. Do you think he can do it? _____

    b. Let *x* represent the number of hours that Andre will walk. Let *y* represent the number of hours he will run. Write an equation using the variables *x* and *y* that shows that Andre's total distance is 18 miles. Use *x* to represent time walking and *y* to represent time running.

    _____

2. Suppose Andre walked the entire distance.

    a. How much time would it take him? _____

    b. Write the ordered pair (*x*, *y*) that would represent walking the entire way.

    _____

    c. Suppose Andre ran the entire distance. How much time would it take him?

    _____

    d. Write the ordered pair (*x*, *y*) that would represent running the entire way.

    _____

    e. Write the ordered pair (*x*, *y*) that would represent walking 2 hours. _____

    f. Find the slope of the line that connects the point in b and d and the point in b and e. What do you now know about the three points?

    _____

    _____

Walk a Mile? (cont.)

Directions: Follow the steps below. The page numbers refer to the TI-Nspire file *lesson04*.

3. On page 2.1, plot the points on the graph.

   a. Why do you think the points lie on a line?

   _____

   b. Draw the line containing these points.

   c. Find the equation of the line. _____

   d. On the graph, what do you call the point where he walked the entire distance?

   _____

   e. On the graph, what do you call the point where he ran the entire distance?

   _____

   f. What do you call the form of the equation shown on the TI-Nspire? Why is it useful?

   _____

   g. The equation that you wrote in 1b is another way to write the equation of a line. It is called *standard form* and is written $Ax + By = C$. Why do you think it is useful?

   _____

   h. How can you easily graph an equation in standard form?

   _____

4. It is possible to rewrite an equation in standard form as an equation in slope-intercept form and graph it that way.

   a. Solve $Ax + By = C$ for y.

   _____

   b. What expressions represent the slope and y-intercept?

   _____

Walk a Mile? *(cont.)*

Directions: Follow the steps below. The page numbers refer to the TI-Nspire file *lesson04*.

---

5. On page 2.2, change the value of variable *A* to 3, variable *B* to 8, and variable *C* to 18.
Define a variable *slope* and a variable *yint* using your answer to 4b. Use the Calculate tool
to evaluate them.

_____

---

6. Enter *slope•x+yint* into *f1(x)*.

  a. Use the Coordinates and Equations tool to find the *x* and *y* intercepts of the line. What
  are the intercepts?

  _____

  b. Do these agree with your earlier answers?

  _____

  _____

---

7. Add a function table. Change the window settings so that you can see the part of the graph
representing Andre's possible walk/run combinations.

  a. Do you think he can complete the distance within the time limit?

  _____

  _____

  b. Change the values of *A* and *B* (the rates at which Andre walks and runs) and *C* (the
  number of miles). How would that change the possibilities?

  _____

  _____

  _____

Name _____

What's My Line?

Directions: Use the TI-Nspire handheld to answer the following questions.

1. Five years after he purchased it, Jamar's car was worth $5,000. It had depreciated an average of $1,800 per year.

    a. Use point-slope form to write an equation that would represent the value of Jamar's car over the five years he owned it.

    _____

    b. Rewrite the equation in slope-intercept form. _____

    c. How much did he pay for the car?_____

    d. If the same depreciation rate continues, in how many years after its purchase will the car be worthless?

    _____

2. Chin is on an exercise program consisting of biking and swimming. At his weight and level of effort, he burns 493 calories per hour when biking and 563 calories per hour when swimming. He wants to burn a total of 1,500 calories in one session of exercising.

    a. Using b for biking and s for swimming, write expressions that describe how many calories he will burn on each.

    _____

    b. Write an equation in standard form showing that he will burn 1,500 calories.

    _____

    c. If he only swam, how long would it take to burn 1,500 calories? _____

    d. If he only biked, how long would it take to burn 1,500 calories? _____

    e. Rewrite the equation in slope-intercept using x and y. Graph it on your handheld.

    _____

    f. Add a function table and look at the possible combinations of biking and swimming. How would you schedule the exercise?

    _____

Systems of Linear Equations

Mathematics Objectives

- Students will solve systems of linear equations in two variables by setting sides equal to one another.

- Students will solve systems of linear equations graphically in two variables.

- Students will use linear combinations to solve systems of linear equations in two variables.

- Students will use matrices in reduced row-echelon form to solve systems of linear equations.

Applications and Skills

Graphs and Geometry
    Function Editor
    Intersection of Lines

Calculator
    Create and Store Matrix
    Matrix Operations
    Reduced Row-echelon Form

Lists and Spreadsheets
    Assign variables to list
    Use list in matrix

Materials

- TI-Nspire handhelds

- TNS file: lesson05.tns

- *How Old Are They?*
  (pages 92–93; page092.pdf)

- *It's a Secret*
  (pages 94–98; page094.pdf)

- *Kookie's Cookies*
  (pages 99–100; page099.pdf)

Starting the Lesson

After loading the TNS file (lesson05.tns) on each handheld, begin the exercise by instructing students to do the following:

1. Turn on the TI-Nspire by pressing (off/on).

2. Press (⌂) and choose **My Documents**.

3. In the folder *Algebra TCM*, choose *lesson05*.

4. Remind students how to navigate through the TNS file. To move forward through the pages, press (ctrl) ▶. To move backward through the pages, press (ctrl) ◀. To choose a particular page, press (ctrl) ▲, position the cursor on the desired page and press (enter). To undo previous steps, press (ctrl) (Z) or (ctrl) (esc). Show students that any time they are using a menu that they wish to exit, they should press (esc).

Note: Page numbers refer to the TI-Nspire file lesson05.

Explaining the Concept

Problem 1—How Old Are They?

Step 1   Distribute copies of *How Old Are They?* (pages 92–93) to students so they can record their findings as appropriate during the instructional steps of this problem.

Step 2   Remind students that to write an equation for *s* in terms of *r*, the equation should be in the form *s =*, with the variable *r* on the right side.

Step 3   For 1c, emphasize that it is possible to set the two equations equal to one another only because Sarita and Angela are the same age.

Step 4   In 1e, point out that the choice of variables is up to the student, but to graph them on the TI-Nspire you must use *x* and *y*. Show students the equations written as the system:

$$\begin{cases} y = 2x + 20 \\ y = 10x - 4 \end{cases}$$

Step 5   Note: Steps 5–8 are needed to complete question 2. In question 2, enter the equations into *f1* and *f2* on page 1.2. Show students how to access the Trace tool by pressing (menu) and choosing **Trace** and then **Graph Trace**. Use the right and left arrows on the NavPad to move along the function. Discuss the ordered pair that accompanies the trace cursor. Use the up or down arrows on the NavPad to show the trace on both functions simultaneously. Emphasize that the trace is showing the points on the graphs that have the same *x*-coordinates. The *y*-coordinate is the function value for each graph. As students trace to *x*-coordinates that are beyond the original window settings, the window will jump to show the new points. Tracing in the opposite direction will return to the window.

——— Step 5 ———

Step 6   On page 1.2, have students add a function table. (See page 245 for detailed instructions on how to add a function table.) Explain that the table shows ordered pairs on each line. Moving the cursor into the *f2* column enables the table to show values for both equations. To fully view both the *f1* and *f2* columns simultaneously, have students perform a custom split. Press (ctrl) (⌂) to display the Tools menu. Choose **Page Layout** and then **Custom Split**. The cursor will

——— Step 6 ———

Note: Page numbers refer to the TI-Nspire file lesson05.

Explaining the Concept *(cont.)*

Problem 1—How Old Are They? *(cont.)*

Step 6
(cont.)
change to this symbol (⊙) and the dividing line between the table and the graph will blink. You can now use the NavPad to drag the dividing line left or right.

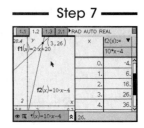
—— Step 7 ——

Step 7
Remind students that each ordered pair is a solution to the equation. Point out that the solution to the system is the ordered pair that is common to both equations.

Step 8
For 2a, explain that tracing is not a reliable way to find the point of intersection because the cursor may not land on the point. One way to find the point of intersection is to scroll through the table. Discuss with students that the point of intersection would occur where both functions have the same *y*-value at a given *x*-value. This may not appear on the table. The other way is to press (menu) and choose **Points & Lines** and then **Intersection Point(s)**. Move the cursor to one of the lines. When the cursor becomes a hand(✋), press (enter). Move to the other line and press (enter) again. Press (enter) one more time to display the point of intersection. Be sure that students identify the values as the ages of Sarita, Angela, and Roberto. Remind students to press (ctrl) (tab) to switch between the graph and the function table.

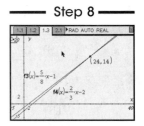
—— Step 8 ——

Step 9
In question 3, have students graph the equations in *f3* and *f4* on page 1.3 and find the intersection as in Step 8. In 3d, discuss the easiest way to solve the equation algebraically. Point out that the simplest way is to multiply both sides by the common denominator of the fractions and then solve the equation. In 3g, most students will think that the graphical solution was easier.

Problem 2—It's a Secret!

Step 1
Distribute copies of *It's a Secret!* (pages 94–98) to students so they can record their findings as appropriate during the instructional steps of this problem.

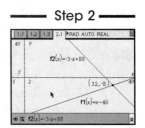
—— Step 2 ——

Step 2
In 1b, survey the students about their preferred methods.

Note: Page numbers refer to the TI-Nspire file lesson05.

Explaining the Concept (cont.)

Problem 2—It's a Secret! (cont.)

Step 3   Help students rewrite the system for questions 1g–1h. Explain that the system resulting from substituting the combined equation has the same solution as the original system and is equivalent to it.

$$\begin{cases} x - y = 40 \\ 3x + y = 88 \end{cases} \quad \begin{cases} x + 0y = 32 \\ 3x + y = 88 \end{cases} \quad \begin{cases} -3x + 0y = -96 \\ 3x + y = 88 \end{cases} \quad \begin{cases} x + 0y = 32 \\ 0x + y = -8 \end{cases}$$

Step 4   For question 2, help the students follow these steps:

$$\begin{cases} 3x + 2y = 10 \\ 2x + 7y = 1 \end{cases} \quad \begin{cases} 21x + 14y = 70 \\ -4x - 14y = -2 \end{cases} \quad \begin{cases} 17x + 0y = 68 \\ 2x + 7y = 1 \end{cases} \quad \begin{cases} x + 0y = 4 \\ 2x + 7y = 1 \end{cases}$$

$$\begin{cases} -2x + 0y = -8 \\ 2x + 7y = 1 \end{cases} \quad \begin{cases} x + 0y = 4 \\ 0x + 7y = -7 \end{cases} \quad \begin{cases} x + 0y = 4 \\ 0x + y = -1 \end{cases}$$

Step 5   Notes: Steps 5–8 are needed to complete question 3. For 3a, open page 2.2 and remind students that these equations are in standard form and that numbers in front of x and y are called the *coefficients*. The numbers without coefficients are called *constants*. The matrix is entered on a calculator page. Use the (tab) key to move between entries in the matrix. To store the matrix, press (tab) to move to the outside of the matrix, then press (ctrl) (sto→ var) (C) (≈ enter).

— Step 5 —

Step 6   Review Least Common Multiple (LCM) with students. Tell students that eliminating variables is easiest if you use the LCM, although any common multiple would work. In 3b, to multiply row 1 by 7, press (menu) and choose **Matrix & Vector**, then **Row Operations**, and finally **Multiply Row**. The command *mRow* can also be typed in. In either case, the syntax is mRow (factor, matrix, row). In this case, it is mRow $(7, c, 1)$. To store the results in a matrix, press (tab) (ctrl) (sto→ var) (D) (≈ enter). If students forget to store the matrix before pressing (≈ enter), they can press (ctrl) (sto→ var) (D) (≈ enter) and the previous answer will be recalled and stored.

— Step 6 —

Step 7   The TI-Nspire can combine, multiply, and add steps from 3c. Press (menu) and choose **Matrix & Vector**, **Row Operations**, and then **Multiply Row & Add**. The syntax is mRowAdd (factor, matrix, row to be multiplied, row to be added). In this case, it is mRowAdd $(-2, d, 2, 1)$. The row to be added is replaced by the sum in the new matrix.

— Step 7 —

Note: Page numbers refer to the TI-Nspire file lesson05.

Explaining the Concept *(cont.)*

Problem 2—It's a Secret *(cont.)*

Step 8   Students should be able to suggest how to complete 3d–3f.

────── Step 8 ──────

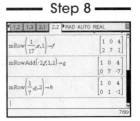

Step 9   For question 4, the handheld can automatically rewrite a matrix in reduced row-echelon form. Press (menu) and choose **Matrix & Vector** and then **Reduced Row–Echelon Form**. Put the name of the matrix in the parentheses. For question 4c, students need to use the blank matrix on page 2.3.

────── Step 9 ──────

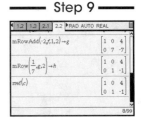

Step 10   Note: Steps 10–12 are needed to complete question 5. For question 5, discuss the dimension of a matrix as the number of rows by the number of columns. Look at the matrix from question 3. It has 2 rows and 3 columns and is a 2 by 3 matrix.

Step 11   To enter the matrix for 5a on page 2.3, press (menu) and choose **Matrix & Vector**, then **Create**, and finally **New Matrix**. The *newMat (2, 3)* creates a 2 by 3 matrix. Fill in the matrix by grabbing it. (Use the up arrow on the NavPad to highlight the matrix and press (enter).) Delete the zeros and replace them with the coefficients and constants.

────── Step 11 ──────

Step 12   Help the students put the equations in 5b into standard form so that they can be entered into a matrix. Students are most successful if they first multiply both sides of each equation by the denominator before attempting to solve.

────── Step 11 ──────

Note   See page 246 for detailed instructions on creating a new matrix. These step-by-step directions may be useful for students to have while working on question 2 in *It's a Secret!* (page 94). It is important to remind students to enter a comma between numbers when building a matrix in order to avoid error messages.

────── Step 12 ──────

Systems of Linear Equations *(cont.)*

Note: Page numbers refer to the TI-Nspire file lesson05.

Applying the Concept

Problem 3—Kookie's Cookies

Step 1   Distribute copies of *Kookie's Cookies* (pages 99–100) to students so they can record their findings.

Step 2   Have students complete question 4 in groups. Then have the groups trade the systems they created and solve each other's systems.

Differentiation

- **Below Grade Level**—Work through question 1 on *Kookie's Cookies* (page 99) and have students take detailed notes. Have students use those notes to aid in solving question 2. Students should work independently to solve question 3. Question 4 should be completed in small groups or as a class.

- **Above Grade Level**—Have small groups create a *PowerPoint* presentation detailing the steps they took to solve question 4 on *Kookies Cookies* (page 99). The *PowerPoint* slide show should include an original problem written and solved by the group. If time permits, each group can then share its *PowerPoint* presentation with the rest of the class.

——— Step 1 ———

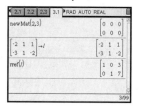

——— Step 1 ———

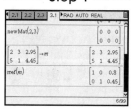

——— Step 1 ———

Extending the Concept

- Look at systems consisting of parallel lines and equations that are multiples of each other.

- Find solutions of nonlinear systems graphically.

- Have students use the elimination method to solve simple quadratic systems.

Name _____

How Old Are They?

Directions: Follow the steps below. The page numbers refer to the TI-Nspire file *lesson05*.

---

1. Angela and Sarita are the same age. Sarita's age is 20 years more than twice the age of her son Roberto. Angela's age is 4 years less than 10 times Roberto's age.

   a. Using *r* to represent Roberto's age and *s* for Sarita's age, write an equation for Sarita's age in terms of Roberto's age.

      _____

   b. Using *r* to represent Roberto's age and *a* for Angela's age, write an equation for Angela's age in terms of Roberto's age.

      _____

   c. Because Angela and Sarita are the same age, set the two right sides of the two equations equal to each other to find Roberto's age. How old is Roberto?

      _____

      _____

   d. Find Angela and Sarita's age. _____

   e. Rewrite the equation from question 1a using *x* for Roberto's age and *y* for Sarita's age.

      _____

   f. Rewrite the equation from question 1b using *x* for Roberto's age and *y* for Angela's age.

      _____

---

2. The two equations using the same variables represent a system of equations. Graph the equations on page 1.2. Look at the function table.

   a. Find the point of intersection of the two lines. This is the solution to the system of equations.

      _____

── Step 2 ──

How Old Are They? *(cont.)*

Directions: Follow the steps below. The page numbers refer to the TI-Nspire file *lesson05*.

---

b. What do the *x* and *y* coordinates represent?

_____

c. Which way was easier to find the solution: solving or graphing the equation?

_____

---

3. Connor and Lavon are the same age. Connor's age is one year less than five-eights of the age of his brother, Leon. Lavon's age is two years less than two-thirds of Leon's age.

a. Write an equation for Lavon's age in terms of Leon's age, using *x* for Leon's age and *y* for Lavon's age.

_____

b. Write an equation for Connor's age in terms of Leon's age, using *x* for Leon's age and *y* for Connor's age.

_____

c. Graph the equations on page 1.3. Find the point of intersection of the two lines.

_____

d. Set the right sides of each equation equal to each other and solve for *x*. What is Leon's age?

_____

e. How old are Connor and Lavon?

_____

f. What do the *x* and *y* coordinates represent?

_____

g. Which way was easier to find the solution: solving the equation or graphing the equation?

_____

——— Step 3c ———

Name

It's a Secret!

Directions: Follow the steps below. The page numbers refer to the TI-Nspire document *lesson05*.

1. Jason is trying to find the answer to the riddle, "What does a skeleton order at a restaurant?" The answer is in code. The letters in the message are determined by solving systems of equations and then using the corresponding letter from the chart in question 6. The first system is:

$$\begin{cases} x - y = 40 \\ 3x + y = 88 \end{cases}$$

Jason knows that he could solve each equation for y and set the equations equal to each other, or he could solve the system graphically. Try each method.

a. Solve each equation for y.

_____

b. Do you think that graphing or solving algebraically would be easier?

_____

c. Graph your equations on page 2.1. What is the solution?

_____

d. Jason knows another method for solving the system. He can solve the system by using linear combinations. He knows that he can combine the equations to find their common solution. Write the equations in their original form, lining up the like terms. Add the like terms of the two equations together. What is the resulting equation? (Notice that the y terms have been eliminated.)

_____

e. Solve the equation for x. Is this the same as the value found by using the methods above?

_____

f. One way to find y is to substitute the value for x into either of the equations in 1a and find the value of y. Do you get the correct answer by doing this?

_____

It's a Secret! *(cont.)*

Directions: Follow the steps below. The page numbers refer to the TI-Nspire document *lesson05.*

---

g. Another way to find the value of y is to eliminate the x terms. To do this, replace the first equation of the original system with your solution from 1e. Write it in the form $x + 0y = 32$. What can you multiply the first equation by so that you can eliminate the x terms?

_____

h. Multiply and then add the like terms together. What happens to the x terms?

_____

i. Solve the equation for y. _____

---

2. The next pair of equations that Jason needs to solve is $\begin{cases} 3x + 2y = 10 \\ 2x + 7y = 1 \end{cases}$.

a. He realizes that nothing will automatically eliminate when he combines the equations. He chooses to eliminate the y terms by multiplying all the terms in the first equation by 7 and all the terms in the second equation by –2. Why did he make this choice?

_____

b. Rewrite the equations, add the like terms, and solve for x. What is the value of x?

_____

c. Jason rewrote the system as $\begin{cases} x + 0y = 4 \\ 2x + 7y = 1 \end{cases}$.

How can he eliminate the x term in the second equation?

_____

d. Eliminate the x terms and find the value of y. _____

e. Rewrite the system in the form $\begin{cases} x + 0y = 4 \\ 0x + y = -1 \end{cases}$.

What are the solutions to the system?

_____

It's a Secret! *(cont.)*

Directions: Follow the steps below. The page numbers refer to the TI-Nspire document *lesson05.*

3. Your TI-Nspire can organize the steps in question 2. Begin by entering the coefficients of the pair of equations from 2a into a matrix. On page 2.2, enter the coefficients and constant terms for the first equation in row 1 and for the second equation in row 2 of the 2 by 3 matrix. Store it as matrix *c*. To eliminate the *y* terms, you need to create coefficients for the *y* terms that are opposites. The easiest way is to find the Least Common Multiple (LCM).

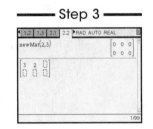

——— Step 3 ———

a. What is the LCM of the coefficients of *y* ? _____

b. Multiply row 1 by 7 so that the coefficient of the *y* term is 14, the LCM. Store the result as matrix *d*.

c. In matrix *d*, multiply the second row by –2 so that the coefficient of the *y* term is –14 and add it to the first row. Store the result as matrix *e*.

d. To solve the first equation for *x*, multiply the first row of matrix *e* by the reciprocal of the coefficient of *x*. Store the result as matrix *f*.

e. To eliminate *x* in the second equation, multiply row one of matrix *f* by the opposite of the coefficient of *x* in the second equation. Add this to the second equation. Solve the result as matrix *g*.

f. To solve the second equation for *y*, multiply the second equation of matrix *g* by the reciprocal of the coefficient of *y*. Store this as matrix *h*.

It's a Secret! *(cont.)*

Directions: Follow the steps below. The page numbers refer to the TI-Nspire document *lesson05.*

---

4. Matrix *h* is in reduced row-echelon form. The first row of this matrix will show the value of *x* and the second row will show the value of *y*.

1 0 *a*
0 1 *b*

a. Do these solutions agree with your solutions in question 2?

_____

b. Use the handheld to rewrite matrix *c* in reduced row-echelon form. Is it the same as matrix *h* ?

_____

c. Enter the coefficients from question 1 into matrix *p* on page 2.3, and use your handheld to rewrite it in reduced row-echelon form. What is the solution to the system?

_____

—— Step 4c ——

---

5. Finish finding the answer to the riddle by entering coefficient matrices for the systems and using reduced row-echelon form to find the solution. Each equation must be in standard form before entering the matrix.

a. $-5x + 4y = 11$
     $3x + 6y = -15$

_____

b. $y = \frac{5}{8}x - 1$
     $y = \frac{2}{3}x - 2$

_____

It's a Secret! (cont.)

Directions: Follow the steps below. The page numbers refer to the TI-Nspire document *lesson05*.

---

6. Write the *x*-coordinates and the *y*-coordinates for questions 1, 2, 5a, and 5b. Then, solve the riddle.

1 (,   ) 2 (,   ) 5a (,   ) 5b (,   )

−8	P		5	M
6	Z		7	O
−3	E		10	T
−1	R		14	B
0	L		20	V
2	U		24	I
4	A		32	S

"What does a skeleton order at a restaurant?"

Answer: A __ __ __ __ __   __ __ __

Name _____

Kookie's Cookies

Directions: Follow the steps below. The page numbers refer to the TI-Nspire document *lesson05*.

1. Jada, Aaron, and Liza stopped in Kookie's Cookie Shop after school. Jada spent $1 more than twice as much as Liza, while Aaron spent $2 less than 3 times as much as Liza. Jada and Aaron spent the same amount of money. Using x for the amount of Liza's purchase and y for the amount of the purchases of Jada and Aaron, write and solve a system of equations representing Jada's and Aaron's purchases in terms of Liza's. How much did each person spend? Page 3.1 can be used for calculations.

   _____

2. Hiro and Ben were also at the cookie shop. Hiro bought 2 brownies and 3 gingersnaps for a total of $2.95. Ben purchased 5 brownies and 1 gingersnap for a total of $4.45. Using x for the number of brownies and y for the number of gingersnaps, write and solve a system of equations for their purchases. How much did the brownies and gingersnaps cost? Page 3.1 can be used for calculations.

   _____

3. Mrs. Cullen bought cookies each Friday for 3 weeks. Each time she bought macaroons, shortbread cookies, and apricot bars.

Cookie Order	Macaroons	Shortbread	Apricot Bars	Total
Week 1	7	5	2	$9.55
Week 2	5	8	1	$8.65
Week 3	0	9	6	$9.90

   Using x for macaroons, y for shortbread, and z for apricot bars, write a system of equations for each week's purchase. Solve the equations. Page 3.1 can be used for calculations.

   _____

   _____

Kookie's Cookies (cont.)

Directions: Follow the steps below. The page numbers refer to the TI-Nspire document *lesson05*.

4. Erik and 4 friends are buying cookies at Kookie's Cookie Shop. They all select at least one cookie from each of the five kinds offered on the menu. None of the friends can place exactly the same order and each must have at least one odd number in the order.   Fill in a cookie order for each.

   a.

Cookie	Chocolate Chip	Oatmeal	Peanut Butter	Sugar	Snicker-doodles
Price per Cookie	75¢	50¢	60¢	40¢	55¢

Cookie Order	Chocolate Chip (x)	Oatmeal (y)	Peanut Butter (z)	Sugar (t)	Snicker-doodles (w)	Total Cost
Erik						
Sven						
Jasper						
Emmett						
Seamus						

   b. Enter the purchases on page 3.2 to see the total of what each of the friends spent. Write a system of equations for their purchases.

   ─── Step 4b ───

   c. Trade your equations with another group and solve that group's equations.

Coefficients and Exponents

Lesson 6

Mathematics Objectives

- Students will relate like terms involving exponents to area.

- Students will combine like terms.

- Students will simplify exponential expressions.

Applications and Skills

Graphs and Geometry
Drag Point
Collect Data

Lists and Spreadsheets
Manual Data Capture
Use of Formulas

Materials

- TI-Nspire handhelds

- TNS file: lesson06.tns

- *Be Square*
(pages 105–107; page105.pdf)

- *Combining Cubes*
(pages 108–109; page108.pdf)

- *Isn't It All the Same?*
(pages 110–111; page110.pdf)

- blank paper

- scissors

- rulers

Starting the Lesson

After loading the TNS file (lesson06.tns) on each handheld, begin the exercise by instructing students to do the following:

1. Turn on the TI-Nspire by pressing (off/on).

2. Press (⌂) and choose **My Documents**.

3. In the folder *Algebra TCM*, choose *lesson06*.

4. Remind students how to navigate through the TNS file. To move forward through the pages, press (ctrl) ▶. To move backward through the pages, press (ctrl) ◀. To choose a particular page, press (ctrl) ▲, position the cursor on the desired page and press (enter). To undo previous steps, press (ctrl) (Z) or (ctrl) (esc). Show students that any time they are using a menu that they wish to exit, they should press (esc).

Note: Page numbers refer to the TI-Nspire file lesson06.

Explaining the Concept

Problem 1—Be Square

Step 1 Distribute copies of *Be Square* (pages 105–107) to students so they can record their findings as appropriate during the instructional steps of this problem.

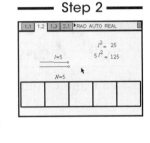

——— Step 2 ———

Step 2 Students often confuse how to combine like terms using exponents. Explain that the diagram on page 1.2 shows squares. To drag the point on the slider, move the cursor to the point. When the cursor turns into a hand, press ⌜ctrl⌟ ⌾ to grab the point. Use the NavPad to drag the point. The values will change as the point moves. The size of the squares and the number of squares will also change.

Step 3 In 1d, the students will be collecting data for the spreadsheet on page 1.3. Have the students look at the spreadsheet. Explain that column A collects the length of one side of one square; column B, the area of one square; column C, the number of squares; and column D, the total area of all the squares. Column E contains the ratio of the value of the number in column D to the number in column B.

——— Step 4 ———

Step 4 Have students return to page 1.2 to collect the data. To collect the data, have them press ⌜ctrl⌟ ⌜.⌟ after each change of l and N.

Step 5 To clear the spreadsheet, have students click on the formula row twice. If they accidentally delete the formula, remind them to press ⌜ctrl⌟ ⌜Z⌟ to undo their last step. As the data is cleared, some warnings may be displayed. The students should click on **OK**. In order to clear the entire spreadsheet, students must do this for the first four columns.

——— Step 5 ———

Step 6 Students will be completing steps for this exercise in groups. In question 2, each student will collect values for different values of l. When they finish, they will compile the data on the chart on page 107 of this book.

Step 7 In question 3, each student should choose an expression from the right of the square chart and show that the values from the chart support the combining of like terms. Point out that this is because the coefficients represent the numbers of squares of the same size.

Coefficients and Exponents (cont.)

Lesson 6

Note: *Page numbers refer to the TI-Nspire file lesson06.*

Explaining the Concept (*cont.*)

Problem 2—Combining Cubes

Step 1   Distribute copies of *Combining Cubes* (pages 108–109) to students so they can record their findings as appropriate during the instructional steps of this problem.

Step 2   This is a quick replay of the squares from the last exercise. The students should be able to complete this with very little direction. Emphasize again that the cubes are like terms because each l^3 represents cubes of the same size. Have students use pages 2.1 and 2.2 for this problem.

────── Step 1 ──────

────── Step 2 ──────

Applying the Concept

Problem 3—Isn't It All the Same?

Step 1   Distribute copies of *Isn't It All the Same?* (pages 110–111) to students so they can record their findings.

────── Step 2 ──────

Step 2   On question 2, ask the students why the size of the square changes. Be sure that they connect the use of the parentheses to the change in size instead of a number of squares. Discuss how many of the small squares would fit into the large square.

Step 3   On question 3b, discuss why the ratio is the square of the coefficient.

────── Step 3 ──────

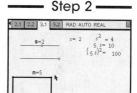

Note: Page numbers refer to the TI-Nspire file lesson06.

Applying the Concept *(cont.)*

Problem 3—Isn't It All the Same? *(cont.)*

Differentiation

- **Below Grade Level**—Allow students to complete the *Isn't It All the Same?* (pages 110–111) activity sheet in groups of three. Provide students with paper, scissors, and rulers so they can concretely construct the squares as a a representation of the ratios presented in the problem.

- **Above Grade Level**—Instruct students to complete the *Isn't It All the Same?* (pages 110–111) activity sheet independently. With remaining time, have students create their own sketches. Then have students switch their sketches with partners. Have the partners write expressions for the sketches.

Extending the Concept

- Look at geometric ways to represent terms like xy or xy^2.

- Discuss like terms in one dimension as line segments.

Name _____

Be Square

Directions: Follow the steps below. The page numbers refer to the TI-Nspire file *lesson06*.

---

1. Page 1.2 contains a diagram showing a number of squares, N, of a given length, l. When you drag the dot on the upper line, you vary the value of l between 0 and 5. Dragging the dot on the lower line changes the value of N between 1 and 5. N and l are always integer values.

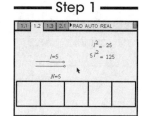

——— Step 1 ———

   a. What does $3l^2 + 2l^2$ equal? Why?

   _____

   b. Drag the open dots to the right and left to change the values of l and N. Sketch the diagram for $5l^2$ when $l = 3$.

   c. What are the values of l^2 and $5l^2$ when $l = 3$?

   _____

   d. Set $N = 1$ and $l = 1$. Collect the data from this setting. Leave $l = 1$ and change N to 2. Collect the data again. Change N to 3, 4, and 5, collecting the data after each change. How is each l^2 term represented on page 1.2?

   e. Look at page 1.3. Column A contains the length of the side of one square; column B, the area of one square; column C, the number of squares shown; column D, the total area of all the squares shown; and column E, the ratio of the total area (column D) to the area of one square (column B). Copy the data onto the chart below.

length	area	nsquar	totalarea	ration
Length L	Area 1 l^2	N	Area N Nl^2	Ratio

Be Square (cont.)

Directions: Follow the steps below. The page numbers refer to the TI-Nspire file *lesson06*.

2. Clear the data from the spreadsheet on page 1.3. Return to page 1.2. Have each member of your group choose 2, 3, 4, or 5 for *l* and repeat the data collection. Enter your data on the chart below. How does the ratio compare to the number of squares?

length	area	nsquar	totalarea	ration
Length l	Area 1 l^2	N	Area N Nl^2	Ratio

_____

_____

3. As a group, combine your data on the chart on the next page.

   a. Choose one of the expressions to the right of the chart. Simplify the expression, then evaluate it for two different values of *l*. Evaluate your simplified expression.

   _____

   _____

   _____

   _____

   b. Why do the exponents stay the same when simplifying $3l^2 + 2l^2 = 5l^2$?

   _____

   _____

   _____

   _____

   _____

Be Square *(cont.)*

Directions: Compile your data from question 2 on *Be Square* in the table below.

Length L	Area 1 l^2	N	Area N Nl^2
1			
1			
1			
1			
1			
2			
2			
2			
2			
2			
3			
3			
3			
3			
3			
4			
4			
4			
4			
4			
5			
5			
5			
5			
5			

$3l^2 + 2l^2$ $\qquad$ $4l^2 + l^2$

$5l^2 - 3l^2$ $\qquad$ $4l^2 - 3l^2$

Name _____

Combining Cubes

Directions: Follow the steps below. The page numbers refer to the TI-Nspire file *lesson06*.

---

1. Does $3l^3 + 2l^3$ equal $5l^3$? Why?

_____

---

2. Look at page 2.1. Drag the open dots to the right and left to change the values of l and N.

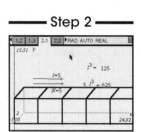

  a. Sketch the diagram for $5l^3$ when $l = 3$.

  b. How is each l^3 represented?

  _____

  c. What are the values of l^3 and $5l^3$?

  _____

  d. Set $N = 1$ and $l = 1$. Collect the data from this setting. Choose another value for N and collect the data. Choose a different value for l and collect the data. Choose one more pair of values and collect the data.

Combining Cubes (cont.)

Directions: Follow the steps below. The page numbers refer to the TI-Nspire file *lesson06*.

3. Look at page 2.2. Column A contains the length of the side of one cube; column B, the volume of one cube; column C, the number of cubes shown; column D, the total volume of all the cubes shown; and column E, the ratio of the total volume to the volume of one cube. Copy the data onto the chart below.

side	volume	nscu	totv	ratio1
Length l	Volume 1 l^3	N	Volume N Nl^3	Ratio

a. How is each l^3 term represented on page 2.1?

_____

b. How does the ratio compare to the number of cubes?

_____

c. Write three algebraic expressions that can be evaluated from your chart. Simplify the expressions and compute the value of each expression for the values from your chart. If needed, return to page 2.1 to evaluate the simplified expressions.

_____

_____

_____

d. Why do the exponents stay the same when simplifying $3l^3 + 2l^3 = 5l^3$?

_____

_____

Name _____

Isn't It All the Same?

Directions: Follow the steps below. The page numbers refer to the TI-Nspire file *lesson06*.

---

1. Does $(3s)^2 + (2s)^2 = (5s)^2$? Why or why not?

_____

_____

_____

---

2. Look at page 3.1. Drag the open dots to the right and left to change the values of *s* and *n*.

a. Sketch the diagram showing $(5s)^2$ when $s = 3$.

—— Step 2 ——

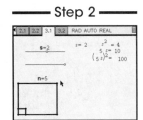

b. What are the values of s^2 and $(5s)^2$ when $s = 3$?

_____

c. Set $n = 1$ and $s = 1$. Collect the data from this setting. Choose another value for *N* and collect the data. Choose a different value for *s* and collect the data. Choose one more pair of values and collect the data.

Isn't It All the Same? *(cont.)*

Directions: Follow the steps below. The page numbers refer to the TI-Nspire file *lesson06*.

3. Look at page 3.2. Column A contains the length of the side of the small square; column B, the area of the small square; column C, the number multiplied times *s;* column D, the length of the large square; column E, the area of the large square; and column F, the ratio of the area of the large square to the area of the small square. Copy the data onto the chart below.

side	ssq	nside	lside	nssq	ration
Length Small s	Area Small s^2	n	Length Large ns	Area Large $(ns)^2$	Ratio $\dfrac{\text{Area large}}{\text{Area small}}$

a. How is each s^2 term represented on page 3.1?

_____

b. How does the ratio compare to the number of squares?

_____

c. Write three algebraic expressions that can be evaluated from your chart. Simplify the expressions and compute the value of each expression for the values from your chart.

_____

_____

_____

_____

_____

d. How is the ratio related to *n*?

_____

Pythagorean Theorem

Mathematics Objectives

- Students will investigate the meaning of the Pythagorean Theorem.

- Students will learn to create Pythagorean Triples.

- Students will use linear combinations to solve systems of linear equations in two variables.

Applications and Skills

Graphs and Geometry
Drag Point
Measure Length
Calculate
Store Variable
Measure Angle

Lists and Spreadsheets
Manual Data Capture
Use of Formulas

Materials

- TI-Nspire handhelds

- TNS file: lesson07.tns

- *Right Away!*
(pages 116–117; page116.pdf)

- *Pick Two*
(pages 118–119; page118.pdf)

- *Pythagorean Trivia*
(pages 120–121; page120.pdf)

Starting the Lesson

After loading the TNS file (lesson07.tns) on each handheld, begin the exercise by instructing students to do the following:

1. Turn on the TI-Nspire by pressing (on).

2. Press (⌂) and choose **My Documents**.

3. In the folder *Algebra TCM*, choose *lesson07*.

4. Remind students how to navigate through the TNS file. To move forward through the pages, press (ctrl) ▶. To move backward through the pages, press (ctrl) ◀. To choose a particular page, press (ctrl) ▲, position the cursor on the desired page and press (enter). To undo previous steps, press (ctrl) (Z) or (ctrl) (esc). Show students that any time they are using a menu that they wish to exit, they should press (esc).

Note: Page numbers refer to the TI-Nspire file lesson07.

Explaining the Concept

Problem 1—Right Away!

Step 1 Distribute copies of *Right Away!* (pages 116–117) to students so they can record their findings as appropriate during the instructional steps of this problem.

Step 2 Remind students of the labeling of the sides and angles of a triangle, using capital letters for vertices and lower-case letters for the opposite sides. Review the Pythagorean Theorem. Emphasize that in a right triangle, the right angle is understood to be C.

Step 3 For question 2 on page 1.2, drag point P. Remember, to grab a point press ⓒⓣⓡⓛ 🖱. Use the right and left arrows on the NavPad to drag the point. Emphasize that the Pythagorean relationship is only true for a right triangle.

Step 4 In question 2d, remind students that the solution to the equation requires the use of $\pm$, but the length of the hypotenuse is always positive.

Step 5 On page 2.1 for question 3, students should measure the length of a by pressing (menu) and choosing **Measurement** and then **Length**. Use the NavPad to move to side a. When the hand and segment BC appear in the figure, press (enter) or 🖱, drag the measurement to the left, and press (enter) or 🖱 again. Repeat for sides b and c.

Step 6 For question 3a, enter the expression by opening a text box. To do this, press (menu) and choose **Actions** and then **Text**. Move the cursor to where you wish to place the expression and press (enter). Type in the expression and press (enter). Calculate the value of the expression by pressing (menu) and choosing **Actions** and then **Calculate**. Point at the expression, press (enter), and then point to the values. Drag the vertices to compare the calculated length with the measured length.

Step 7 For questions 3a through 3e, repeat the steps above. Emphasize that the Pythagorean relationship is independent of the lengths of a, b, and c.

—— Step 3 ——
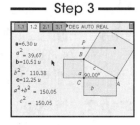

—— Step 3 ——
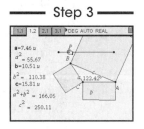

—— Step 3 ——
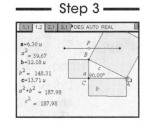

—— Step 5 ——

—— Step 7 ——
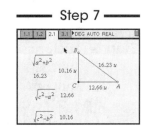

Note: Page numbers refer to the TI-Nspire file lesson07.

Explaining the Concept *(cont.)*

Problem 2—Pick Two

Step 1   Distribute copies of *Pick Two* (pages 118–119) to students so they can record their findings as appropriate during the instructional steps of this problem.

Step 2   In 1b on page 3.1, replace the values for *m* and *n* by pressing (enter) twice. Press (clear) to erase the current value and type in the new value.

Step 3   In 1b, evaluate $n^2 - m^2$, $2mn$, and $n^2 + m^2$ as in step 6 of *Right Away!* In 1d, to store the values, move to the value, and press (enter) (sto var). Choose **Store Var**, the letter of the variable, and then press (enter). The bold letters indicate that the letters stand for variables. (Note: When using the Calculate tool for this problem, the values will be stacked on top of each other. The students will need to grab and drag the values so that they are beside the expression evaluated.)

—— Step 3 ——

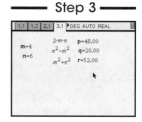

Step 4   To set up the spreadsheet on page 3.2, use the NavPad to move the cursor into the formula cell for column A. This is the rectangle under the name. Press (menu), choose **Data**, then **Data Capture**, and finally **Manual Data Capture**. Now, press (sto var). Use the NavPad to select *p*. If the handheld displays a message, use the drop-down menu to select *variable reference*. Press (enter) to make the selection and then press (enter) again to complete the choice. Repeat, putting *q* in column B and *r* in column C. Point out to the students that the columns also have names in addition to the letters.

—— Step 4 ——

Step 5   In 1h, point out to students that when they press (ctrl) (.), they are putting the current values of *p*, *q*, and *r* into the columns on the spreadsheet. Each time they press (ctrl) (.), they will collect another data set.

—— Step 6 ——

Step 6   Before students begin to work on question 2, remind them to press (⊗) twice to change the values of *m* and *n*. If they only press (⊗) once, the variable will be entirely deleted.

—— Step 7 ——

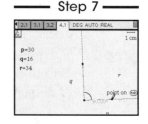

Step 7   In question 2c, the formula $a^2 + b^2$ refers to columns A and B. To enter the formula, click in the formula cell of column D and type the formula. Press (enter). In column E, enter the formula c^2. Press (enter).

Note: Page numbers refer to the TI-Nspire file lesson07.

Explaining the Concept (cont.)

Problem 2—Pick Two (cont.)

Step 8 On page 4.1 for question 3b, students should recognize the right triangle. Insist that they measure the right angle to verify it. To measure the angle, press (menu) and choose **Measurement** and then **Angle**. Click on the three points that make the angle, with the second point being the vertex of the angle. Press (enter) to display the measurement.

Step 9 For 3f, make a list of students' Pythagorean Triples.

Applying the Concept

Problem 3—Pythagorean Trivia

Step 1 Distribute copies of *Pythagorean Trivia* (pages 120–121) to students so they can record their findings.

Step 2 Have students construct objects to make square corners.

Step 3 Make a grid of the classroom and find distances between places in the room.

Differentiation

- **Below Grade Level**—Work through question 1 on *Pythagorean Trivia* (page 120) as a whole group. Then, have students work in smaller groups to create their own trivia problem. Supply students with yarn or string and a measuring tape. Students can then act out the problem using these manipulatives.

- **Above Grade Level**—Allow students to use a coordinate plane and construct their own right triangles. Encourage students to plot the points in quadrants 2, 3, or 4 and find the length of the hypotenuse using the Pythagorean Theorem.

Extending the Concept

- Investigate the converse of the Pythagorean Theorem.

Name _____

Right Away!

Directions: Follow the steps below. The page numbers refer to the TI-Nspire document *lesson07*.

---

1. What does the Pythagorean Theorem say about the side lengths of a triangle?

   _____

---

2. On page 1.2, drag point P to the right and left. Watch the values of a, b, c, $a^2 + b^2$, c^2, and the measure of $\angle C$.

   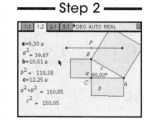
   ———— Step 2 ————

   a. When does $a^2 + b^2 = c^2$?

   _____

   _____

   b. With $\angle C$ set at 90°, drag point A to the right and left, and then point B up and down. As the values of a, b, and c change, what happens to the values of $a^2 + b^2$ and c^2?

   _____

   _____

   c. Describe the Pythagorean Theorem in terms of the areas of the squares.

   _____

   _____

   _____

   _____

   d. Solve the Pythagorean Theorem for the length of the hypotenuse.

   _____

Right Away! *(cont.)*

Directions: Follow the steps below. The page numbers refer to the TI-Nspire document *lesson07*.

3. On page 2.1, measure the lengths of *a*, *b*, and *c*. Let $a = \overline{BC}$, $b = \overline{CA}$, and $c = \overline{AB}$. Enter your expression from question 2d into a text box. Use the Calculate tool to evaluate it for the values of *a* and *b*. Drag points A and B and compare the measured length of *c* with the calculated length.

Step 3

   a. Was your solution correct? Why or why not?

   _____

   _____

   _____

   b. Use the Pythagorean Theorem to solve for *a*.

   _____

   c. Enter your expression for *a*. Use the Calculate tool to evaluate it for the values of *b* and *c*. Drag points A and B. Compare the measured length of *a* with the calculated length. Was your solution correct?

   _____

   _____

   _____

   d. Use the Pythagorean Theorem to solve for *b*.

   _____

   e. Enter your expression for *b*. Use the Calculate tool to evaluate it for the values of *b* and *c*. Drag points A and B. Compare the measured length of *b* with the calculated length. Was your solution correct?

   _____

   _____

Name _____

Pick Two

Directions: Follow the steps below. The page numbers refer to the TI-Nspire document *lesson07*.

1. There are sets of three numbers that have special properties. Given two of the numbers, you can find the third.

   a. Pick a whole number for n and a smaller whole number for m. What numbers did you choose?

   _____

   b. On page 3.1, replace m and n with the numbers from 1a. Then, use the Calculate tool to evaluate $2mn$, $n^2 - m^2$, and $n^2 + m^2$.

   c. What values did you get for $2mn$, $n^2 - m^2$, and $n^2 + m^2$?

   _____

   d. Store $2mn$ to variable p, $n^2 - m^2$ to variable q, and $n^2 + m^2$ to variable r.

   e. On page 3.2, set up column A to manually collect data from variable p.

   f. Set up column B to manually collect data from variable q.

   g. Set up column C to manually collect data from variable r.

   h. Return to page 3.1 and collect this data for p, q, and r.

   ——— Step 1b ———

   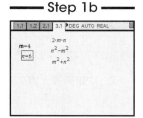

   ——— Step 1e ———

2. Change the values for m and n. Be sure that m and n are integers and $m < n$. Collect the values for p, q, and r.

   a. What are the values? _____

   b. Continue choosing numbers for m and n. Collect values until you have 10 sets of data.

   c. Return to page 3.2. In column D, enter the formula $a^2 + b^2$. In column E, enter the formula c^2. What do you notice about the values in columns D and E?

   _____

Pick Two *(cont.)*

Directions: Follow the steps below. The page numbers refer to the TI-Nspire document *lesson07*.

3. Choose two sets of values with small numbers for *p*, *q*, and *r* from page 3.2.

  a. What values did you choose?

  _____

  b. On page 4.1, change the values of *p*, *q*, and *r* to one of the sets of values you chose in 3a. What kind of triangle does this appear to be?

  _____

  c. Measure an angle to verify the kind of triangle. What is the measure of this angle?

  _____

  d. Try the other set of data. What kind of triangle is this?

  _____

  e. Look at columns D and E from the spreadsheet on page 3.2. How can you tell that all of the values of *p*, *q*, and *r* would create triangles like this?

  _____

  _____

  _____

  f. Numbers like this are called Pythagorean Triples. Use the rules from question 1 to find three more Pythagorean Triples.

  _____

  _____

  _____

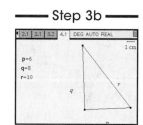

——— Step 3b ———

Name _____

Pythagorean Trivia

Directions: Use the TI-Nspire handheld to answer the following questions.

1. Emily and her father are building a deck.

   a. They need to make a square corner. Emily brings her father a rope with four knots tied in it as shown below. Why can the rope be used to make a square corner?

   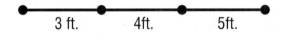

   3 ft.   4ft.   5ft.

   _____

   _____

   _____

   b. Use the numbers 2 and 4 to create another set of numbers that would work.

   _____

   c. They want to put a board for support diagonally across the deck as shown below. At what length should they cut the board?

   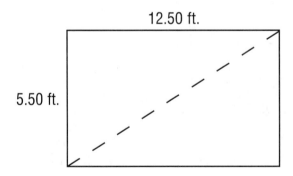

   12.50 ft.

   5.50 ft.

   _____

Pythagorean Trivia (cont.)

Directions: Use the TI-Nspire handheld to answer the following questions.

---

d. They want one portion of the deck to be a right triangle with a hypotenuse of 6.5 feet and one leg of 1.5 feet. How long should the other side be?

_____

---

2. Now write your own Pythagorean Trivia problem. Use question 1 as your model. Be sure to include any necessary sketches.

Generating Parabolas

Mathematics Objectives

- Students will express the area of rectangles in terms of distances in the coordinate plane.

- Students will generate quadratic functions from the area of rectangles.

- Students will develop vertex form for the equation of parabolas.

Applications and Skills

Graphs and Geometry
　　Drag Point
　　Trace
　　Graph Using Text Box
　　Function Editor
　　Scatter Plot
　　Manual Manipulation of Graph

Lists and Spreadsheets
　　Automatic Data Capture

Materials

- TI-Nspire handhelds

- TNS file: lesson08.tns

- *In the Area*
  (pages 126–128; page126.pdf)

- *A Moving Experience*
  (pages 129–132; page129.pdf)

- *Where Are They Now?*
  (pages 133–134; page133.pdf)

Starting the Lesson

After loading the TNS file (lesson08.tns) on each handheld, begin the exercise by instructing students to do the following:

1. Turn on the TI-Nspire by pressing (off/on).

2. Press (⌂) and choose **My Documents**.

3. In the folder *Algebra TCM*, choose *lesson08*.

4. Remind students how to navigate through the TNS file. To move forward through the pages, press (ctrl) ▶. To move backward through the pages, press (ctrl) ◀. To choose a particular page, press (ctrl) ▲, position the cursor on the desired page and press (enter). To undo previous steps, press (ctrl) (Z) or (ctrl) (esc). Show students that any time they are using a menu that they wish to exit, they should press (esc).

Note: Page numbers refer to the TI-Nspire file lesson08.

Explaining the Concept

Problem 1—In the Area

Step 1 Distribute copies of *In the Area* (pages 126–128) to students so they can record their findings as appropriate during the instructional steps of this problem.

Step 2 The figure on 1.2 shows a square whose size will be changed as point P is dragged. On 1a, emphasize the relationship between the *x*-coordinate of point P and the area. Help students think about the ordered pairs they are generating in the form (*x*, Area). Show them how to express the length of the square as the difference of $|x - 0|$ to represent the distance between *x* and the origin.

Step 3 On page 1.3, the scatter plot appears simultaneously as the students *slowly* drag point P. To move to the right side of the page, press ⌃ ⭾. To trace on the scatter plot, press ⓜ and choose **Trace** and then **Graph Trace**. Move from point to point using the left and right arrows on the NavPad. For 2b, discuss the relationships of the horizontal and vertical coordinates to the diagram of the square. It will be helpful to describe the axes as horizontal and vertical to emphasize the difference between the left and right sides of the page.

Step 4 For 2c, on the right side of the page, press ⓜ and choose **Actions** and then **Text**. Press ⏎. In the box, use the keypad to enter the formula x^2. Use either the ⓧ² or the ⓥ key. Use ② for the exponent. To graph, grab the text and drag it to the *x*-axis. The page displays the graph and its equation. Point out that the lowest point of the parabola is called the *vertex*. It is also possible to graph the function using the Function Editor, but with the limited space on the split screen, the text box is easier.

Step 5 To clear the data on the spreadsheet for question 3, move to page 1.4 and use the up arrow on the NavPad to move the cursor into the rectangle below the list name (the formula row), and then press ⏎ twice. The scatter plot will be removed, but the graph of the function remains on page 1.3. If a student accidentally deletes the formulas, enter the following expressions into the edit lines of List A and List B respectively: *capture('xc,1)*; *capture('areaa,1)*.

Note: Page numbers refer to the TI-Nspire file lesson08.

Explaining the Concept *(cont.)*

Problem 1—In the Area *(cont.)*

Step 6 Question 3 changes the width to twice the length. To change the value of n, move the cursor near the value of n. When the hand appears (☝), press ⏎ twice. Press ⌫ to remove the previous value and enter the new value for n. Press ⏎. Help the students write the formula for the area.

— Step 6 —
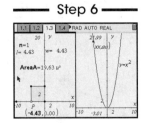

Step 7 In question 4, students should notice that the graph is narrower than the previous graph. Show students that it is also possible to drag a graph to match the new data. To do this, move the cursor to the parabola until this symbol (✻) appears. Then grab it and drag it. The equation is updated as the graph moves, but it is not very accurate. As students complete question 5, they should notice that the value of n determines the width of the graph. Help them compare the width to a standard of $y = x^2$. Explain that $y = ax^2$ is the standard form for the equation of a parabola with the vertex at the origin.

— Step 6 —
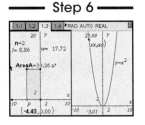

Problem 2—A Moving Experience

Step 1 Distribute copies of *A Moving Experience* (pages 129–132) to students so they can record their findings as appropriate during the instructional steps of this problem.

— Step 2 —
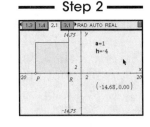

Step 2 Open page 2.1. Discuss finding the distance between two points on the x-axis as the absolute value of the difference of the x-coordinates. Help students see that the distance between point P and R is $|x - -4|$. With $a = 1$, this is the width as well.

— Step 3 —
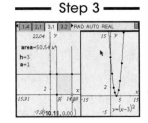

Step 3 For question 3, be sure that students try positive and negative values for h. Point out that $y = a(x - h)^2$ describes any parabola with vertex at $(h, 0)$. Look at equations like $y = -2(x + 4)^2$ and $y = 3(x - 4)^2$ to be sure that students understand that $(x + 4)$ is the same as $|x - -4|$.

— Step 3 —
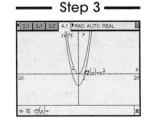

Step 4 Students should notice on page 4.1 that the y-coordinates for $y = x^2 - 4$ are all four units less than those on the graph of $y = x^2$. Have them drag the graph of $y = x^2$ until it coincides with $y = x^2 - 4$. (Note: The screen shot for this step can be found on page 125.)

Note: Page numbers refer to the TI-Nspire file lesson08.

Explaining the Concept *(cont.)*

Problem 2—A Moving Experience *(cont.)*

Step 5   On question 8, discuss the effect of the $k - 5$.

Step 6   Question 9 combines all of the earlier discoveries. Emphasize that the equation $y = a(x - h)^2 + k$ is called the vertex form of the equation of a parabola. Give students several equations in vertex form and ask them to give the vertex and describe the graph of the parabola.

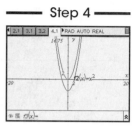

——— Step 4 ———

Applying the Concept

Problem 3—Where Are They Now?

Step 1   Distribute copies of *Where Are They Now?* (pages 133–134) to students so they can record their findings. Have students work with partners to find the solutions.

Step 2   Have the partners take turns giving each other either graphs or equations.

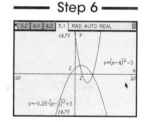

——— Step 5 ———

——— Step 6 ———

Differentiation

- **Below Grade Level**—Work through question 1 on *Where Are They Now?* (page 133) in a step-by-step manner. Have the pairs take notes. Ask for a volunteer pair to work out question 2 on the board or overhead. Have the pairs solve questions 3–8.

- **Above Grade Level**—After completing the activity sheet, have each student write an equation of his or her own and sketch two graphs. Only one graph should show the correct parabola for the equation. Have each student swap his or her equation and graphs with a partner. The partners should find the vertex and pick which graph is correct.

Extending the Concept

- Investigate the standard form of a parabola and its relation to vertex form.

Name _____

In the Area

Directions: Follow the steps below. The page numbers refer to the TI-Nspire document *lesson08*.

1. Look at page 1.2. Move point P to the right and left along the *x*-axis. The square formed has length and width equal to the distance between the origin and point P.

   ─── Step 1 ───

   a. What is the relationship between the length of the square and the *x*-coordinate?

   _____

   _____

   b. What is the relationship between the length and the width?

   _____

   _____

   c. Describe the relationship between the position of P and the area of the square.

   _____

   _____

   d. Write a formula for the area in terms of the *x*-coordinate. It does not matter if *x* is positive or negative when you write the formula. Why?

   _____

   _____

   _____

   _____

In the Area (cont.)

Directions: Follow the steps below. The page numbers refer to the TI-Nspire document *lesson08*.

---

2. On page 1.3, the diagram is repeated with a graph on the right side. The graph will display a scatter plot with the *x*-coordinate of point P on the horizontal axis and the area of the rectangle on the vertical axis.

—— Step 2 ——

    a. Sketch your prediction of what the scatter plot will look like and then slowly drag point P to the right and left.

    b. Trace on the scatter plot. What do the *x* and *y* coordinates represent?

    _____

    c. Enter the formula for the area from 1b into a text box and drag it to the *x*-axis. Does the graph match the scatter plot?

    _____

    d. The graph is called a *parabola*. What is the equation of the parabola?

    _____

---

3. On page 1.4, clear the data from the spreadsheet. Return to page 1.3. Change the value of *n* from 1 to 2. Move point P to the right and left and look at the length, width, and area.

    a. What is the new relationship between the length and the width of the rectangle?

    _____

    b. Write a formula for the area of the rectangle.

    _____

In the Area (cont.)

Directions: Follow the steps below. The page numbers refer to the TI-Nspire document *lesson08*.

c. How do you think the graph of the data from this rectangle will differ from the previous one?

_____

_____

d. Move point P slowly to the right and left. Enter the formula from question b onto the right side and drag it to the *x*-axis. How does it compare to the previous graph?

_____

e. What is the equation of this parabola?

_____

4. Clear the values from the spreadsheet on page 1.4 and return to page 1.3. Pick a number for *n* so that the graph will be steeper than the previous graphs.

a. What number did you choose for *n*, and what is the relationship between the length and the width?

_____

b. Write a formula for the area of the rectangle. Check your prediction by moving point P.

_____

c. In general, how does the value of *n* predict the steepness of the graph?

_____

_____

d. What is the equation of this parabola?

_____

Name _____

A Moving Experience

Directions: Follow the steps below. The page numbers refer to the TI-Nspire document *lesson08*.

1. On page 2.1, the *x*-coordinate of point R is determined by the value of *h*. The length of the side of the rectangle is the distance between points P and R. The width of the rectangle is determined by the value of *a* multiplied by the length. Page 2.1 begins with point R at (–4, 0) and the length equal to the width. Move point P to the right and left and watch the area change.

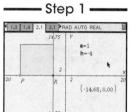

—— Step 1 ——

   a. What is the relationship between the length of the rectangle and the *x*-coordinate?

   _____

   _____

   b. What is the relationship between the length and the width?

   _____

   _____

   c. Describe the length of the rectangle in terms of *x* and –4. What *x*-coordinate causes the length to equal 0?

   _____

   _____

   d. Write a formula for the area in terms of the *x*-coordinate.

   _____

A Moving Experience (cont.)

Directions: Follow the steps below. The page numbers refer to the TI-Nspire document *lesson08*.

2. On page 3.1, the diagram is repeated with a graph on the right side. The graph will display a scatter plot with the *x*-coordinate of point P on the horizontal axis and the area of the rectangle on the vertical axis. *Slowly* drag point P to the right and left.

—— Step 2 ——

a. What are the coordinates of the vertex?

_____

b. Graph your formula on the scatter plot. Did it work?

_____

c. How does the *x*-coordinate of R appear in the formula?

_____

3. Clear the data on page 3.2. Return to page 2.1. Try different values for *h* and *a*. Be sure to try *h* = 0.

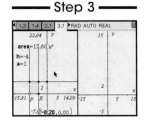
—— Step 3 ——

a. Choose a value for *h* that will give a formula of $(x - 3)^2$. Try it.

_____

b. Clear the data. Change the value of *a* to 2. How do you think this will change the graph? Will the vertex change?

_____

c. Try several values for *a* and *h*. Describe the graph of $y = a(x - h)^2$. Where is the vertex?

_____

A Moving Experience *(cont.)*

Directions: Follow the steps below. The page numbers refer to the TI-Nspire document *lesson08*.

---

4. Page 4.1 shows the graph of $y = x^2 - 4$ and $y = x^2$. Use the Trace tool to find the points where x is 0, 2, and −2 on both graphs. What is true about the y-coordinates of the points on $y = x^2 - 4$ as compared to those on $y = x^2$?

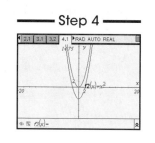

——— Step 4 ———

_____

_____

---

5. On a separate sheet of paper, sketch a graph of your prediction of the graph of $y = 3x^2 - 5$. Check it on page 4.2.

---

6. On a separate sheet of paper, sketch a graph of your prediction of the graph of $y = .5x^2 + 2$. Check it on page 4.2.

---

7. On a separate sheet of paper, sketch a graph of your prediction of the graph of $y = -x^2 + 2$. Check it on page 4.2.

---

8. Describe the graph of any equation of the form $y = ax^2 + k$. Where is the vertex?

_____

_____

---

9. On page 5.1, graph $y = (x - 4)^2 - 3$. What is its vertex?

_____

A Moving Experience (cont.)

Directions: Follow the steps below. The page numbers refer to the TI-Nspire document *lesson08*.

10. Sketch your prediction of the graph of $y = -.25(x - 2)^2 + 3$ below. Check it on page 5.1.

Name _____

Where Are They Now?

Directions: For each equation, give the vertex, describe it (wider or narrower than $y = x^2$), and tell whether it opens up or down. Then, give the letter of the matching graph. The graphs are located on the next page.

	Vertex	Describe	Match
1. $y = -x^2 + 4$			
2. $y = 3(x + 2)^2$			
3. $y = x^2$			
4. $y = 2(x + 3)^2$			
5. $y = -2x^2$			
6. $y = -4(x - 2)^2 - 3$			
7. $y = \frac{1}{2}(x - 2)^2$			
8. $y = x^2 - 4$			

Where Are They Now? *(cont.)*

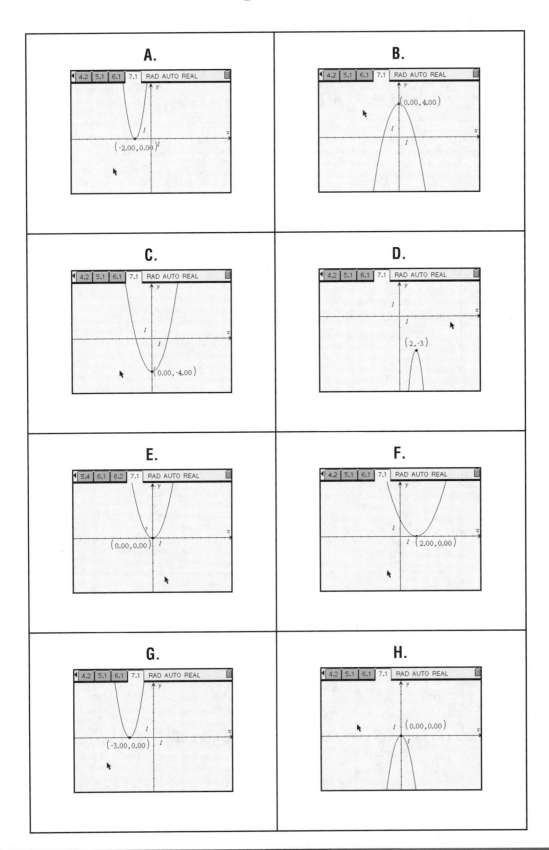

Mathematics Objectives

- Students will graph one-variable inequalities.

- Students will solve one-variable inequalities.

- Students will write one-variable inequalities.

TI-Nspire Applications

Graphs and Geometry
  Inequalities
  Coordinates and Equations
  Intersection
  Scatter Plot
  Variables
  Draw Ray
  Draw Line
  Graph in Text Box
  Perpendicular Line

Lists and Spreadsheets
  Formulas
  Sequence

Calculator
  Truth Test

Materials

- TI-Nspire handhelds

- TNS file: lesson09.tns

- *Glazed Over*
  (pages 141–143; page141.pdf)

- *Back and Forth*
  (pages 144–145; page144.pdf)

- *Carnegie Hall*
  (Practice, Practice, Practice)
  (page 146; page146.pdf)

Starting the Lesson

After loading the TNS file (lesson09.tns) on each handheld, begin the exercise by instructing students to do the following:

1. Turn on the TI-Nspire by pressing (off/on).

2. Press (⌂) and choose **My Documents**.

3. In the folder *Algebra TCM*, choose *lesson09*.

4. Remind students how to navigate through the TNS file. To move forward through the pages, press (ctrl) ▶. To move backward through the pages, press (ctrl) ◀. To choose a particular page, press (ctrl) ▲, position the cursor on the desired page and press (enter). To undo previous steps, press (ctrl) (Z) or (ctrl) (esc). Show students that any time they are using a menu that they wish to exit, they should press (esc).

Note: Page numbers refer to the TI-Nspire file lesson09.

Explaining the Concept

Problem 1—Glazed Over

Step 1   Distribute copies of *Glazed Over* (pages 141–143) to students so they can record their findings as appropriate during the instructional steps of this problem.

Step 2   Note: Steps 2–5 are needed to complete question 1b. On page 1.2, in the formula cell titled *dozen*, enter in the number of dozens by using a sequence. Move the cursor into the cell below the title (the formula row) and press ⟨enter⟩ or ⟨≈⟩ and *dozen:=* will appear in the cell. Type in *seq(n,n,25,300,25)* and press ⟨enter⟩. This creates a sequence that begins at 25, ends at 300, and increases in steps of 25. The first *n* of *n,n* denotes the expression. The second indicates the variable. (If you used *2n,n* the sequence would be completed with 1•2•25 = 50, 2•2•25 = 100, then 3•2•25 = 150, etc.)

—— Step 2 ——

Step 3   Help students generate the formula *cost=2.75•dozen*. Type in the formula by moving to the formula row and pressing ⟨enter⟩ or ⟨≈⟩. Have students type *2.75×dozen* and press ⟨enter⟩. (The names of the columns are also available by pressing ⟨sto var⟩. Use the NavPad to move to the desired variable and press ⟨enter⟩.) The column for income is titled *salesd*. Type in the formula *salesd:=3×dozen*.

—— Step 3 ——

Step 4   Discuss the meaning of profit as the difference of the income and the costs. So long as this is positive, it is a profit. Help the students enter the formula *profit:=salesd–cost*.

—— Step 4 ——

Step 5   For question 1b, show students that changing the number for the price of a dozen in the *salesd* column updates the *profit* column as well. After they look at the effect of changing the price, make sure they set the price at $5 per dozen.

Step 6   Note: Steps 6–9 are all a part of question 1c and are needed to complete 1d. For question 1c, remind the students to press ⟨ctrl⟩ ⟨I⟩ to insert a new page and to choose **Add Graphs & Geometry**. To set the graph mode to scatter plot, press ⟨menu⟩ and choose **Graph Type** and then **Scatter Plot**. To choose the list for *x*, press ⟨≈⟩ and then use the NavPad to move to *dozen*. Press ⟨≈⟩ to select the list. Press ⟨tab⟩ to move to the *y* list. Select *profit* for this list. (Note: It was necessary to name the columns on the spreadsheet so that they could be selected for the scatter plot.)

—— Step 6 ——

Note: Page numbers refer to the TI-Nspire file lesson09.

Explaining the Concept *(cont.)*

Problem 1—Glazed Over *(cont.)*

Step 7 You can hide the scatter plot entry line by pressing (ctrl)(G). Remind the students that pressing (menu) and choosing **Window** and then **Zoom–Data** automatically creates a suitable window for the data. Draw a line through the data points by pressing (menu) and choosing **Points & Lines** and then **Line**. Move the cursor to any data point and press (enter) or (⌘). Then, move to another data point and press (enter) or (⌘) again. Press (esc) to exit the menu. Depending on the points selected, the line may not extend through all of the points. It will become longer when you use it to find the point of intersection in Step 11.

Step 8 Discuss why the data is linear. Find the equation of the line. (See page 245 for more detailed instructions on using the Coordinates and Equations tool.) Discuss why the slope of the line is 2.25. The *y*-intercept may be displayed in the form of *1.16E-12*. Explain that this means $1.16 \cdot 10^{-12}$ and that this happens because TI-Nspire technology uses very good approximations rather than using algebra to find the equation of the line. Ask them why the *y*-intercept is really zero.

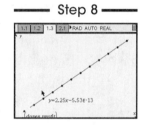

——— Step 8 ———

Step 9 Type the equation *y > 260* in a text box. (See page 243 for detailed instructions on how to use a text box to graph an equation.) Ask the students why the shading appears above the line. Emphasize that it is shaded above because that is where the *y*-values are greater than 260.

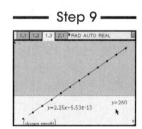

——— Step 9 ———

Step 10 Discuss the ordered pairs of the scatter plot above the line *y* = 260 and below it. Ask which points indicate a profit of more than $260.

Step 11 Find the point of intersection of the lines. (See page 230 for detailed instructions on finding an intersection point.) Find the coordinate of the point. (See page 234 for detailed instructions on finding the coordinates of a point.) Look at the *x*-coordinate of the point compared to the *y*-coordinate of the point of intersection. Remind students that they could find the *x*-value by solving the equation $2.25x = 260$.

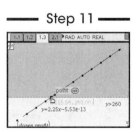

——— Step 11 ———

Note: Page numbers refer to the TI-Nspire file lesson09.

Explaining the Concept *(cont.)*

Problem 1—Glazed Over *(cont.)*

Step 12 In 1f, to draw a vertical line through the point of intersection, press (menu) and choose **Constructions** then **Perpendicular**. Point to the *x*-axis and press (⌖) and then to the point of intersection of the lines. Press (⌖) again. If students have trouble finding the *x*-axis, remind them to press (ctrl) (G) to remove the scatter plot entry line. Use the Coordinates and Equations tool to find the equation of the vertical line. Point out that that the points to the right of the vertical line have *x*-coordinates greater than 115.56. Describe which values of *x* are associated with profits above $260. Show the students how to write the inequality $x > 115.56$. Ask them what inequality they could write using whole numbers. Point out that so long as whole dozens of doughnuts are involved, the relationship could be expressed as $x \geq 120$.

Step 13 In question 1i, discuss that solving $2.25x > 260$ is the same as solving $2.25x = 260$.

Step 14 In 1j, find the *x*-intercept of the vertical line by finding its intersection with the *x*-axis. (See step 11.) Draw the ray along the *x*-axis going right from the *x*-intercept. Press (menu) and choose **Points & Lines** and then **Ray**. Begin on the *x*-intercept and click on the *x*-axis near the edge of the screen. Hover over the ray and press (ctrl) (menu) and then choose **Attributes**. Click the triangle on the upper square until the line weight is thick to illustrate the ray.

Step 15 Graph the solution to the inequality $x > 115.56$ on a number line. Point out that an open circle is used because of > and a closed circle, indicating inclusion of the point would be used if it were ≥. Discuss that any point on the ray is a solution to the inequality, but only integers and multiples of 12 could be solutions to the doughnut problem.

115.56

— Step 12 —

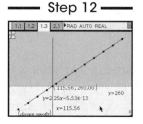
— Step 12 —

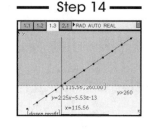
— Step 14 —

Note: Page numbers refer to the TI-Nspire file lesson09.

Explaining the Concept *(cont.)*

Problem 1—Glazed Over *(cont.)*

Step 16 Discuss all of the ways that students can show the solution to the equation: With the intersection of $y = 2.25x$ and $y = 260$ and shading above the horizontal line; with the vertical line, indicating all the points to the right; and the number line. Discuss checking a solution on the calculator page with *true* indicating a solution and *false* indicating not a solution.

— Step 16 —

Problem 2—Back and Forth

Step 1 Distribute copies of *Back and Forth* (pages 144–145) to students so they can record their findings as appropriate during the instructional steps of this problem.

Step 2 Have the students look at the values of A and B and their relative positions on page 2.2. Help them write the inequalities. Emphasize the connection of the right/left orientation with the correct inequality sign. Ask them to write all of the inequalities in this exercise with A first.

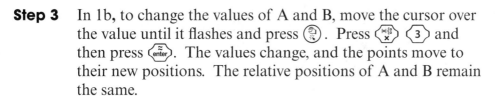
— Step 3 —

Step 3 In 1b, to change the values of A and B, move the cursor over the value until it flashes and press ⊙. Press ⊠ ③ and then press ⏎. The values change, and the points move to their new positions. The relative positions of A and B remain the same.

— Step 4 —

Step 4 In 1c, the relative positions of A and B are switched. B is now on the left, and the inequality is now A > B. (Note: The window has to be changed to Xmin = –60 and Xmax = 5.)

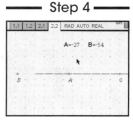
— Step 5 —

Step 5 Have students repeat 1b and 1c with division instead of multiplication. They do not need to write all the inequalities, but rather just describe the effect. After repeating Step 1c, the window settings need to be Xmin = –10 and Xmax = 10.

Step 6 Question 2 repeats question 1 using one positive and one negative number. Question 3 repeats question 1 using two negative numbers. Emphasize that the sign of the factor or divisor determines when the inequality sign is reversed. The negative number reverses the right/left relationship.

— Step 6 —

Note: Page numbers refer to the TI-Nspire file lesson09.

Explaining the Concept (cont.)

Problem 2—Back and Forth (cont.)

Step 7   Ask the students if they think that adding or subtracting will reverse the inequality signs. Have them try adding and subtracting positive and negative numbers to reinforce that it is only multiplying and dividing by negative numbers that reverses inequalities.

Applying the Concept

Problem 3—Carnegie Hall (Practice, Practice, Practice)

Step 1   Distribute copies of *Carnegie Hall (Practice, Practice, Practice)* (page 146) to students so they can record their findings.

Step 2   Have students solve each inequality graphically and algebraically.

Note: To graph in a text box, they must use the variable x. For questions 3 and 4, instruct them to graph the two sides of each inequality and then identify where the correct graph is. Remind them that they may have to change the window settings to see the points of intersection.

Differentiation

- **Below Grade Level**—Solve questions 1 and 3 on *Carnegie Hall (Practice, Practice, Practice)* (page 146) as a group. Then have students work in pairs to solve questions 2 and 4.

- **Above Grade Level**—After completing *Carnegie Hall (Practice, Practice, Practice)* (page 146), have students create a How-To Guide for solving question 4. They should include detailed step-by-step instructions and pictures showing how they solved the inequality.

Extending the Concept

- Investigate the intersection and union of inequalities.

Name _____

Glazed Over

Directions: Follow the steps below. The page numbers refer to the TI-Nspire document *lesson09*.

The Brookville PTA is planning a fundraiser. They are going to sell Crunchy Crisp doughnuts on a Saturday morning outside the football stadium of the local university. If they order any number of glazed doughnuts between 25 dozen and 300 dozen, their cost for the doughnuts will be $2.75 per dozen. They need to decide how much to charge for the doughnuts and how many to order. They would like to make more than $260. They plan to sell all of the doughnuts they order.

1. On page 1.2, in column A *(dozen)*, enter a formula that will enter values between 25 and 300, increasing by 25 in each cell. In column B *(cost)*, enter a formula for the cost of purchasing that number of dozens of doughnuts. In column C, *(salesd)*, write a formula for the total number of dollars taken in from the sale. Start with a price of $3 per dozen. In column D, *(profit)*, write a formula for the profit from the sale.

    Step 1

1.1	1.2	2.1	2.2	RAD AUTO REAL
dozen	cost	salesd	profit	
=seq(n,n,2				
25				
50				
75				
100				
125				
B1				

    a. What are your formulas?

    _____

    _____

    _____

    _____

    b. The fundraising committee is considering charging $3.00 per dozen doughnuts. Use the spreadsheet data to explain why the goal will not be reached by doing this.

    _____

    _____

    _____

    _____

    _____

    _____

Glazed Over (cont.)

Directions: Follow the steps below. The page numbers refer to the TI-Nspire document *lesson09*.

c. Insert a new page and make a scatter plot. Use *dozen* for the *x*-axis and *profit* for the *y*-axis. In a text box, enter the inequality $y > 260$ and drag it to the *x*-axis to graph it. Draw a line through the data points. Why is the shading above the line?

_____

_____

_____

d. Where are the points of the scatter plot that indicate the profit is more than $260?

_____

e. What is the intersection of the lines? Which portion of the scatter plot indicates the values for which the profit is greater than $260?

_____

f. Draw a vertical line through the point of intersection and find its equation. On which side of the vertical line do all of the points of the solution lie? Write an inequality for these *x*-values. How could you find this number algebraically?

_____

g. On which side of the vertical line do all of the solutions of $2.25x > 260$ lie?

_____

h. Write an inequality that describes the *x*-values of the points for which the profit would be more than $260.

_____

i. How can you solve the inequality $2.25x > 260$ algebraically? How does it differ from solving $2.25x = 260$?

_____

_____

Glazed Over (cont.)

Directions: Follow the steps below. The page numbers refer to the TI-Nspire document *lesson09.*

j. Find the *x*-intercept of the vertical line. What do all of the points to the right of the *x*-intercept represent? Draw the ray pointing to the right along the *x*-axis that starts at the *x*-intercept. What is true about all the *x*-values on the ray?

_____

_____

_____

k. Make a number-line sketch of the solution.

l. Is *x* = 120 a solution to the inequality 2.25*x* > 260? Insert a calculator page and type in 2.25•120 > 260. What happens when you press enter? What does it mean?

_____

_____

_____

m. What will happen when you try 2.25•120 < 260?

_____

_____

Name _____

Back and Forth

Directions: Follow the steps below. The page numbers refer to the TI-Nspire document *lesson09*.

1. Move to page 2.2. Write all inequalities with the value of A on the left side.

— Step 1 —

a. Write an inequality using 3 and 6 and another using A and B. On the number line, which point is on the left, point A or point B?

_____

_____

_____

b. Multiply the values of A and B times 3 and rewrite the inequalities. On the number line, which point is on the left, point A or point B?

_____

_____

_____

c. Multiply the values of A and B times −3 and rewrite the inequalities. On the number line, which point is on the left, point A or point B?

_____

_____

_____

d. Repeat steps b and c using division instead of multiplication. What happened when you multiplied or divided by a negative number?

_____

_____

_____

Back and Forth (cont.)

Directions: Follow the steps below. The page numbers refer to the TI-Nspire document *lesson09*.

---

2. On page 2.2, change the value of A to –4 and the value of B to 2.

   ─── Step 2 ───

   a. Write an inequality using –4 and 2 and another using A and B. On the number line, which point is on the left, point A or point B?

   _____

   _____

   b. Multiply the values of A and B times 2 and rewrite the inequalities. On the number line, which point is on the left, point A or point B?

   _____

   _____

   c. Multiply the values of A and B times –2 and rewrite the inequalities. On the number line, which point is on the left, point A or point B?

   _____

   _____

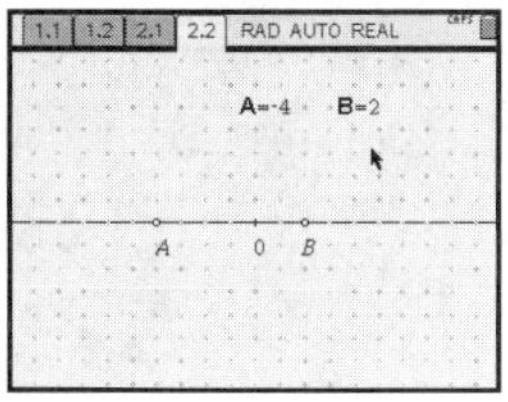

3. On page 2.2, change the value of A to –8 and the value of B to –4. Look at the effect of multiplying and dividing the values of A and B by positive and negative numbers. What causes an inequality sign to be reversed?

   _____

   _____

   _____

   _____

Name _____

Carnegie Hall (Practice, Practice, Practice)

Directions: Solve each inequality algebraically and graphically. Show all of the steps and sketch the graph. Show each solution on a number line. Check your solution on a Calculator page.

1. $2w + 4 \geq 9$

2. $7 - 3m > -28$

3. $24 - k \leq -4k + 15$

4. $-3(2 - 2m) \leq 2(m + 4)$

Two-Variable Linear Inequalities

Mathematics Objectives

- Students will graph two-variable linear inequalities.
- Students will solve two-variable linear inequalities.
- Students will write two-variable linear inequalities.
- Students will solve systems of two-variable linear inequalities.

Applications and Skills

Graphs and Geometry
    Inequalities
    Coordinates and Equations
    Intersection
    Scatter Plot
    Variables
    Draw Line
    Perpendicular Line

Lists and Spreadsheets
    Formulas

Data and Statistics
    Scatter Plot
    Dot Plot
    Movable line
    Drag points

Calculator
    Truth Test

Materials

- TI-Nspire handhelds
- TNS file: lesson10.tns
- *The Prize*
  (pages 153–155; page153.pdf)
- *The Cost*
  (pages 156–157; page156.pdf)
- *Cross Section*
  (pages 158–159; page158.pdf)

Starting the Lesson

After loading the TNS file (lesson10.tns) on each handheld, begin the exercise by instructing students to do the following:

1. Turn on the TI-Nspire by pressing (off/on).
2. Press (⌂) and choose **My Documents**.
3. In the folder *Algebra TCM*, choose *lesson10*.
4. Remind students how to navigate through the TNS file. To move forward through the pages, press (ctrl) ▶. To move backward through the pages, press (ctrl) ◀. To choose a particular page, press (ctrl) ▲, position the cursor on the desired page and press (enter). To undo previous steps, press (ctrl) (Z) or (ctrl) (esc). Show students that any time they are using a menu that they wish to exit, they should press (esc).

Note: Page numbers refer to the TI-Nspire file lesson10.

Explaining the Concept

Problem 1—The Prize

Step 1   Distribute copies of *The Prize* (pages 153–155) to students so they can record their findings as appropriate during the instructional steps of this problem.

Step 2   On page 1.2, to enter the formula in Column C, move the cursor to the formula cell below the column name (the formula row) and press ⊙. Type in the formula *jsales:=4*⊗*cc+3*⊗*pb*. Students can type in the *cc* and the *pb*, but it is also possible to access the names of the columns by pressing ⌨ and using the NavPad to move to the desired variable and pressing ⏎.

──── Step 2 ────

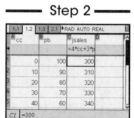

Step 3   The Data and Spreadsheet environment provides an easy way to make scatter plots and dot plots. It is possible to make only one graph on each section, but it is also possible to drag any points whose values are not defined in terms of another variable. In this exercise, it is possible to drag the points on the scatter plot, but not the dot plot. When the points on the scatter plot are dragged, the values on the spreadsheet change, and the points on the dot plot move in concert. It may be necessary to adjust the window settings. (See page 236 for detailed instructions on adjusting the window settings.)

──── Step 4 ────

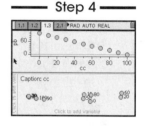

Step 4   On page 1.3, to configure the scatter plot, click at the lower part of the upper section and choose *cc* from the menu. Click at the left and choose *pb*.

──── Step 5 ────

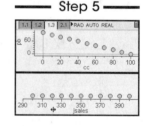

Step 5   Remember, to move between the two sections of the page, press ⌨ ⌨. Configure the dot plot by clicking at the bottom of the page section and choosing *jsales* from the menu.

──── Step 6 ────

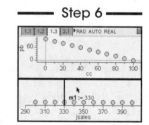

Step 6   Add a movable line to the dot plot. (See page 241 for detailed instructions on how to add a movable line.) Because this is a dot plot with values on just the horizontal axis, the line is automatically a vertical line. Grab the line and drag it to 330.

Note: Page numbers refer to the TI-Nspire file lesson10.

Explaining the Concept *(cont.)*

Problem 1—The Prize *(cont.)*

Step 7 In 1d, show the students how to click on a point on the dot plot that they wish to move. This will highlight this point and the corresponding point on the scatter plot. Then, press ⌷ctrl⌷ ⌷tab⌷ to move to the scatter plot and grab the point. As you drag this point, watch the dot plot to see where the other point is positioned. Tell the students to press ⌷esc⌷, then ⌷ctrl⌷ ⌷tab⌷. Now press ⌷⌷ and the points will be released. If they do not do this, they will be dragging the previous point and the new point.

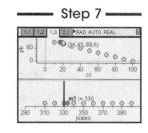
—— Step 7 ——

Step 8 Encourage the students to place the points on the dot plot relatively close to the vertical line with the points on the scatter plot spread out. This will make the line in question 1f more obvious.

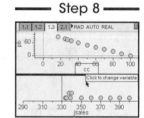
—— Step 8 ——

Step 9 In 1f, on page 1.3, add a moveable line. (See page 241 for detailed instructions on how to add a movable line.) Because this is a scatter plot, the line is oblique. To change the slope, move the cursor toward one end of the line. When the cursor looks like this (**⌣**), press ⌷ctrl⌷ ⌷⌷. Use the NavPad to tilt the line. The exact equation of this line is not important. It depends upon the students' positioning of the points. It should provide a connection to the line that they will graph in question 2. Discuss that there are pairs of numbers of boxes of Cashew Crunches and Peanut Butter Cups that meet the condition of valuing more than \$330. All of their points should be above the line.

—— Step 9 ——

Step 10 For question 2, add a new Graphs and Geometry page. Add a scatter plot by pressing ⌷menu⌷ and choosing **Graph Type** and then **Scatter Plot**. Move the cursor to the *x* and then press ⌷⌷. Choose *cc* on the drop-down menu. Press ⌷⌷. Press ⌷tab⌷ to move to the *y* drop-down menu and choose *pb*. Adjust the window settings. (See page 236 for detailed instructions on adjusting window settings.) Remind students that pressing ⌷tab⌷ moves between the Function Editor and the graph.

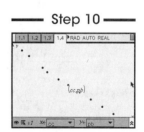
—— Step 10 ——

Note: Page numbers refer to the TI-Nspire file lesson10.

Explaining the Concept *(cont.)*

Problem 1—The Prize *(cont.)*

Step 11   Remind students that these are the same points from their scatter plots on the previous page and that they all meet the condition $4x + 3y > 330$. Point out that solving $4x + 3y = 330$ for y yields an equivalent equation. Although this equation is probably not the same as the equation from the Data and Statistics scatter plot, it should be close. Change to the Function Editor by pressing (menu) and choosing **Graph Type** and then **Function**. Type the equation in $f1(x)$. All of the points on the scatter plot should be above the line. Have the students compare their graphs.

Step 12   In 2e, hide $f1(x)$ from the inserted graph screen by moving the cursor to the line on the screen. Press (≈enter) (ctrl) (menu). Choose **Hide/Show**. Move to the Function Editor and $f2(x)$. When = is replaced with >, the $f2(x)$ changes to a y. Close the Function Editor by pressing (ctrl) (G).

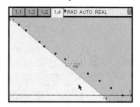

Step 13   In 2f, to draw a point any place on the dashed line, press (menu). Choose **Points & Lines** and then **Point**. To draw a vertical line through the point, change the window settings so that the *ymin* is set to –5. This displays the *x*-axis and allows it to be chosen to create the perpendicular. Press (menu) and choose **Construction** and then **Perpendicular**. Select the point and then the *x*-axis to create the perpendicular. Create another point on the vertical line and use the Coordinates and Equations tool to find the ordered pair of each point. (See page 245 for detailed instructions on how to use this tool.) As students drag the point to the right and left on the dashed line, and the other point up and down, they should observe that the *y*-coordinate of any point in the shaded region is greater than the coordinate on the dashed line.

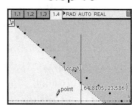

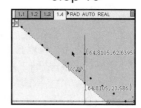

Step 14   In 3a, put a point any place in the shaded region by pressing (menu) and choosing **Points & Lines** and then **Point**. Use the Coordinates and Equations tool to find the coordinates of the point. To store the coordinates, move the cursor until the *x*-coordinate flashes, press (ctrl) (menu), and then choose **Store**. Type the name of the variable *c,* and it will fill the Var space. Repeat these directions for the *y*-coordinate to store it in *p*.

Note: Page numbers refer to the TI-Nspire file lesson10.

Explaining the Concept *(cont.)*

Problem 1—The Prize *(cont.)*

Step 15 In 3a, the handheld will return the response *true* when the point is in the shaded region and *false* when it is not. Discuss that the *true* means that the point is a solution to the inequality and that in the problem situation, it means that the sales were more than $330.

—— Step 15 ——
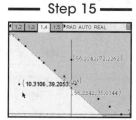

Problem 2—The Cost

Step 1 Distribute copies of *The Cost* (pages 156–157) to students so they can record their findings as appropriate during the instructional steps of this problem.

—— Step 15 ——
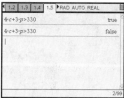

Step 2 Students should use the skills from *The Prize* to complete most of these questions. Question 1 uses ≤. The symbol is located in the symbol template and can be accessed by pressing (ctrl) (≤β°). Ask the students why this graph has a solid line and the line in *The Prize* problem was a dashed line.

—— Step 3 ——
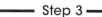

Step 3 In 1e, have them put a point on the graph page and use the Coordinates and Equations tool to find the ordered pair. To change the ordered pair, move to the coordinate and press (enter) twice. Press (clear) to delete the numbers and then type in the new coordinate and press (enter).

Step 4 Solving the equation in question 2 requires reversing the inequality sign. Be sure the students understand why this happens. Make sure they test the points and discuss the shading.

—— Step 4 ——

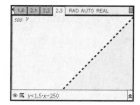

Applying the Concept

—— Step 4 ——

Problem 3—Cross Section

Step 1 Distribute copies of *Cross Section* (pages 158–159) to students so they can record their findings.

Step 2 Have students solve each inequality graphically and algebraically. Help them choose appropriate windows.

Note: *Page numbers refer to the TI-Nspire file lesson10.*

Applying the Concept *(cont.)*

Problem 3—Cross Section *(cont.)*

Differentiation

- **Below Grade Level**—Work through question 1 on *Cross Section* (page 158) with students. As you work through parts a–g on question 1, have students write notes and hints to themselves on question 2 (page 159) so they will remember what steps to take to answer the question. Allow students to work in pairs, using their notes, to solve question 2.

- **Above Grade Level**—After completing *Cross Section* (page 158), have students work in pairs to write their own real-world problems. Students' questions should mirror those in their activity sheets. After the pairs have solved their own problems, have them switch problems with another pair and solve each other's problems. If time permits, have each pair read their newly-created problem to the group. Then, have the group vote for the most creative and original problem.

Extending the Concept

- Look at examples of Linear Programming.
- Investigate quadratic inequalities.

Name _____

The Prize

Directions: Follow the steps below. The page numbers refer to the TI-Nspire document *lesson10*.

1. The junior class is selling candy to raise money for a dance. They have two kinds of candy bars: Cashew Crunches selling for $4.00 per box and Peanut Butter Cups selling for $3.00 per box. Jada can win a prize if she sells more than $330 worth of candy.

   a. Page 1.2 shows some possible numbers of boxes of each kind of candy. Column A *(cc)*, contains the number of boxes of Cashew Crunches. Column B *(pb)*, contains the number of boxes of Peanut Butter Cups. In column C *(jsales)*, write a formula for the total of Jada's sales. What is your formula?

   _____

   b. Jada is trying to plot a strategy for her sales and would like to look at the possibilities graphically. On page 1.3, create a scatter plot on the upper portion, using *cc* along the horizontal axis and *pb* on the vertical axis. Use Zoom-Data to create a window that shows all of the data.

   c. On the lower portion of page 1.3, make a dot plot using *jsales*. Add a movable line at *jsales = 330*. Which dots represent the values for which Jada will win a prize?

   _____

   d. Drag the points in the scatter plot so that all of the *jsales* points are greater than $330. Is there a higher or lower limit for the points in the scatter plot?

   _____

   e. Look at the *jsales* values on page 1.2. Are they all larger than $330?

   _____

   f. Add a movable line on page 1.3 to the scatter plot in a place that you think approximates the limit from question 1d. What is the equation of the line? Are all of the points of the scatter plot above or below the line?

   _____

--- Step 1a ---

--- Step 1c ---

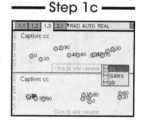

The Prize (cont.)

Directions: Follow the steps below. The page numbers refer to the TI-Nspire document *lesson10*.

2. Insert a Graph and Geometry page and make a scatter plot with *cc* as the *x*-coordinate and *pb* as the *y*-coordinate. Rewrite the formula for *jsales* using *x* for *cc* and *y* for *pb*.

   a. Write an equation, setting the expression equal to $330.

   _____

   b. Solve the equation for *y*. How does this equation compare to the movable line from page 1.3?

   _____

   c. Graph the equation on the same page with the scatter plot. Where are all the points on the scatter plot in relation to the line?

   _____

   d. Return to page 1.3 and move the points to different places with *jsales* still more than $330. Are the points still above the line on the scatter plot?

   _____

   e. Hide *f1(x)* on the inserted graph screen. Open the Function Editor. Change the = sign in *f2(x)* to > and then enter the equation from 2b. Why is the line dashed?

   _____

   f. Put a point on the dashed line and draw a vertical line through it. Put another point on the vertical line in the shaded region and find the coordinates of both points. Drag the point on the dashed line. What is always true about the *y*-coordinates of the two points?

   _____

   g. Where are all of the points from the scatter plot in relation to the shaded region?

   _____

The Prize (cont.)

Directions: Follow the steps below. The page numbers refer to the TI-Nspire document *lesson10*.

---

3. Put a point in the shaded region. Store its *x*-coordinate as *c* and its *y*-coordinate as *p*. Insert a Calculator page and type in $4c + 3p > 330$.

  a. What does the handheld say?

  _____

  b. Drag the point to another place in the shaded region. On the handheld, evaluate the expression again. What does the handheld say?

  _____

  c. Where should the point be to get the response *false*? Move the point and test your theory.

  _____

  _____

  _____

  _____

  _____

Name _____

The Cost

Directions: Follow the steps below. The page numbers refer to the TI-Nspire document *lesson10*.

---

1. The junior class is sponsoring a dance. They are decorating with streamers. Blue streamers costs $3.00 per roll, and gold streamers costs $4.00 per roll. They have budgeted $54.00 for streamers.

    a. Using *x* for the number of rolls for blue streamers and *y* for the number of rolls of gold streamers, write an expression for the cost of streamers.

    _____

    b. Write an inequality showing that they may spend, at most, $54.00.

    _____

    c. Find an ordered pair that fits in the budget and another pair that does not. Test them on the Calculator page on 2.1.

    _____

    d. Solve the inequality for *y*. When you graph the inequality, will the shading be above or below the line? Graph the inequality on page 2.2.

    _____

    _____

    e. Where should the point that worked from question 1c appear on the graph? Plot the point to test your answer.

    _____

    _____

The Cost (cont.)

Directions: Follow the steps below. The page numbers refer to the TI-Nspire document *lesson10*.

2. None of the juniors are going to pay admission to the dance. The dance committee estimates that this will cost about $2.00 for each junior who attends. They will make $3.00 for each of the other students who attend the dance. The committee hopes to make a profit of more than $500.

   a. Using x for the number of freshmen, sophomores, and seniors, and y for the number of juniors, write an expression for the amount of money they will net from the dance.

   _____

   b. Write an inequality showing that they will make more than $500.

   _____

   c. Write an ordered pair that shows they will make more than $500 and another showing they will not. Test them on the Calculator page on 2.1.

   _____

   d. Solve the inequality for y and graph it on page 2.3. Where is the shaded region? Check your points from question 2c.

   _____

3. Insert 3 Graph and Geometry pages and graph the following inequalities. Sketch the solutions to the inequalities below. Be sure to show a dashed or solid line. Give the ordered pair of a point that is a solution and another that is not a solution.

   a. $y \le \frac{2}{5}x + 2$

   b. $4x - 5y > 10$

   c. $2x + 3y \le 6$

Name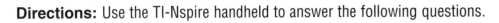

Cross Section

Directions: Use the TI-Nspire handheld to answer the following questions.

1. Tamika got a $50 gift certificate for Edge, a book and music store. She is going to use it to buy gifts for her 5 cousins. Depending on her purchases, some of the cousins may receive more than one item. The CDs cost $12 each, and the books she wants are $6.50 each. Use x for the number of CDs and y for the number of books she could buy.

   a. Write an inequality describing the total number of CDs and books she could purchase.

   _____

   b. Write an inequality describing the total cost of the gifts.

   _____

   c. Write a system of inequalities that describes the conditions on Tamika's purchases.

   _____

   d. Solve the inequalities for y and the system graphically. Sketch the graph below.

   e. Give the coordinates of a point that satisfies the problem situation and explain what they mean in terms of the problem.

   _____

   _____

   f. Give the coordinates of a point that is a solution to the system of inequalities but does not satisfy the conditions of the problem situation.

   _____

   g. Give the coordinates of a point that is not a solution to the system. _____

Cross Section (cont.)

Directions: Use the TI-Nspire handheld to answer the following questions.

2. Anthony is earning money to buy an HD television set for his room. The cheapest set he can find costs $300, but he would buy a bigger one if he had enough money. He earns $5 per hour babysitting and $8 per hour at the local fast-food restaurant. He would like to work no more than 100 hours. Use *x* to represent the number of hours he will babysit and *y* to represent the number of hours he will work at the restaurant.

   a. Write an inequality describing the total number of hours he will work.

   _____

   b. Write an inequality describing the total amount of money he will earn.

   _____

   c. Write a system of inequalities that describes the conditions Anthony is trying to meet.

   _____

   d. Solve the inequalities for *y* and the system graphically. Sketch the graph below.

   e. Give the coordinates of a point that satisfies the problem situation and explain what they mean in terms of the problem.

   _____

   f. Give the coordinates of a point that is a solution to the system of inequalities but does not satisfy the conditions of the problem situation.

   _____

   g. Give the coordinates of a point that is not a solution to the system. _____

Absolute Value

Mathematics Objectives

- Students will identify absolute value as distance.

- Students will define absolute value as x.

$$|x| = \begin{cases} x, & x \geq 0 \\ -x, & x < 0 \end{cases}$$

- Students will graph absolute-value equations.

- Students will identify the vertex of the graph of an absolute-value equation.

- Students will solve equations and inequalities with absolute value.

Applications and Skills

Graphs and Geometry
 Coordinates and Equations
 Intersection
 Scatter Plot
 Variables
 Draw Line/Segment
 Perpendicular Line
 Function Graphing
 Change Segment Width
 Slider

Lists and Spreadsheets
 Automatic Data Capture

Materials

- TI-Nspire handhelds

- TNS file: lesson11.tns

- *Change of Direction*
  (pages 165–167; page165.pdf)

- *Above and Below*
  (pages 168–169; page168.pdf)

- *Check Up*
  (pages 170–171; page170.pdf)

Starting the Lesson

After loading the TNS file (lesson11.tns) on each handheld, begin the exercise by instructing students to do the following:

1. Turn on the TI-Nspire by pressing (off on).

2. Press (⌂) and choose **My Documents**.

3. In the folder *Algebra TCM*, choose *lesson11*.

4. Remind students how to navigate through the TNS file. To move forward through the pages, press (ctrl) ▶. To move backward through the pages, press (ctrl) ◀. To choose a particular page, press (ctrl) ▲, position the cursor on the desired page and press (enter). To undo previous steps, press (ctrl) (Z) or (ctrl) (esc). Show students that any time they are using a menu that they wish to exit, they should press (esc).

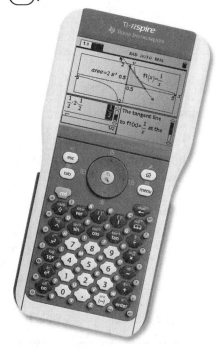

Note: Page numbers refer to the TI-Nspire file lesson11.

Explaining the Concept

Problem 1—Change of Direction

Step 1 Distribute copies of *Change of Direction* (pages 165–167) to students so they can record their findings as appropriate during the instructional steps of this problem.

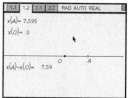
——— Step 2 ———

Step 2 In question 1, the car is used to demonstrate the difference between position and displacement. Absolute value describes distance. The total distance traveled is the sum of the absolute values of each coordinate on the number line.

Step 3 In question 2, $x(A)$ is the coordinate of point A and $x(O)$ is the coordinate of point O. In this question, the coordinate of point O is zero. In later problems, it will be moved to other positions. Grab point A and drag it to the right and left. Direct the students' attention to the changing value of $x(A) - x(O)$. Ask why sometimes it is positive and why sometimes it is negative.

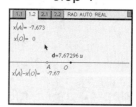
——— Step 4 ———

Step 4 Measure the distance between $x(A)$ and $x(O)$ in 2b. (See page 228 for detailed instructions on measuring the length of a segment.) To store the measurement as variable d, move the cursor to the measurement. When it flashes, press ⌢sto⌣var⌣ then choose **Store Var** and type d. Press ⌢enter⌣. Have the students slide point A again. Help them recognize $x(A) - x(O)$ is the same as d.

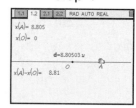
——— Step 4 ———

Step 5 In 2d, open a text box and enter $|x|$. (See page 226 for detailed instructions on using a text box.) Remember the absolute-value symbol is in the math expressions template which can be accessed by pressing ⌢ctrl⌣ ⌢|◻|◻/◻ x⌣. Use the NavPad to move to the symbol and press ⌢enter⌣. Press Ⓧ to insert x as the argument of the absolute value. To evaluate $|x|$ using $x(A)$, use the Calculate tool. (See page 233 for detailed instructions on using this tool.) Drag the value near the $|x|$ and press ⌢enter⌣.

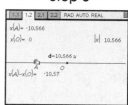
——— Step 5 ———

Step 6 As they slide point A right and left, make certain that the students recognize that the absolute value is the same as the distance and that it is never negative.

——— Step 7 ———

Step 7 In 2h, remind students how to insert a new page by pressing ⌢ctrl⌣ Ⓘ.

Note: Page numbers refer to the TI-Nspire file lesson11.

Explaining the Concept *(cont.)*

Problem 1—Change of Direction *(cont.)*

Step 8   In 2j, make sure students recognize that the absolute value of a negative number is equal to its opposite. They should read $|-x|$ as the absolute value of the opposite of x. Using the negative of x becomes confusing in this situation. The opposite is also useful in describing the definition of more complicated expressions.

Step 9   In question 3, it is necessary to drag point A *slowly* to collect the data uniformly. Emphasize that the points on the x-axis are the coordinates from the number line and the y-coordinates are the absolute values of those numbers.

——— Step 9 ———

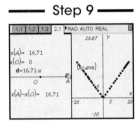

Step 10   In 3a, move to the right side of the page. Press (menu) and choose **Points and Lines** and then **Line**. If students dragged point A slowly, the points should be linear. (If they need to drag it again, tell them to move to the next page, move the cursor into the formula cell, and press (enter) twice. This will clear all the data.) To draw the line, move the cursor to a point on the scatter plot and press (⊙) or (enter). Move to a second point and press (⊙) or (enter) again.

——— Step 10 ———

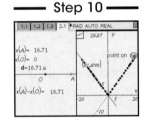

Step 11   Find the equation of the lines. (See page 245 for detailed instructions on using the Coordinates and Equations tool.) So long as the points were collected uniformly, the lines should be $y = x$ and $y = -x$. The TI-Nspire may show a very small number as a y-intercept, such as *1.4E–12*.

——— Step 11 ———

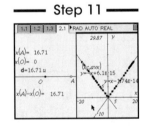

Step 12   Discuss the portions of each line that make up the absolute-value graph. Emphasize that the determination is made according to $x > 0$ or $x < 0$ and that the point $(0, 0)$ is called the *vertex* of the graph.

Step 13   In 3e, point out that the definition of absolute value is an example of a piecewise function, where the function is made up of pieces of two or more functions. Hide each line. (See page 238 for detailed instructions on hiding lines.) Press (tab) to move into the Function Editor to graph $f1(x) = |x|$. (Remember, the absolute value symbol is in the math expressions template which is accessed by pressing (ctrl) (⌊ᵃᵇⁱⱼ⌋).)

——— Step 13 ———

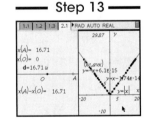

Note: Page numbers refer to the TI-Nspire file lesson11.

Explaining the Concept *(cont.)*

Problem 2—Above and Below

Step 1 Distribute copies of *Above and Below* (pages 168–169) to students so they can record their findings as appropriate during the instructional steps of this problem.

Step 2 Insert a Graphs and Geometry page.

Step 3 In 1a, find the points of intersection. (See page 230 for detailed instructions on finding an intersection point.) Point out that the *x*-coordinates of the points are the solutions to the equation |*x*| = 4.

————— Step 3 —————

Step 4 In 1b, to use the definition of absolute value to solve the equation, have students write the following:

$$|x| = \begin{cases} 4, & x \geq 0 \\ -4, & x < 0. \end{cases}$$

Show how these are related to the graph.

————— Step 5 —————

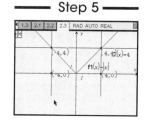

Step 5 Draw the perpendicular lines. (See page 230 for detailed instructions on constructing perpendicular lines.) Find the points as in Step 4. Show that these are the points on the number line that are 4 units away from 0.

————— Step 6 —————

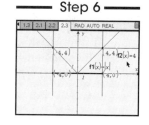

Step 6 In 1d, draw the line segment by pressing (menu) and choosing **Points & Lines** and then **Segment**. You will then need to press ⊙ on each endpoint. Press (enter). Use the NavPad to point to the line segment. Change the weight of the line by pressing (ctrl) (menu). Choose **Attributes**. Stay in the upper square in the drop-down menu and press the right arrow on the NavPad. Press (enter). Ask the students about the values of the coordinates of any point on the line segment. This is the graph of the solution to the inequality |*x*| < 4. If you wish, show students that this could be expressed in interval notation as (–4, 4).

Step 7 In 1f, show them that shading the number line to the right of 4 and to the left of –4 graphs the solution of |*x*| > 4. In interval notation, this would be written (–∞,–4), (4, ∞).

Step 8 In 1g–1i, help the students make the connection between the use of *a* and 4.

Note: Page numbers refer to the TI-Nspire file lesson11.

Explaining the Concept *(cont.)*

Problem 2—Above and Below *(cont.)*

Step 9   In question 2, it is important to emphasize that the vertex is at the center of the region on the *x*-axis and its coordinate is –3. The solutions to the equation are 4 units to the right and left of –3 which could be found with –3 + 4 and –3 – 4.

Step 10   In question 3, help students identify the number at the center of the region and find the distances to the right and left.

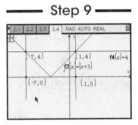
——— Step 9 ———

——— Step 10 ———

Applying the Concept

Problem 3—Check Up

Step 1   Distribute copies of *Check Up* (pages 170–171) to students so they can record their findings.

Step 2   Have students solve the questions graphically and algebraically.

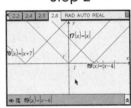
——— Step 2 ———

Differentiation

- **Below Grade Level**—After discussing questions 1 and 2 of *Check Up* (page 170) as a whole group, have students work in pairs to complete the activity sheet. You may consider solving all of the part a's with students. This will provide them with an example to follow.

- **Above Grade Level**—After completing the activity sheet in pairs, have students write their own inequality problems based on the ages of their family members. Students should use question 7 as a model. Students can then create *PowerPoint* slide shows that explain how to reach the solution. Encourage the use of pictures of the family members referred to in the inequality problem, fun fonts, and animation. Have students present the *PowerPoint* slide shows to the class.

Extending the Concept

- Investigate absolute-value functions of the form $y = a \mid x - b \mid$, equations of the form $a \mid x - b \mid$, and inequalities of the form $a \mid x - b \mid < c$ and $a \mid x \mid - b \mid < c$.

Name _____

Change of Direction

Directions: Follow the steps below. The page numbers refer to the TI-Nspire document *lesson11*.

1. A toy car is on a straight track, going forward and backward. Think of the track as a number line. Draw it below, and label the middle of the track as the number 0. The car starts 8 inches to the right of center and moves to the center. It then moves 5 inches to the left of center. It moves back to the center and then two more inches to the right.

a. Where did the car end up?

_____

_____

b. How far did it travel?

_____

_____

c. Why are the answers to questions 1a and 1b different?

_____

_____

_____

Change of Direction (cont.)

Directions: Follow the steps below. The page numbers refer to the TI-Nspire document *lesson11*.

2. On page 1.2, slide point A to the right and left on the line. *x(A)* is the coordinate of point A, and *x(O)* is the coordinate of point O.

   —— Step 2 ——

   a. What does $x(A) - x(O)$ represent?

   _____

   b. Measure the distance between O and A. Store the value as *d*. Move point A to the right and left again. Is the distance ever negative? Can it be zero?

   _____

   _____

   c. What is the relationship between *d* and $x(A) - x(O)$? When does the relationship change?

   _____

   _____

   d. In a text box, enter |*x*|. Calculate its value using *x(A)*. Slide point A to the right and left. When is the value of |*x*| the same as *x(A)*? What is its value when they are not the same?

   _____

   _____

   e. What is the relationship between |*x*| and *d*?

   _____

   f. If $x \geq 0$, what will be true about the value of |*x*|?

   _____

   g. If $x < 0$, what will be true about the value of |*x*|?

   _____

Change of Direction (cont.)

Directions: Follow the steps below. The page numbers refer to the TI-Nspire document *lesson11*.

---

   h. Find the values for $|-2|$, $|0|$, $|8|$, and $|-1.2|$. Check your answers on a Calculator page.

   _____

   i. There is a mystery number that is 3 units from the origin on a number line. What are the possibilities for its value?

   _____

   j. What question do you ask to determine which value to choose?

   _____

   k. Fill in the blanks. $|x| =$ _____ when $x \geq 0$, and $|x| =$ _____ when $x < 0$.

---

3. On page 2.1, as you *slowly* slide point A to the right and left, you will be collecting data for the scatter plot on the right side of the page. The values on the *x*-axis are $x(A)$, and those on the *y*-axis are $|x|$.

   a. Draw lines through the right and left branches of the graph. Use the Coordinates and Equations tool to find the equations of the lines. What are the equations?

   _____

   b. What part of the line $y = x$ makes up the right side of the absolute value graph?

   _____

   c. What part of the line $y = -x$ makes up the left side of the absolute value graph?

   _____

   d. The formal definition of absolute value is $|x| = \begin{cases} x, & x \geq 0 \\ -x, & x < 0. \end{cases}$

   Explain what that means.

   _____

   _____

   e. Hide the lines and graph $y = |x|$. Sketch the graph on a separate piece of paper.

Name _____

Above and Below

Directions: Use the TI-Nspire handheld to answer the questions below.

1. Insert a Graphs and Geometry page and graph the equations $y = |x|$ and $y = 4$.

   a. Find the points of intersection. What are the solutions to the equation $|x| = 4$?

   _____

   b. Use the definition of absolute value $|x| = \begin{cases} x, & x \geq 0 \\ -x, & x < 0 \end{cases}$ to find the solutions to the equation $|x| = 4$.

   _____

   c. Draw lines perpendicular to the x-axis through the points of intersection. Find the points of intersection with the x-axis. Sketch the x-axis below, showing the x-values of the intersection points.

   d. On the graph, draw a line segment between the points on the x-axis. Use attributes to make the line weight medium. On the section of $y = |x|$ immediately above the line segment, where is it in relation to the graph of $y = 4$?

   _____

   e. What is the solution to the inequality $|x| < 4$?_____

   f. What is the solution to the inequality $|x| > 4$?_____

   g. What are the solutions to any equation of the form $|x| = a$? _____

   h. Draw a number line and show the solution to the inequality $|x| < a$. _____

   i. Draw a number line and show the solution to the inequality $|x| > a$. _____

Above and Below *(cont.)*

Directions: Use the TI-Nspire handheld to answer the questions below.

---

2. Insert a Graphs and Geometry page and graph the equations $y = |x + 3|$ and $y = 4$.

   a. What is the vertex of the absolute value graph, and how could you determine it from the equation?

   _____

   b. What are the points of intersection of the two graphs? What are the solutions to the equation $|x + 3| = 4$?

   _____

   c. Draw lines perpendicular to the *x*-axis through the points of intersection of the two graphs.

   d. Find the points of intersection of the perpendicular lines with the *x*-axis. What is the distance between each point and the vertex of the graph of $y = |x + 3|$?

   _____

   e. One of the points is 4 units to the right of the vertex and the other is 4 units to the left of the vertex. How could you find the solutions without the graph?

   _____

   f. Draw a number line and sketch the solution to the inequality $|x + 3| < 4$.

   g. Draw a number line and sketch the solution to the inequality $|x + 3| > 4$.

---

3. Find the solutions to $|x - 2| = 5$, $|x - 2| < 5$, and $|x - 2| > 5$. Check your solutions graphically.

   _____

---

4. What is the solution to the inequality $|x + 3| > -4$?

   _____

Name _____

Check Up

Directions: Use the TI-Nspire handheld to answer the questions below.

---

1. Explain why the following statement is true: "The absolute value of a number is never negative."

   _____

---

2. Find a number b so that the equation $|x| = b$ has only one solution.

   _____

---

3. Sketch the graphs of the equations. Give the coordinates of the vertex of each graph.

   a. $y = |x|$ **b.** $y = |x + 7|$ **c.** $y = |x - 4|$

Check Up (cont.)

Directions: Use the TI-Nspire handheld to answer the questions below.

4. Find the solutions to the equations.

    a. $|x| = 0$ **b.** $|x + 7| = 0$ **c.** $|x - 4| = 0$

    _____   _____   _____

5. Find the solutions to the equations.

    a. $|x| = 3$ **b.** $|x + 7| = 3$ **c.** $|x - 4| = 3$

    _____   _____   _____

6. Show the solutions to the inequalities on number lines.

    a. $|x + 7| > 3$

    b. $|x + 7| < 3$

    c. $|x - 4| > 3$

    d. $|x - 4| < 3$

7. José's age is within 4 years of his sister Isabella's age. Isabella is 8 years old. Write an inequality using absolute value to describe José's age.

_____

Factors, Zeros, and Roots

Mathematics Objectives

- Students will find solutions to, zeros of, and *x*-intercepts of graphs of factorable quadratic functions.

- Students will recognize the relationships between the zeros of functions, the *x*-intercepts of the graph of the function, and the solutions to $f(x) = 0$.

- Students will use the graph of a function to factor and solve quadratic equations.

Applications and Skills

Create New Folder/Document

Create New Problem/Page

Graphs and Geometry
Function Editor
Intersection Point
Coordinates and Equations
Graph Trace

Calculator
Store
Define Function

Materials

- TI-Nspire handhelds

- *Zeros Are Something Else* (page 178; page178.pdf)

- *Take It Apart* (page 179; page179.pdf)

- *Too Square* (pages180–181; page180.pdf)

- cardboard pieces

- scissors

- markers

- small rubber balls

Starting the Lesson

Note: There is no TNS file for this lesson. The students will be creating a new TNS file during this lesson.

Begin the exercise by instructing students to do the following:

1. Turn on the TI-Nspire by pressing (off/on).

2. Press (⌂) and choose **New Document**.

3. Remind students how to navigate through the TNS file. To move forward through the pages, press (ctrl) ▶. To move backward through the pages, press (ctrl) ◀. To choose a particular page, press (ctrl) ▲, position the cursor on the desired page and press (enter). To undo previous steps, press (ctrl) (z) or (ctrl) (esc). Show students that any time they are using a menu that they wish to exit, they should press (esc).

Note: Page numbers refer to the TI-Nspire file lesson12.

Explaining the Concept

Problem 1—Zeros Are Something Else

Note: The language in this lesson refers to functions, their graphs, and zeros. The word *equation* is used for mathematical sentences like $(x - 2)(x + 4) = 0$.

Step 1   Distribute copies of *Zeros Are Something Else* (page 178) to students so they can record their findings as appropriate during the instructional steps of this problem.

Step 2   When the students press ⌂ and choose **New Document**, the screen may display a prompt asking whether they wish to save the changes to the current document. Choosing *Yes* saves it in its current form. Choosing *No* keeps the current document in its last saved form. Choosing *Cancel* returns to the current document. Have students use the NavPad to highlight their choice and then press ⏎.

Step 3   When the new document opens, have students choose **Add Graphs & Geometry** and press ⏎.

Step 4   The equation entry line at the bottom of the page displays $f1(x)=$. Enter $x^2 - 1$. Students most likely perceive this expression as being the same as the variable y. Explain that the TI-Nspire names functions *f1, f2, f3*, etc., to allow the use of more than one equation at a time. In mathematics, they are usually named *f, g, h,* etc.

Step 5   Show them how to exit the entry line by pressing (tab) twice. If the equation of the function needs to be moved, they can move the cursor near the equation until the hand (☝) appears. Then they can grab it and drag it to the desired place.

——— Step 5 ———

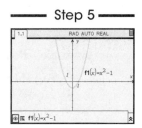

Step 6   Ask students to describe the graph of $f1(x)$. Have them find the intercepts. (See page 230 for detailed instructions on finding intersection points.) Both x-intercepts will appear as points.

Step 7   Find the coordinates of the points. (See page 245 for detailed instructions on how to use the Coordinates and Equations tool.) Discuss that the x-intercept is the x-coordinate of the point where the graph crosses the x-axis and the y-coordinate is zero.

——— Step 7 ———

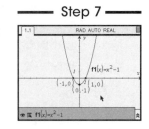

Note: Page numbers refer to the TI-Nspire file lesson12.

Explaining the Concept (cont.)

Problem 1—Zeros Are Something Else (cont.)

Step 8   Ask students to return to the equation entry line by pressing (tab), and then have them graph $(x) = x^2 - 4$. Have them predict the x-intercepts and then find them. Show the students that they can also check their prediction by using the Trace tool. (See page 234 for detailed instructions on using the Trace tool.) The trace tool will probably open on the graph of $f1$. To move to $f2(x)$, press the down arrow on the NavPad. Have students use the right and left arrows to explore points on the graph. Then, type in the predicted x-coordinate of an intercept and press (enter). The point is now displayed. Pressing (enter) again pastes the point and its ordered pair on the page. Continue until all three intercepts have been located. Remind students to grab and drag the text around the screen so that it is readable.

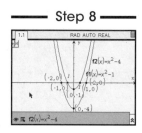
——— Step 8 ———

Step 9   Have students add a function table. (See page 245 for detailed instructions on adding a function table.) Discuss the meaning of the table. Ask them to find the values of $f1(x)$ when x is 2, when x is 5, and when x is 10 by using the NavPad to move up and down the table. Explain that there is a simpler way to ask the value of $f1(x)$ when x is 10, and that is to say "Find $f1$ of 10." This is written as $f1(10)$. Explain that this is called *function notation*. Ask students to find $f1(7)$ with and without the chart.

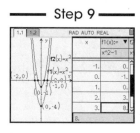
——— Step 9 ———

Step 10   To view $f2$ on the table, press (tab) to move to the top of the table. Press ⌨ to open the cells. Use the right arrow on the NavPad to move into the right-hand column. Press (tab) to move down to the table. Press ⌨ to open the cells. Ask students to find $f2$ of several different values of x. Ask them to identify x values where $f1(x) = 0$ and $f2(x) = 0$.

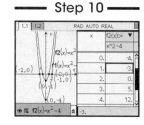
——— Step 10 ———

Step 11   Have students add a new Calculator page. All of the functions and variables defined on any page of a problem are available for use in the entire problem. So, it is possible to evaluate functions on the Calculator page. Type in $f1(1)$ and press (enter). Then type in $f2(-2)$ and press (enter). Remind students that they have found the value of the function for the given x-value.

——— Step 11 ———

Note: *Page numbers refer to the TI-Nspire file lesson12.*

Explaining the Concept (cont.)

Problem 1—Zeros Are Something Else (cont.)

Step 12 Show students how to define a function on the Calculator page. Press (menu) and choose **Actions** and then **Define**. Have them type in $f3(x) = x^2 - 9$ and press (enter). Have them find $f3(3)$ and $f3(-3)$.

——— Step 12 ———

Step 13 Explain that 3 and –3 are called *zeros* of the $f3(x)$ because $f3(3)$ and $f3(-3)$ equal zero.

Step 14 Ask students how to verify that 2 is a zero of $f2(x)$.

Step 15 Ask them to predict any other zeros of $f1(x)$. Have them verify their answers.

Step 16 Have students return to page 1.1.

Step 17 Ask students how the x-intercepts of the graphs are related to the zeros of the functions. Have them predict the x-intercepts of the graph of $f3(x) = x^2 - 9$.

Step 18 To graph $f3(x)$, first press (ctrl) (tab) to move to the side of the page containing the graph. Remind students to press (tab) to access the entry line. Because they defined $f3$ on the Calculator page, $x^2 - 9$ is already shown on the entry line. (If necessary, use the up and down arrows on the NavPad to move to $f3$.) To activate the graph, press (enter).

Step 19 Ask students to find the x-intercepts of the graph of $f3(x)$ by using either the Intersection or Trace tools.

——— Step 19 ———

Step 20 Ask students why the value of the x-intercept of the graph of a function is equal to the zero of the function. Emphasize that the value of the y-coordinate of a point on a graph is equal to the value of the function.

Step 21 Instruct students to save their work by pressing (ctrl) (S) and typing the filename *lesson12*.

Problem 2—Take It Apart

Step 1 Distribute copies of *Take It Apart* (page 179) to students so they can record their findings as appropriate during the instructional steps of this problem.

Factors, Zeros, and Roots (cont.)

Note: *Page numbers refer to the TI-Nspire file lesson12.*

Explaining the Concept (cont.)

Problem 2—Take It Apart (cont.)

Step 2 Have students insert a new problem by pressing (ctrl) ▲. Then have them press (ctrl) (menu) and choose **Insert Problem**. Press ⚟ to open the new problem, and then press (menu). Choose **Add Graphs & Geometry**. Ask students to name a function in the form $f(x) = (x - a)(x - b)$, with zeros of 3 and –2, and express it in both factored and simplified forms. Have some of the students graph the factored form while others graph the simplified form in $f1(x)$. Compare their graphs.

Step 3 Have students enter $2(f1(x))$ in $f2(x)$ and graph the function.

Step 4 Have students hide $f1$ and $f2$. Ask them to write a function with zeros of 2.5 and –1. Graph it in $f4(x)$.

Step 5 Ask them to use only integers to write an equation with solutions of 2.5 and –1. Have them solve the equation by graphing it.

Step 6 Have students insert a new problem. Ask them to guess the solutions to the equation $x^2 - 7x + 12 = 0$. Ask them how they could verify their solutions.

Step 7 After they have found the solutions of 4 and 3 either by graphing the function $f(x) = x^2 - 7x + 12$ or by using the Calculator page to verify the zeros, ask them to rewrite the function and the equation as $(x - 3)(x - 4) = 0$ and $f(x) = (x - 3)(x - 4)$. Explain that this is called *factored form*.

Step 8 Hide the previous graphs. Ask students what function to graph in order to find the solutions to $x^2 - 11x + 30 = 0$. Have them graph it, rewrite the function and the equation in factored form, and find the solutions.

Step 9 Hide the previous graph. Ask students to find the solutions to the equation $2x^2 - 7x - 4 = 0$ graphically, and rewrite the equation in factored form. The solutions are –0.5 and 4, and students will probably write $(x + 0.5)(x - 4) = 0$. Ask them to simplify the product by multiplying. (Note: The screen shot for this step is on page 177.)

——— Step 2 ———

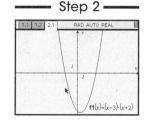

——— Step 3 ———

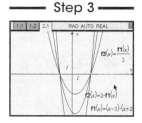

——— Step 5 ———

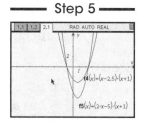

——— Step 7 ———

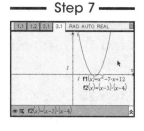

——— Step 8 ———

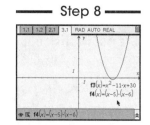

Note: Page numbers refer to the TI-Nspire file lesson12.

Explaining the Concept (cont.)

Problem 2—Take It Apart (cont.)

—— Step 9 ——

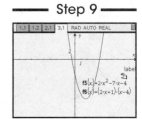

Step 10 Ask students how they could write an equivalent equation or an equation with the same solutions that would simplify to $2x^2 - 7x - 4 = 0$. To see a complete graph of the function, change the window settings. Also, remind students to press ⌃(ctrl) (S) to save their work.

Applying the Concept

Problem 3—Too Square

Step 1 Distribute copies of *Too Square* (pages 180–181) to students so they can record their findings.

Step 2 Students should use the TI-Nspire to complete *Too Square*. They can insert a new problem in the Lesson 12 TNS file. Remind students to press ⌃(ctrl) (S) to save their work.

Differentiation

- **Below Grade Level**—Place students in small groups. Provide each group with cardboard pieces, markers, and scissors so that students can act out and solve question 1 on *Too Square* (page 180). Have students work in pairs to solve question 2.

- **Above Grade Level**—After they complete their activity sheets, place students in pairs. Have them create their own problems about the acceleration of gravity and the function that describes the height of projectiles. Provide students with a ball to aid in creating their problems.

Extending the Concept

- Ask students to find the zeros of quadratic equations that are not factorable.

- Have students investigate the acceleration of gravity and the function that describes the height of projectiles.

- Look at advanced factoring techniques.

Name _____

Zeros Are Something Else

Directions: Answer the following questions using the TI-Nspire handheld.

---

1. What are the *x*-intercepts of the graph of $f1(x) = x^2 - 1$?

_____

---

2. What are the *x*-intercepts of the graph of $f2(x) = x^2 - 4$?

_____

---

3. What are the advantages to using function notation?

_____

_____

---

4. For what values of *x* on the table are $f1(x) = 0$ and $f2(x) = 0$?

_____

---

5. What is the zero of a function?

_____

_____

---

6. What are the zeros of $f1(x) = x^2 - 1$, $f2(x) = x^2 - 4$, and $f3(x) = x^2 - 9$?

_____

---

7. What are the *x*-intercepts of the graph of $f3(x) = x^2 - 9$?

_____

---

8. How are the zeros of a function related to the *x*-intercepts of the graph of the function?

_____

_____

Name _____

Take It Apart

Directions: Answer the following questions using the TI-Nspire handheld.

---

1. What function in the form $f(x) = (x - a)(x - b)$ has zeros of 3 and –2?

   _____

2. What is the simplified form of the function in Question 1?

   _____

3. Do the functions in Questions 1 and 2 have the same graph?

   _____

4. How do the graphs and the x-intercepts of $2(f1(x))$ compare to $f1(x)$?

   _____

5. What function in the form $f(x) = (x - a)(x - b)$ has zeros of 2.5 and –1?

   _____

6. What function with integer values has zeros of 2.5 and –1?

   _____

7. What do you think are the solutions to $x^2 - 7x + 12 = 0$? How can you check?

   _____

8. Write the factored form of the equation $x^2 - 11x + 30 = 0$ and find its solutions.

   _____

9. Find the solutions to the equation $2x^2 - 7x - 4 = 0$ and write them in factored form.

   _____

Name _____

Too Square

Directions: Answer the following questions using the TI-Nspire handheld.

1. The area of a rectangular piece of cardboard is 80 in.² Julie cuts one-inch squares out of each corner and then turns up the edges to make an open-topped box. The width of the box is two inches less than the length. Use *x* to represent the original length of the cardboard.

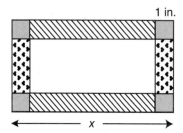

1 in.

x

   a. Write an expression for the length of the box. _____

   b. Write an expression for the width of the box. _____

   c. Write an expression for the area of the bottom of the box.

   _____

   d. Write an expression for the area of one of the ▨▨▨▨ regions.

   _____

   e. Write an expression for the area of one of the ✦✦✦ regions.

   _____

   f. What is the area of one of the ▨ regions? _____

   g. Write an expression for the total area of the cardboard. Set it equal to 80.

   _____

   h. Rewrite the equation in the form $x^2 + bx + c = 0$. _____

   i. Factor the equation and find the solutions. _____

   j. What do the solutions represent? _____

Too Square (cont.)

Directions: Answer the following questions using the TI-Nspire handheld.

2. José throws a ball straight up in the air, releasing the ball 6 feet from the ground. The initial velocity of the ball was 29 ft./sec. The function $f(t) = -16t^2 + 29t + 6$ gives the ball's distance above the ground at the time (t), seconds after the release of the ball.

a. What is the distance above the ground when the ball hits the ground?

_____

_____

_____

b. Why would one of the zeros of the function equal the number of seconds that would elapse before the ball hits the ground?

_____

_____

_____

c. What are the zeros of the function? Which one makes sense for the number of seconds that will elapse before the ball hits the ground?

_____

_____

_____

d. Use the zeros to factor $f(t) = -16t^2 + 29t + 6$.

_____

_____

_____

_____

Completing the Square/Quadratic Formula

Mathematics Objectives

- Students will explore the geometric interpretation of completing the square.

- Students will learn to solve equations of the form $x^2 + bx + c = 0$ by completing the square.

- Students will use completing the square to develop the quadratic formula.

- Students will learn to solve equations of the form $x^2 + bx + c = 0$ by using the quadratic formula.

Applications and Skills

Graphs and Geometry
    Sliders
    Measure Area
    Translation
    Rotation
    Text
    Calculate

Calculator
    Use of Variables from Graph page

Materials

- TI-Nspire handhelds

- TNS file: lesson13.tns

- *Everywhere A Square*
  (pages 187–188; page187.pdf)

- *Complete It*
  (pages 189–190; page189.pdf)

- *Formalize It*
  (pages 191–192; page191.pdf)

Starting the Lesson

After loading the TNS file (lesson13.tns) on each handheld, begin the exercise by instructing students to do the following:

1. Turn on the TI-Nspire by pressing (off/on).

2. Press (⌂) and choose **My Documents**.

3. In the folder *Algebra TCM*, choose *lesson13*.

4. Remind students how to navigate through the TNS file. To move forward through the pages, press (ctrl) ▶. To move backward through the pages, press (ctrl) ◀. To choose a particular page, press (ctrl) ▲, position the cursor on the desired page and press (enter). To undo previous steps, press (ctrl) (Z) or (ctrl) (esc). Show students that any time they are using a menu that they wish to exit, they should press (esc).

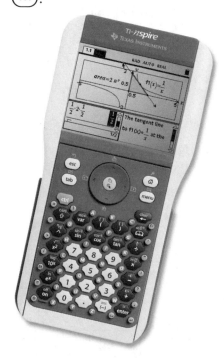

Completing the Square/Quadratic Formula (cont.)

Note: Page numbers refer to the TI-Nspire file lesson13.

Explaining the Concept

Problem 1—Everywhere a Square

Step 1   Distribute copies of *Everywhere a Square* (pages 187–188) to students so they can record their findings as appropriate during the instructional steps of this problem.

Step 2   On page 1.2, point out that the length of the side of the square and the length of the rectangle are the same and are labeled with the variable x. The height of the rectangle is b. Discuss that the total area of the square and rectangle are 140 square units.

— Step 2 —

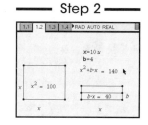

Step 3   The next steps use geometric transformations to demonstrate completing the square. Discuss translation and rotation with the students as transformations in which the dimensions and areas are unchanged.

Step 4   Show students how to translate the top portion of the rectangle by pressing (menu) and choosing **Transformation** and then **Translation**. Select the upper rectangle and then the lower-left corner of the upper rectangle by pressing (⊙). Drag the rectangle to the upper-left corner of the square and press (⊙) again. Ask students to hide the upper portion of the rectangle by selecting it and pressing (ctrl) (menu) and then choosing **Hide/Show**. Ask how the total area of the figures compares to the area of the original figures.

— Step 4 —

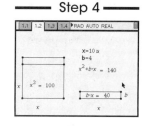

Step 5   To rotate the lower rectangle, press (menu) and choose **Transformation** and then **Rotation**. Select the rectangle. Then, move the cursor to the lower-left corner of the rectangle until the double arrows (↺) appear. Press (enter) three times. These keystrokes indicate the object to be rotated, select the point about which the object is rotated, and define the angle of rotation. After the third time, move the cursor to the left, and the new figure appears. (See page 232 for more detailed instructions on rotating a figure.) Press (enter). Hide the lower rectangle. Page 1.3 repeats the final image on 1.2.

— Step 5 —

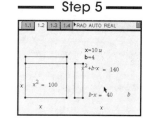

Step 6   Page 1.3 displays the rotated figure. Translate the rotated rectangle as in Step 4, choosing the new rectangle, its lower-left corner, and then the lower-left corner of the square. Hide the original rectangle. The diagram on page 1.4 repeats the final image from 1.3.

— Step 6 —

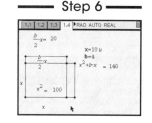

Note: Page numbers refer to the TI-Nspire file lesson13.

Explaining the Concept *(cont.)*

Problem 1—Everywhere a Square *(cont.)*

Step 7 To find the area of the shaded square on page 1.5, press (menu) and choose **Measurement** then **Area**. Select the square and press (enter) twice. Have students verify their expressions for area by evaluating the expression for the current value of *b*.

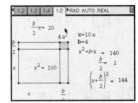
——— Step 7 ———

Step 8 In question 1g, press (menu) and choose **Shapes** and then **Polygon** to draw the large square. Select each vertex of the large square in turn by pressing (enter). At the fourth vertex, press (enter) twice. (Use the Polygon tool or the Rectangle tool because the Regular Polygon tools do not allow you to choose all four of the vertices.) Find the area as in Step 7.

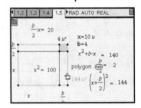
——— Step 8 ———

Step 9 For question 1i, open page 1.2. To change the values of *b*, move the cursor to the current value until it flashes and press (enter) twice. Press (clear) to delete the previous value and enter the new value, pressing (enter) when finished. Be sure that the students choose odd and even values for *b*. It is possible to change the values of *x* as well, but the labels on the diagram will not follow these changes. Be certain that students recognize that the original area is always equal to $\left(x + \dfrac{b}{2}\right)^2 - \dfrac{b^2}{4}$.

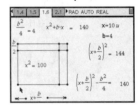
——— Step 9 ———

Problem 2—Complete It

Step 1 Distribute copies of *Complete It* (pages 189–190) to students so they can record their findings as appropriate during the instructional steps of this problem.

Step 2 In 1a, remind students to grab the open circle to operate the sliders. The graph of the parabola will change as the values of the parameters *a, b,* and *c* are changed.

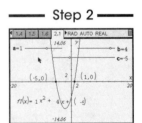
——— Step 2 ———

Step 3 For 1b, discuss the difference between function notation and *y* = notation. For 1c, remind students that the *x*-intercepts are the *x*-coordinates where the graph crosses the *x*-axis and that they occur where the *y*-value is zero.

Step 4 For 1d, discuss the relationship between the algebraic equation $x^2 + 4x - 5 = 0$ and the *x*-intercepts of the graph of $f(x) = x^2 + 4x - 5$. (See Step 5 on page 185 for the steps to completing the square for this equation.)

Note: Page numbers refer to the TI-Nspire file lesson13.

Explaining the Concept (cont.)

Problem 2—Complete It (cont.)

Step 5   For 2d through 2f, students should have the steps for completing the square to solve $x^2 + 4x - 5 = 0$. This is located to the right. If necessary, expand $(x + 2)^2$ to show the algebraic connection to the diagrams of the previous problem. Point out that the $\pm$ is necessary to get both solutions to the equation.

——— Step 5 ———
$$x^2 + 4x = 5$$
$$x^2 + 4x + 4 - 4 = 5$$
$$(x + 2)^2 - 4 = 5$$
$$(x + 2)^2 = 9$$
$$x + 2 = \pm 3$$
$$x + 2 = 3 \text{ or } x + 2 = -3$$
$$x = 1 \text{ or } x = -5$$

Step 6   For question 3a, discuss that the solutions do not come out even. To show this, have students move the cursor so that it hovers over the value of the x-intercept and then press ⊕. Pressing the plus sign increases the number of decimal places displayed while pressing ⊖ decreases the number.

Step 7   For question 3c, the steps for the student solution are located to the right. Help students write these steps without simplifying them.

——— Step 7 ———
$$x^2 + 3x - 8 = 0$$
$$x^2 + 3x = 8$$
$$x^2 + 3x + \tfrac{3^2}{4} - \tfrac{3^2}{4} = 8$$
$$(x + \tfrac{3}{2})^2 - \tfrac{3^2}{4} = 8$$
$$(x + \tfrac{3}{2})^2 = 8 + \tfrac{3^2}{4}$$
$$x + \tfrac{3}{2} = \pm \sqrt{(8 + \tfrac{3^2}{4})}$$
$$x = -\tfrac{3}{2} \pm \sqrt{(8 + \tfrac{3^2}{4})}$$

Step 8   Press (ctrl) (I) to insert a new Calculator page. When students press (A) (enter), (B) (enter), and (C) (enter), they will see the values of a, b, and c that were used on the previous page. Help students type in the last expression for x. Remind them that the TI-Nspire cannot enter $\pm$ and that they should use the + first and then re-evaluate the expression with the –. The handheld will return an exact value with a radical expression. To get a decimal approximation, press (ctrl) (enter). Show students how to use the NavPad to move up to the previous entry and press (enter) to recall the previous expression and change the + to a –.

Step 9   Remind students that the values for a, b, and c are stored in the memory. Show students how to recall the last expression and replace the 3 with c and the –8 with b. When they press (enter), they should get the same value as their previous computation. Recalling this statement and changing the – to a + yields the other solution.

Step 10   To reinforce the power of the formula, copy one of the formulas and paste the expression in a text box on the previous page. Repeat for the other expression. Then evaluate each formula using the Calculate tool. (See page 233 for detailed instructions on how to use the Calculate tool.)

Note: *Page numbers refer to the TI-Nspire file lesson13.*

Applying the Concept

Problem 3—Formalize It

Step 1   Distribute copies of *Formalize It* (pages 191–192) to students so they can record their findings.

Step 2   For question 1c, help students with the steps of completing the square with the new equation $x^2 + \frac{1}{2}x - 3 = 0$. These steps are located to the right (Step 2a). For 1d, have them identify the values of a, b, and c from 1c. Show the rewritten expression on the right (Step 2b). Help them enter the expression into a text box and use the Calculate tool to evaluate the expression. (See page 233 for detailed instructions on how to use the Calculate tool.)

Step 3   Explain to students that the quadratic formula is usually used in its simplest form (located to the right). Have them enter this in a text box with the − sign, and use the Calculate tool to evaluate it. It is necessary to use a multiplication sign between the a and the c in the discriminant.

Step 4   In 4b, explain that $b^2 - 4ac$ is called the *discriminant of the quadratic* and its value determines the number of solutions of the quadratic.

Step 5   For 5b, discuss why the negative discriminant causes the quadratic formula to yield the error message. Emphasize the relationship of no solution with the absence of an x-intercept on the graph.

—— **Step 2a** ——

$$x^2 + \tfrac{1}{2}x - 3 = 0$$

$$\left(x + \frac{1}{2 \cdot 2}\right)^2 - \left(\frac{1}{2 \cdot 2}\right)^2 = 3$$

$$\left(x + \frac{1}{2 \cdot 2}\right)^2 = 3 + \left(\frac{1}{2 \cdot 2}\right)^2$$

$$x + \frac{1}{2 \cdot 2} = \sqrt{\pm 3 + \left(\frac{1}{2 \cdot 2}\right)^2}$$

$$x = -\frac{1}{2 \cdot 2} \pm \sqrt{3 + \left(\frac{1}{2 \cdot 2}\right)^2}$$

—— **Step 2b** ——

$$x = \frac{-b}{2a} - \sqrt{-\frac{c}{a} + \left(\frac{b}{2a}\right)^2}$$

—— **Step 3** ——

Simplified Form of the Quadratic Equation

$$\frac{-b \pm \sqrt{b^2 - 4ac}}{2a}$$

Differentiation

- **Below Grade Level**—After working through question 1 on *Formalize It* (page 191–192) as a group, have students work in small groups to solve question 2 and in pairs for question 3. Solve question 4 as a group.

- **Above Grade Level**—After students have completed *Formalize It* (pages 191–192), have them use the sliders to explore with various values of a, b, and c, including positive and negative values and zero.

Extending the Concept

- Look at complex solutions to quadratic equations.

Name _____

Everywhere a Square

Directions: Follow the steps below. The page numbers refer to the TI-Nspire document *lesson13*.

---

1. Look at page 1.2. The diagram shows a representation of a square and a rectangle. The length of the side of the square is the variable *x* and is equal to the length of the rectangle. The height of the rectangle is *b*. Both *x* and *b* can be changed.

    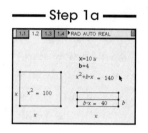
    —— Step 1a ——

   a. Look on page 1.2 to see how the variables *x* and *b* represent the sum of the areas of the square and the rectangle.

   b. What are the current values of *x* and *b,* the areas of the square and the rectangle, and the sum $x^2 + bx$?

      _____

   c. Translate the upper half of the rectangle to the top of the square. Hide the top half of the rectangle. What are the expressions for and the current value of the area of the rectangle that you moved? Rotate the remaining half of the rectangle.

      _____

      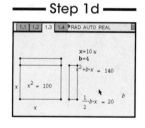
      —— Step 1d ——

   d. Page 1.3 shows the same figure as page 1.2 following the translation and rotation. Translate it to the right side of the square. Hide the previous rectangle.

   e. Page 1.4 shows the same figure as page 1.3 following the rotation and transformation.

      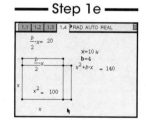
      —— Step 1e ——

   f. On page 1.5, find the area of the shaded square. What is the translation?

      _____

   g. What is the expression for the area of the large square? Evaluate the expression using the current values of *b* and *x.*

      _____

Everywhere a Square *(cont.)*

Directions: Follow the steps below. The page numbers refer to the TI-Nspire document *lesson13*.

---

h. What is the difference of the area of the large square and the area of the original pieces?

_____

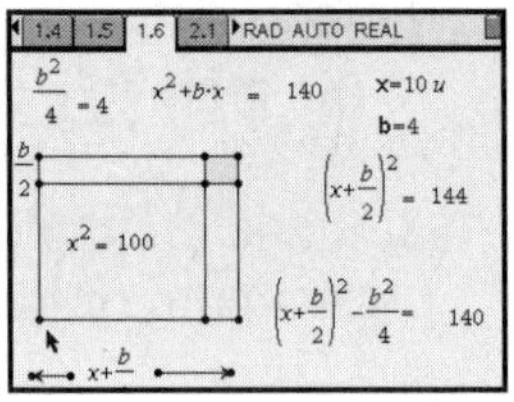

i. Look at page 1.6. What expression shows the difference of the area of the large square and the area of the shaded square? Return to page 1.2 and change the value of b, using integer values. Look at pages 1.3 through 1.6 and complete the chart below. What is true about the columns $\left(x + \frac{b}{2}\right)^2$ and $\left(x + \frac{b}{2}\right)^2 - \frac{b^2}{4}$?

_____

_____

—— Step 1i ——

x	b	$x^2 + bx$	$\left(x + \frac{b}{2}\right)^2$	$\frac{b^2}{4}$	$\left(x + \frac{b}{2}\right)^2 - \frac{b^2}{4}$

Note: The procedure outlined above is called *completing the square*. It can be used to solve quadratic equations.

Name _____

Complete It

Directions: Follow the steps below. The page numbers refer to the TI-Nspire document *lesson13*.

---

1. Solve the equation $x^2 + 4x - 5 = 0$ graphically.

   a. On page 2.1, use the sliders to set $a = 1$, $b = 4$, and $c = -5$.

   b. What is the function that is graphed?

   _____

   c. What are its *x*-intercepts? _____

   d. What are the solutions to the equation? _____

--- Step 1a ---

[graph screen showing:]
1.4 1.5 1.6 2.1 ▶RAD AUTO REAL
14.06 y
a=2   b=1
                                          c=-6
(-2,0)   2   (1.5,0)   x
20   2   20
f1(x)= 2 x² + 1 x + (-c)
-14.06

---

2. Solve the equation $x^2 + 4x - 5 = 0$ using *completing the square*.

   a. Quadratic equations are usually written in the form $ax^2 + bx + c = 0$. This is called *standard form*. What are *a*, *b*, and *c* in the equation $x^2 + 4x - 5 = 0$?

   _____

   b. Add 5 to each side so that the equation is in the form $x^2 + bx = -c$. What are the values of $\frac{b}{2}$ and $\frac{b^2}{4}$?

   _____

   c. Rewrite the equation in the form $x^2 + bx + \frac{b^2}{4} - \frac{b^2}{4} = -c$ and then $\left(x + \frac{b}{2}\right)^2 - \frac{b^2}{4} = -c$.

   _____

   d. Return to page 1.6. What does the left side of the equation $\left(x + \frac{b}{2}\right)^2 - \frac{b^2}{4}$ represent?

   _____

   e. Add $\frac{b^2}{4}$ to each side so that the equation is in the following form:

   $\left(x + \frac{b}{2}\right)^2 - \frac{b^2}{4} + \frac{b^2}{4} = -c + \frac{b^2}{4}$.

   f. Take the square root of both sides. Do not forget the ±. Simplify the expressions.

   _____

Complete It (cont.)

Directions: Follow the steps below. The page numbers refer to the TI-Nspire document *lesson13*.

---

3. Use the equation $x^2 + 3x - 8 = 0$.

   a. Use the sliders on page 2.1 to graph the function $f(x) = x^2 + 3x - 8$. What are the values of a, b, and c?

   _____

   b. What are the approximate solutions to the equation?

   _____

   c. Show the steps of completing the square for solving the equation without simplifying.

   _____

   d. Insert a Calculator page. Evaluate the expression from question 3c.

   _____

   e. Look at the expression you entered. Identify the values for b and c. Now, use the NavPad to capture the last entry, and rewrite the expression using b and c instead of the numbers. Then change the + to a – to find the other solution. This is called the *quadratic formula* for the case when a is equal to one.

   _____

   f. Copy each of the formulas. Paste them into a text box on the previous page and calculate the value of each. Use the sliders to change the values of b and c. What is true about the values of the x-intercepts and the values of the formula as you change b and c?

   _____

   g. What happens if the graph has no x-intercepts?

   _____

Name _____

Formalize It

Directions: Follow the steps below. The page numbers refer to the TI-Nspire document *lesson13*.

---

1. Use the equation $2x^2 + x - 6 = 0$.

   a. What are a, b, and c? On page 3.1, use the sliders to graph the corresponding function.

   _____

   b. What equation with $a = 1$ has the same solutions as $2x^2 + x - 6 = 0$?

   _____

   c. Use the Completing the Square tool to solve the equation from part b.

   _____

   d. By rewriting the expression using a, b, and c from part b you get the expression to the right. Enter this expression into a text box. Use the Calculate tool to find the value of the expression. Which x-intercept have you found?

   _____

   e. The expression from completing the square simplifies to

$$\frac{-b \pm \sqrt{b^2 - 4ac}}{2a}$$

   This is known as the *quadratic formula*. Enter this expression into a text box. The expression must be entered by pressing the following sequence of keys: 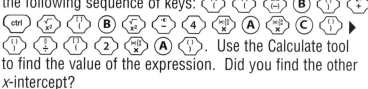. Use the Calculate tool to find the value of the expression. Did you find the other x-intercept?

   _____

—— Step 1a ——

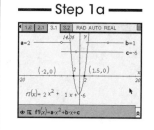

—— Step 1d ——

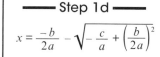

$$x = \frac{-b}{2a} - \sqrt{-\frac{c}{a} + \left(\frac{b}{2a}\right)^2}$$

Formalize It (cont.)

Directions: Follow the steps below. The page numbers refer to the TI-Nspire document *lesson13.*

---

2. Use the equation $3x^2 + 4x - 5 = 0$.

  a. What are a, b, and c?

  _____

  b. Using the Calculator page 3.2 and the quadratic formula, find the solutions to the

  equation. _____

  c. Return to page 3.1 and use the sliders to graph the equations. Check the x-intercepts and the values of the expressions in the text boxes.

---

3. Use the equation $x^2 + 4x = 0$.

  a. What are a, b, and c?

  _____

  b. On the Calculator page, use the quadratic formula to solve $x^2 + 4x = 0$ using both

  the $+$ and the $-$ signs. Check your solution with the sliders. _____

---

4. Use the equation $4x^2 + 4x + 1 = 0$.

  a. Use the sliders to solve the equation. How many x-intercepts does this graph have?

  _____

  b. On the Calculator page, use the quadratic formula to solve the equation. Use the discriminant $b^2 - 4ac$ to explain why both solutions are the same.

  _____

---

5. Use the sliders to create a parabola that has no x-intercepts.

  a. What happens to the calculated values? _____

  b. Move to the Calculator page and use the quadratic formula to solve the equation. What is the value of the discriminant? Why do you get an error message when using the quadratic formula?

  _____

  _____

Mathematics Objectives

- Students will model exponential growth.

- Students will graph equations of the form $y = ab^2$.

- Students will solve problems using exponential equations.

- Students will solve problems using compound interest.

- Students will solve problems involving exponential decay.

Applications and Skills

Graphs and Geometry
Coordinates and Equations
Scatter Plot
Function Graphing
Intersection Point

Lists and Spreadsheets
Formula
Cell Formula

Materials

- TI-Nspire handhelds

- *Uncle Buck$*
  (pages 198–200; page198.pdf)

- *More Buck$*
  (pages 201–202; page201.pdf)

- *Compound Buck$*
  (pages 203–205; page203.pdf)

Starting the Lesson

Note: There is no TNS file for this lesson. The students will be creating a new TNS file during this lesson.

To begin the exercise, instruct students to do the following:

1. Turn on the TI-Nspire by pressing (off/on).

2. Press (⌂) and choose **New Document**.

4. Remind students how to navigate through the TNS file. To move forward through the pages, press (ctrl) ▶. To move backward through the pages, press (ctrl) ◀. To choose a particular page, press (ctrl) ▲, position the cursor on the desired page and press (enter). To undo previous steps, press (ctrl) (Z) or (ctrl) (esc). Show students that any time they are using a menu that they wish to exit, they should press (esc).

Note: Page numbers refer to the TI-Nspire file lesson14.

Explaining the Concept

Problem 1—Uncle Buck$

Step 1   Distribute copies of *Uncle Buck$* (pages 198–200) to students so they can record their findings as appropriate during the instructional steps of this problem.

Step 2   The students are creating an interactive spreadsheet that they will be able to adjust for different initial values and multiplication factors. Have students open a new Lists and Spreadsheet document. Have them name the first column *day* and the second column *dollars*. In the formula cell under *day*, have the students type in *seq(n,n,0,10)*.

—— Step 2 ——

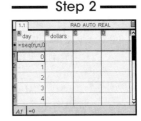

Step 3   Students enter *1* into cell B1 for the initial value and *2* in cell C1 to serve as the multiplication factor. Type in the formula *=C1•B1* into cell B2. Explain to students that the spreadsheet will multiply the contents of these cells even if they are changed. Ask students to change values for C1 and B1 to see that the formula keeps working. Have them change the values back to 1 and 2.

—— Step 3 ——

Step 4   Help students work out that the formula for each cell in *dollars* is C1 times the B cell above. The number for the B cell is the same as the adjacent number in *day*.

—— Step 4 ——

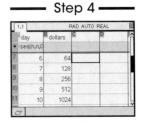

Step 5   On the chart on question 2a, help students identify the total number of times that 2 has been used as a factor for each value in *dollars*. They should notice that it is the same as the number in *day*. For the powers of two, discuss the meaning of 2^0. To write the formula in 2b, help them see that they are just replacing the number for *day* with *x*.

Step 6   To create the scatter plot in question 2c, have students insert a new Graphs and Geometry page. Then, press (menu) and choose **Graph Type** and then **Scatter Plot**.

Step 7   The pop-up menu for *x* is automatically highlighted. Press and move to *day*, press to select it. Move to *y* by pressing (tab). Press and move to *dollars*. Press to select it. Press (tab) until the cursor has moved to the graph. Use the Zoom Data option by pressing (menu) and choosing **Window** and then **Zoom–Data**. Press (ctrl) (G) to close and open the Function Editor.

—— Step 7 ——

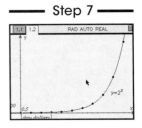

Note: Page numbers refer to the TI-Nspire file lesson14.

Explaining the Concept

Problem 1—Uncle Buck$ (cont.)

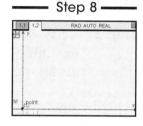

Step 8   In 2d, have the students find the intersection of the *y*-axis. (See page 230 for detailed instructions on finding an intersection point.) The point of intersection is not obvious because it was also a point on the scatter plot. Hide the graph and the scatter plot. (See page 238 for detailed instructions on hiding graphs.) Find the coordinates. (See page 245 for detailed instructions on using the Coordinates and Equations tool.) Emphasize that the *y*-coordinate of the ordered pair (0, 1) is the *y*-intercept because the *x*-coordinate is 0. Ask the students to explain why this is the initial value, the value on day 0.

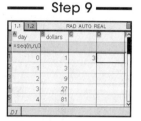

Step 9   In 3a, explain that when the students change spreadsheet cell C1 to 3 on page 1.1, all of the formulas in *dollars* use 3 for the factor and each value is 3 times the previous value.

Step 10   Students should notice that $y = 3^x$ and $y = 5^x$ have the same *y*-intercept as $y = 2^x$ but are steeper.

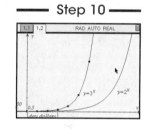

Step 11   In question 4, students should see that changing cell B1 changes the *y*-intercept of the graph and requires an equation of the form $y = ab^x$.

Step 12   Instruct students to save this work by pressing (ctrl) (S) and typing the filename *lesson14*.

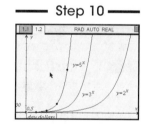

Problem 2—More Buck$

Step 1   Distribute copies of *More Buck$* (pages 201–202) to students so they can record their findings as appropriate during the instructional steps of this problem.

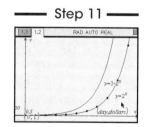

Step 2   Column D, *dollar1*, will contain the total amount the student has each day. It is designed to help students get ready for the idea of compound interest. The formula for each cell in *dollar1* will multiply the number above it times the factor in C1. The formula in D2 is $= c1 \cdot d1 + d1$.

Note: Page numbers refer to the TI-Nspire file lesson14.

Explaining the Concept *(cont.)*

Problem 2—More Buck$ *(cont.)*

—— **Step 3** ——

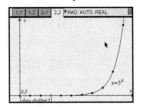

Step 3   In the table on question 3, help students with the *Sum* column. They should see that each term is 2•(above) + 1•(above) and, using the distributive property, this is 3•(above). This is a very important step before students consider compound interest in *Compound Buck$*.

Step 4   Students will need to resize column D to see the values in the lower cells. To resize the column, move the cursor to the top of the column until the column is highlighted. Press (menu) and choose **Actions**, then **Resize**, and finally **Resize Column Width**. Move the cursor to the right until there is enough room to see the lower values and then press (enter).

—— **Step 5** ——

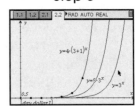

Step 5   Since students are using the same spreadsheet from *Uncle Buck$*, have them insert a Graphs and Geometry page for the scatter plot of *day vs. dollar1*.

—— **Step 6** ——

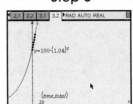

Step 6   Help students see that these equations are of the form $y = a(b + 1)^x$. The *+ 1* comes from the adding in of the previous sum. On question 5, ask the students another way to write $y = 4(4)^x$.

Step 7   Remind students to save their work by pressing (ctrl) (S).

Problem 3—Compound Buck$

—— **Step 2** ——

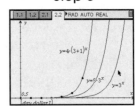

Step 1   Distribute copies of *Compound Buck$* (pages 203–205) to students so they can record their findings.

Step 2   This investigation uses the TI-Nspire skills and the mathematics from *Uncle Buck$* and *More Buck$*. Since students are using the same document, have them insert a new problem. Students will name lists and create formulas as they did in previous exercises. The formula in cell B2 should be *=B1+C1•B1*.

—— **Step 3** ——

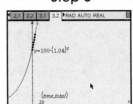

Step 3   In question 1d, the scatter plot looks almost linear when the Zoom-Data option is used. Have students change the window settings so that the Ymin is 0, the Ymax is 150, the Xmin is –50, and the Xmax is 200.

Note: Page numbers refer to the TI-Nspire file lesson14.

Applying the Concept

Problem 3—Compound Buck$ *(cont.)*

Step 4 In question 2, help students see the factoring as .04(above) + above = 1.04 (above), and then write the exponential expression. Show them that the equation is $y = 100(1.04)^x$ where x is the number of years that have elapsed. Discuss the use of compound interest in banking.

Step 5 In question 3, point out that interest rates are always expressed in terms of annual rates. If the interest is compounded twice a year, then the customer will receive that rate every six months. In the formula $A = P(1 + \frac{r}{n})^{nt}$, point out that the rate is divided by n just as the 4% was divided by 2 for semi-annual, and the number of years is multiplied by n because it represents the number of compounding periods that have elapsed.

——— Step 5 ———

Step 6 In question 3e, remind students that they can find out when the account will exceed $500 by graphing $y = 500$ on the same graph and finding the point of intersection. (See page 230 for detailed instructions on finding an intersection point.) Note: The window settings will need to be adjusted.

——— Step 6 ———

Differentiation

- **Below Grade Level**—Have students work in small groups to complete *Compound Buck$* (pages 203–205). Observe groups closely providing instruction as needed.

- **Above Grade Level**—After completing *Compound Buck$* (pages 203–205) have students write a paragraph explaining in detail how they answered question 3. Then, have students exchange paragraphs with partners. They should use one another's paragraphs to check their own work and see if they answered the question correctly.

Extending the Concept

- Have students find examples of graphs showing exponential growth in newspapers and magazines.

Name _____

Uncle Buck$

Directions: Answer the following questions using the TI-Nspire handheld.

1. Your Uncle Bucks is rich, but not very good at math. He asks you how much money you have in your pocket. When you say $1, he says that he will give you twice that amount tomorrow, twice that amount the next day, twice that amount the next day, etc., for 10 days. But, he will only give you the money if you can figure out the amount he would give you on the tenth day.

   a. Create a new document and create a Lists and Spreadsheet page.

   b. Give the name *day* to Column A and the name *dollars* to Column B.

   c. Use a sequence to fill the whole numbers 0 through 10 in the *day* column.

   d. In cell B1, type in the amount of money you have at the beginning (Day 0). What number did you put in cell B1?

   _____

   e. In cell C1, type in the factor that each day's money will be multiplied by. What number did you put in cell C1?

   _____

   f. Cell B2 should contain the number 2. How could you use the contents of cells B1 and C1 to obtain that number? Type that formula into cell B2.

   _____

   g. How could you use the cells C1 and B2 to find the value in B3? Type that formula into cell B3.

   _____

   h. In general, how do you find each cell from the preceding one?

   _____

   i. What day is B11? _____

   j. How much would your uncle be giving you on Day 10? _____

Uncle Buck$ *(cont.)*

Directions: Answer the following questions using the TI-Nspire handheld.

2. Fill in the chart. In the *Factors of 2* column, put the total number of times that 2 has been used as a factor in *Dollars* to get that number. Write each number of dollars as a power of 2.

Day	Dollars	Factors of 2	Power of 2
0			
1			
2			
3			
4			
5			
6			
7			
8			
9			
10			

   a. What would be the power of 2 for Day 20? _____

   b. What is the formula for Day x? _____

   c. Make a scatter plot with *day* on the x-axis and *dollars* on the y-axis. Use your formula from 2b to write a function to match the graph. Graph it on the same page as the scatter plot.

   d. What is the y-intercept of the graph of the function, and what does it mean in terms of the problem?

   _____

   _____

   _____

Uncle Buck$ (cont.)

Directions: Answer the following questions using the TI-Nspire handheld.

---

3. Return to the spreadsheet on page 1.1. Change the number in cell C1 to 3.

   a. What happens to the value of the money each day? _____

   b. Write a formula for the amount of money received on Day *x* and graph it in *f2(x)* on page 1.2.

   _____

   c. What is its *y*-intercept? _____

   d. How does the graph compare to the previous one? _____

   e. What would the formula be if the money were multiplied by 5 each day?

   _____

   f. Check the formula on page 1.2. What is the *y*-intercept?

   _____

---

4. Return to the spreadsheet and return the number in cell C1 to 2. Change the number in cell B1 to 3.

   a. Your money is doubled each day. How much money did you begin with? _____

   b. How do the dollars compare to those in your chart in question 2? Write a formula that describes the number of dollars on day *x*. Check your formula on the scatter plot.

   _____

   c. What is the *y*-intercept of this graph? What does it mean in terms of the problem?

   _____

   d. What is the equation if you start with $10 and the money is doubled each day?

   _____

   e. These equations are of the form $y = ab^x$. This is the general form for an exponential equation. What do *a* and *b* represent?

   _____

Name _____

More Buck$

Directions: Answer the following questions using the TI-Nspire handheld.

1. In *Uncle Buck$*, you investigated how much money Uncle Bucks would give you each day if you began with $1, and he gave you twice as much money as he did the previous day.

   Suppose that you began with $1 and he doubled the total of all your money each day.

   a. Use your spreadsheet from *Uncle Buck$*. Create a new problem page and create a Lists and Spreadsheet page.

   b. Give the name *day* to Column A and the name *dollar1* to Column D.

   c. In the *day* column, type in the whole numbers 0 through 10.

   d. In cell D1, type in the amount of money you have at the beginning (Day 0).

   e. In cell C1, type in the factor (②) that each day's money will be multiplied by.

2. Your money on day one includes your original dollar, plus the two from doubling.

   a. How much would you have? _____

   b. How can you use the spreadsheet to compute the total for day one?

   _____

   c. How would you compute the total in day two?

   _____

   d. In general, how do you compute each day?

   _____

   _____

   _____

   _____

More Buck$ *(cont.)*

Directions: Answer the following questions using the TI-Nspire handheld.

3. Complete the chart below.

Day	Dollar1	Sum	Combine	Power of 3
0		1		
1		$2 \cdot 1 + 1 \cdot 1$	3	3^1
2		$2 \cdot 3 + 3 \cdot 1$	$3 \cdot 3$	3^2
3		$2 \cdot 3^2 + 1 \cdot 3^2$	$3 \cdot 3^2$	3^3
4				
5				
6				
7				
8				
9				
10				

  a. What is the formula for day *x*? _____

  b. Make a scatter plot with *day* on the *x*-axis and *dollar1* on the *y*-axis. Check your formula by graphing.

4. Suppose you start with $5 on Day 0.

  a. Which cell do you change? _____

  b. What formula describes the *dollar1* in terms of *day*? _____

  c. Check the formula on a scatter plot.

5. Suppose you start with $4 and your money is tripled each day.

  a. Which cells do you change? _____

  b. Does a formula of the form $y = b^x$ work for this? Check on your scatter plot.

  _____

  c. Remember that you began with $4 instead of $1. How could you adapt the formula? Try it on your graph.

  _____

Name _____

Compound Buck$

Directions: Answer the following questions using the TI-Nspire handheld.

In a savings account, the amount of interest depends upon how much money is in the account at the time interest is computed. This kind of interest is called *compound interest.* The amount of time that passes between when interest is compounded varies with different kinds of accounts.

1. Aileen puts $100 in a savings account. The interest rate is 4% and the interest is compounded yearly. This means that after one year, 4% of the amount in the account is added to whatever was previously in the account. Aileen leaves all of the money in the account for five years.

   a. On the Lists and Spreadsheet page, give the name *Time* to column A. Enter the whole numbers 0 through 6. Give the name *Total* to the column B. Enter 100 into cell B1. Put 0.04 into cell C1.

   b. How can you use the spreadsheet to find the value in cell B2?

   _____

   _____

   _____

   c. In general, how do you find the value in each cell?

   _____

   _____

   _____

   d. Make a scatter plot with *Time* on the *x*-axis and *Total* on the *y*-axis. What kind of function does the shape of the scatter plot resemble?

   _____

   _____

   _____

Compound Buck$ (cont.)

Directions: Answer the following questions using the TI-Nspire handheld.

2. Fill in the chart below.

Time	Total	Sum	Combine	Simplify
0	100			
1	104	.04(100) + 100	(1+.04)(100)	(1.04)(100)
2	108.16	.04(1.04)(100) + (1.04)(100)	(1+.04)(1.04)(100)	$(1.04)^2$(100)
3				
4				
5				
6				

a. Write an equation that describes the total in the account (*y*) in terms of the number of years (*x*). Check the equation by graphing it on the scatter plot.

_____

b. Change the original deposit to $1,000 and the interest rate to 2.5%. What equation describes the total in the account (*y*) in terms of the number of years, (*x*)?

_____

c. The general formula for interest compounded yearly is $A = P(1 + r)^t$ where *A* stands for the total amount of money in the account, *P* represents the original deposit (called the principal), *r* stands for the rate (expressed as a decimal), and *t* stands for the number of years that have elapsed. Identify the principal, rate, and time in Questions 2a and 2b.

_____

_____

_____

_____

_____

Compound Buck$ (cont.)

Directions: Answer the following questions using the TI-Nspire handheld.

3. Interest can be compounded for other amounts of time. Semi-annual interest is compounded twice a year.

   a. If the interest rate were 4%, what would the semi-annual interest rate be?

   _____

   b. How many times would the interest be compounded in 5 years?

   _____

   c. Set up a spreadsheet that will compute the amount in an account with an original deposit of $100. Be sure to include the half years.

   d. The general formula for compound interest is $A = P(1 + \frac{r}{n})^{nt}$ where n is the number of times per year the interest is compounded. Write the equation for $100 at 4% semi-annually. How does this correspond to your spreadsheet?

   _____

   _____

   _____

   _____

   e. When would the amount in the account exceed $500?

   _____

   _____

Exponential Decay

Mathematics Objectives

- Students will model exponential decay.

- Students will graph equations of the forms $y = a\left(\frac{1}{b}\right)^x$ and $y = ab^{-x}$.

- Students will apply negative exponents.

- Students will recognize the graphs of $y = ab^{-x}$ and $y = ab^x$ as reflections about the y-axis.

- Students will solve problems involving exponential decay.

Applications and Skills

Graphs and Geometry
    Coordinates and Equations
    Scatter Plot
    Variables
    Function Graphing
    Function Table
    Slider

Lists and Spreadsheets
    Formula
    Cell Formula
    Random Number

Materials

- TI-Nspire handhelds

- TNS file: lesson15.tns

- *Heads or Tails?*
  (pages 210–214; page210.pdf)

- *Mirror Image*
  (pages 215–218; page215.pdf)

- *Exponentially Speaking*
  (pages 219–221; page219.pdf)

Starting the Lesson

After loading the TNS file (lesson15.tns) on each handheld, begin the exercise by instructing students to do the following:

1. Turn on the TI-Nspire by pressing (off/on).

2. Press (⌂) and choose **My Documents**.

3. In the folder *Algebra TCM*, choose *lesson15*.

4. Remind students how to navigate through the TNS file. To move forward through the pages, press (ctrl) ▶. To move backward through the pages, press (ctrl) ◀. To choose a particular page, press (ctrl) ▲, position the cursor on the desired page and press (enter). To undo previous steps, press (ctrl) (Z) or (ctrl) (esc). Show students that any time they are using a menu that they wish to exit, they should press (esc).

Note: Page numbers refer to the TI-Nspire file lesson15.

Explaining the Concept

Problem 1—Heads or Tails?

Step 1　Distribute copies of *Heads or Tails?* (pages 210–214) to students so they can record their findings as appropriate during the instructional steps of this problem.

Step 2　In question 1, discuss students' expectations on the results of flipping 500 coins. Discuss the difference between the expected value and what will actually happen.

Step 3　Page 1.2 contains a simulation of coin flipping. It is based on 0 representing tails and 1 representing heads. In this way, the number of heads on a set will be the same as the sum of the numbers in a list. Initially, the spreadsheet contains error messages because the initial values need to be set.

Step 4　Columns C–P are named for how many sets of flips have occurred. Each column contains a formula in the form *=randint(0,1,n)* which generates random integers. The *0* and *1* indicate that only the integers 0 and 1 will be chosen. (If the first two numbers were 5 and 10, then numbers 5, 6, 7, 8, 9, and 10 could be chosen.) The *n* determines how many random numbers will be generated. In *flip0*, *n* is equal to cell b1, the original number of coins.

—— Step 4 ——

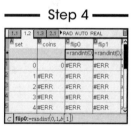

Step 5　Cell b2 is equal to the sum of *flip0* that will represent the number of heads in *flip0*. The value of cell b2 is used to determine the number of random 0s and 1s generated in *flip0*. This pattern is used for determining the rest of the flips.

Step 6　In question 3, have students move into cell b1, type in *500*, and press (enter). The simulation is completed immediately. A domain error may occur if all of the *flips* columns are not used. Each *flips* list shows 0s and 1s representing tails and heads. Column B, *Coins*, displays the sum from each *flips* list. (Note: There is a possibility of receiving an error message because all the flips may not be needed to get to one coin.)

—— Step 6 ——

Step 7　When comparing the results, students should see that their results are all different. The lower cells may contain *#ERR* if the number of coins reached 0 before the last few *flips* were activated. Very rarely, there may be two or more coins left after the 14th simulation. This will not affect the rest of the simulation. Press (ctrl) (R) to rerun the simulation.

—— Step 7 ——

Note: Page numbers refer to the TI-Nspire file lesson15.

Explaining the Concept *(cont.)*

Problem 1—Heads or Tails? *(cont.)*

——— Step 8 ———

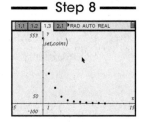

Step 8 In 4, discuss how the number of coins students begin with influences how closely the experimental results approximate the expected results. On the chart, help students recognize that each row changes by another factor of one-half. This also increases the exponent of one-half by one. Return to the top of the chart and discuss what the exponent zero means.

——— Step 9 ———

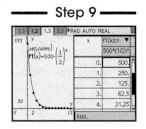

Step 9 In question 5, graph the function on page 1.3 by pressing (ctrl) (G) to show and hide the Function Editor. Press (^) to insert the exponent. The graph of $y = 500\left(\frac{1}{2}\right)^x$ has a y-intercept of 500. Emphasize that 500 is the initial value and is the number of trials when x is 0. For 5c, remind students how to insert a function table by pressing (menu) and choosing **View** and then **Add Function Table**.

——— Step 10 ———

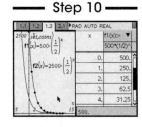

Step 10 In question 6, students will need to adjust the Ymax value by pressing (menu) and choosing **Window** and then **Window Settings**. In questions 6 and 7, students should notice that the graphs have the same shape as the previous one but with different y-intercepts equal to the initial value. Also, remind students that they need to press (ctrl) (tab) to switch between the graph and the table.

Problem 2—Mirror Image

——— Step 10 ———

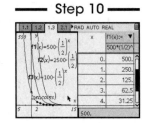

Step 1 Distribute copies of *Mirror Image* (pages 215–218) to students so they can record their findings as appropriate during the instructional steps of this problem.

Step 2 Help students identify the use of negative exponents on the chart. Look at the function table on page 1.3. Use the cursor to move up to see the negative values of x. In questions 1b–1f, emphasize that a negative exponent indicates a reciprocal, that is to say that $x^{-1} = \left(\frac{1}{x}\right)$ and $\left(\frac{1}{x}\right)^{-1} = x$.

——— Step 2 ———

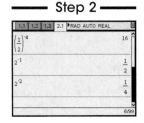

Step 3 In question 2, the slider is used to emphasize what happens as the value of the exponent changes from positive to negative. To use the slider, move the cursor to the open dot and press (ctrl) (·). In 2c, press (menu) and choose **Points & Lines** and then **Point On** to place points on the graph. Press (·) or (enter) twice to select each point. To find the reflection, press (menu)

Note: Page numbers refer to the TI-Nspire file lesson15.

Explaining the Concept *(cont.)*

Problem 2—Mirror Image *(cont.)*

Step 3
(cont.)
and choose **Transformation** and then **Reflection**. For each point, click on the *y*-axis and then the point. Discuss that a mirror image of an object appears to be the same distance from the mirror as the object, but in the opposite direction. Then apply the reasoning to the points as the object and the *y*-axis as the mirror. Press (menu) and choose **Actions** and then **Coordinates and Equations** to find the coordinates of the points of reflection.

Step 4 In 2e, students should recognize that the graphs are mirror images or reflections of each other.

Step 5 In question 3, emphasize the use of the negative exponent to indicate the reciprocal.

Applying the Concept

Problem 3—Exponentially Speaking

Step 1 Distribute copies of *Exponentially Speaking* (pages 219–221) to students so they can record their findings.

Step 2 Students may need help with question 2 to see that the *b* in $y = ab^x$ is 0.9.

Differentiation

- **Below Grade Level**—Work through question 1 on *Exponentially Speaking* (page 219) as a group. Allow the students to work in pairs to solve questions 2–3 (pages 220–221). Provide guided instruction as needed.

- **Above Grade Level**—After completing the activity sheet, have students work in pairs to write a real-world problem on exponential decay.

Extending the Concept

- Have students find examples of graphs showing exponential decay in newspapers and magazines.

—— Step 3 ——

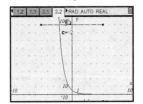

—— Step 3 ——

—— Step 3 ——

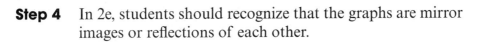

—— Step 4 ——

—— Step 5 ——

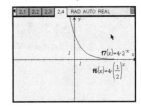

Name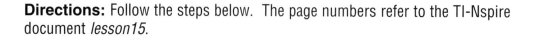

Heads or Tails?

Directions: Follow the steps below. The page numbers refer to the TI-Nspire document *lesson15*.

1. Elise's teacher wants her to investigate random events. She is to begin with 500 coins, flip each coin, and remove the ones that land tails up. She is to take the remaining coins and flip them, again removing those that land tails up. Her teacher wants her to continue this until there is only one coin remaining.

   a. How many coins do you think would be left after the first set of coin flips?

   _____

   b. How many after the next set of flips? _____

   c. How many flips do you think will be necessary for her to complete this task?

   _____

2. Elise thinks her teacher's experiment will take too much time so she devises an investigation on her TI-Nspire. On page 1.2, column A is named *set*. It stands for the number of sets of flips Elise would have made. Column B is named *coins*. It stands for the number of coins flipped in that set.

   a. How many coins is Elise starting with? _____

   b. The rest of the columns will create the flipped coins. Look at column C. The name of the list is *flip0*. This is the result of flipping before any coins are removed. The formula is *=randint (0,1,b1)*. This means that the TI-Nspire will generate a list of random 0s and 1s. The *b1* is the number in cell B1, the number of coins Elise is simulating. The 0 stands for tails and 1 stands for heads. If Elise simulates 500 coins, how many 1s do you predict will appear for the first toss?

   _____

   _____

—— Step 2 ——

set	coins	flip0	flip1
		=randint(0,	=randint(0,
0	0	#ERR	#ERR
1	#ERR	#ERR	#ERR
2	#ERR	#ERR	#ERR
3	#ERR	#ERR	#ERR
4	#ERR	#ERR	#ERR

C | flip0:=randint(0,1,b 1)

Heads or Tails? *(cont.)*

Directions: Follow the steps below. The page numbers refer to the TI-Nspire document *lesson15*.

---

c. If there were that number of 1s, what would be the sum of all the numbers in *flip0*?

_____

d. Click on cell B2. The formula for B2 is *=sum(flip0)*. This will paste the sum of list *flip0* into the cell. If the first toss produced the number of coins landing on heads that you predicted, what number would be pasted into cell B2?

_____

e. What will the formula in *flip1* do?

_____

_____

_____

f. What will the formula in cell B3 do?

_____

_____

_____

g. Look at the formulas in the rest of the columns and in *coins*. Explain how Elise's simulation will work.

_____

_____

_____

_____

Heads or Tails? *(cont.)*

Directions: Follow the steps below. The page numbers refer to the TI-Nspire document *lesson15*.

---

3. Change the value of cell B1 to 500.

   a. Is the number in cell B2 equal to your prediction in question 2b?

   _____

   b. Compare your results with others in your group. Are they the same as yours?

   _____

   c. Look at the lower part of *coins* and all of the *flip* lists. Compare these with others in your group. Why does *#ERR* appear in some of the cells?

   _____

   d. Put the cursor in cell B1 and press ⌃ctrl Ⓡ to rerun the simulation. Do the results change?

   _____

   e. Look at the scatter plot on page 1.3. Compare it to those in your group. Sketch the basic shape of all the scatter plots.

Heads or Tails? *(cont.)*

Directions: Follow the steps below. The page numbers refer to the TI-Nspire document *lesson15*.

4. The results from the simulation are experimental results that should approximate the expected results.

   a. Theoretically, what part of the flips in each set should be heads?

   _____

   b. Complete the chart.

Set (x)	Coins	Product	Exponential Expression
0	500	500	$500\left(\frac{1}{2}\right)^0$
1	250	$500\left(\frac{1}{2}\right)$	$500\left(\frac{1}{2}\right)^1$
2	125	$500\left(\frac{1}{2}\right)\left(\frac{1}{2}\right)$	$500\left(\frac{1}{2}\right)^2$
3			
4			
5			
6			

   c. If you follow the pattern, would the number of coins ever equal zero?

   _____

   d. Write an equation using *y* for coins and *x* for the set that describes the pattern.

   _____

   _____

   _____

Heads or Tails? *(cont.)*

Directions: Follow the steps below. The page numbers refer to the TI-Nspire document *lesson15*.

5. Graph the formula from question 4d on the scatter plot on page 1.3.

    a. What is the *y*-intercept of the graph? Which point in the simulation is it describing?

    _____

    b. How could you have recognized the *y*-intercept from the equation $y = 500\left(\frac{1}{2}\right)^x$?

    _____

    c. Use a function table to look at points whose *x*-coordinates are negative. What is happening to the *y*-coordinates?

    _____

6. On page 1.2, change cell B1 to 2,500.

    a. What equation should approximate the scatter plot?

    _____

    b. On page 1.3, adjust the window and graph the new equation in *f2(x)*.

    c. How does the new graph compare to the old one?

    _____

7. Return to page 1.2 and change cell B1 to 100.

    a. What equation should approximate the scatter plot?

    _____

    b. On page 1.3, graph the new equation in *f3(x)*.

    c. You have been looking at equations of the form $y = a\left(\frac{1}{2}\right)^x$. This is an example of *exponential decay*. How does the initial value of *a* affect the graph?

    _____

Name _____

Mirror Image

Directions: Follow the steps below. The page numbers refer to the TI-Nspire document *lesson15*.

1. In *Heads or Tails?* the chart described the expected values for the exponential decay if each value is half of the previous one.

   a. Look at page 1.3 and think about the pattern of decreasing values.
      Fill in the values for *y* on the chart.

x	y	Exponential Expression
−4		
−3		
−2		
−1		
0	500	$500\left(\frac{1}{2}\right)^{0}$
1	250	$500\left(\frac{1}{2}\right)^{1}$
2	125	$500\left(\frac{1}{2}\right)^{2}$

   b. On the Calculator page on 2.1, evaluate $\left(\frac{1}{2}\right)^{-1}, \left(\frac{1}{2}\right)^{-2}, \left(\frac{1}{2}\right)^{-3}$, and $\left(\frac{1}{2}\right)^{-4}$.
      What does the negative exponent do?

   _____

   c. What do you think the values of 2^{-1}, 2^{-2}, and 2^{-3} are? Write your predictions below.
      Then, check them on the Calculator page on 2.1. Revise your work if necessary.

   _____

   d. What does a negative exponent do?

   _____

   e. Rewrite $\left(\frac{1}{3}\right)^{4}$ and 5^{2} with negative exponents. Check your answers on page 2.1.

   _____

   f. Rewrite 4^{-6} and $\left(\frac{3}{8}\right)^{-2}$ with positive exponents. Check your answers on page 2.1.

   _____

Mirror Image (cont.)

Directions: Follow the steps below. The page numbers refer to the TI-Nspire document *lesson15*.

2. On page 2.2, use the slider to investigate the graph of $y = 5 \cdot 2^{cx}$ as values of c change from –5 to 5.

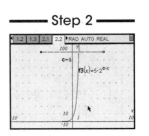
— Step 2 —

a. Make a sketch showing the general shape of the graph when c is positive.

b. Make a sketch showing the general shape of the graph when c is negative.

c. Graph $y = 5(2)^x$ on page 2.3. Choose three points on the graph and reflect them across the y-axis. Find the coordinates of all six points.

_____

_____

d. What is true about the x-coordinates and y-coordinates of each point and its reflection?

_____

Mirror Image *(cont.)*

Directions: Follow the steps below. The page numbers refer to the TI-Nspire document *lesson15*.

e. On the same page, graph $y = 5(2)^{-x}$. What is the relationship between the graphs of $y = 5(2)^x$ and $y = 5(2)^{-x}$?

_____

f. Change the 5 to 3 in both equations. Does the same relationship apply?

_____

g. Change the 2 to 4 in both equations. Does the same relationship apply?

_____

h. Make a sketch of the graph of an equation of the form $y = ab^x$. Include its *y*-intercept. How does it change as the value of *b* increases?

_____

i. Make a sketch of the graph of an equation of the form $y = ab^{-x}$. Include its *y*-intercept. How does it change as the value of *b* increases?

_____

Mirror Image *(cont.)*

Directions: Follow the steps below. The page numbers refer to the TI-Nspire document *lesson15*.

---

3. On page 2.4, graph $y = 4\left(\frac{1}{2}\right)^x$.

    a. Which sketch from questions 2h and 2i does it resemble?

    _____

    _____

    b. Rewrite $y = 4\left(\frac{1}{2}\right)^x$ as an equation where $b = 2$.

    _____

    c. Graph it on page 2.4. Are the graphs the same?

    _____

    d. Use the definition of negative exponents to explain why $y = a\left(\frac{1}{b}\right)^x$ is the same as $y = ab^{-x}$.

    _____

    _____

    _____

    _____

Name _____

Exponentially Speaking

Directions: Use the TI-Nspire handheld to answer the following questions.

1. The NCAA basketball tournament begins with 64 teams and ends with one national champion.

   a. Explain how the tournament is an example of exponential decay.

   _____

   _____

   _____

   b. Write a function that models the tournament with and without negative exponents. What part of the equation describes which round of the tournament is being referred to?

   _____

   _____

   _____

   _____

   c. Suppose the tournament were expanded to 128 teams. What equation would model the tournament?

   _____

Exponentially Speaking (cont.)

Directions: Use the TI-Nspire handheld to answer the following questions.

2. Jacob borrowed $1,000 from his brother. Each month, he pays back 10% of what he still owes.

   a. How much will he pay his brother at the end of the first month? How much will he still owe?

   _____

   b. How much will he pay his brother at the end of the second month? How much will he still owe?

   _____

   c. If he pays 10% of what he owes each month, what percent of his previous debt remains?

   _____

   d. Write an equation that models how much he owes at the end of month x.

   _____

   e. How much will he still owe after 10 months?

   _____

Exponentially Speaking (cont.)

Directions: Use the TI-Nspire handheld to answer the following questions.

3. A colony of bacteria is dying. It starts with 5,000 bacteria. Use x to represent the number of days that elapse.

   a. If half of the colony dies each day, write an equation that models the number of bacteria remaining on day x. How many would there be on day 6?

   _____

   _____

   b. Suppose half of the colony dies every other day. If x still represents the number of days that have elapsed, how should the exponent change?

   _____

   c. Write an equation that would model that number of bacteria remaining on day x. How many would remain on day 6?

   _____

   _____

   d. Suppose that half of the colony dies every 5th day. Write an equation that would model that number of bacteria remaining on day x. How many would remain on day 20?

   _____

   _____

Burrill, G. 2008. The role of handheld technology in teaching and learning secondary school mathematics. Paper presented at 11th International Congress of Mathematical Education. Monterey, Mexico

Florian, J.E., and C.B. Dean. 2001. *Standards in Classroom Practice Research Synthesis: Chapter 2, Mathematics Standards in Classroom Practice.* McREL Publishing.

Marzano, R. J. 2003. *What Works in Schools: Translating Research into Action.* Alexandria, VA: Association for Supervision and Curriculum Development.

National Council of Teachers of Mathematics. 2000. *Principles and Standards for School Mathematics: Number and Operations Standard.*

National Council of Mathematics Teachers. 2003. *NCTM Position Statement: The Use of Technology in the Learning and Teaching of Mathematics.* October.

National Council of Mathematics Teachers. 2005. *NCTM Position Statement: Highly Qualified Teachers.* July.

Seely, C. 2004. *Engagement as a Tool for Equity. NCTM News Bulletin.* Reston, VA: National Council of Teachers of Mathematics. November.

SRI International. 2006. TI-Nspire math and science learning handhelds: What research says and what educators can do. Menlow Park, CA: SRI International.

Sutton, J. and A. Krueger. 2002. *EDThoughts: What We Know About Mathematics Teaching and Learning.* Aurora, CO: Mid-continent Research for Education and Learning.

Waits, B. and F. Demana. 1998. *The Role of Graphing Calculators in Mathematics Reform.* Colombus, OH: The Ohio State University. (ERIC Document Reproduction Service No. ED458108).

Waits, B. and H. Pomerantz. 1997. *The Role of Calculators in Math Education.* Colombus, OH: The Ohio State University. Prepared for the Urban Systemic Initiative/ Comprehensive partnership for Mathematics and Science Achievement (USI/CPMSA). Retrieved September 12, 2006 from *http://education.ti.com/educationportal/sites/US/ nonProductSingle/research_therole.html*

Keystroke Hints

Keystroke	Action
(ctrl)(Z) or (ctrl)(esc)	undoes last action can be used repeatedly to go back several steps
(CAPS ⇧)(esc)	redoes last action
(⌂)	allows you to add applications, manage documents, move to home screen, or view system information
(tab)	moves fields in application or expression template
(ctrl)	alternates between primary and secondary functions on keyboard
(ctrl)(tab)	moves to next application in split screen
(ctrl) ▼	from My Documents, displays Page Sorter from Page Sorter, displays page
(ctrl) ▶	moves to next page
(ctrl) ◀	moves to previous page
(ctrl) ▲	from page, displays Page Sorter from Page Sorter, displays My Documents
(⊙)	selects object
(ctrl)(⊙)	grabs object
(≈ enter)	completes operation
(ctrl)(7)	moves to Problem 1 in Page Sorter moves to top of list in My Documents
(ctrl)(1)	moves to last problem in Page Sorter moves to bottom of list in My Documents
(ctrl)(9)	pages up in Page Sorter
(ctrl)(3)	pages down in Page Sorter
(esc)	closes any open menus or dialog boxes
(menu)	opens application menu for current application
(ctrl)(menu)	right click—offers options for current application or selected object
(ctrl)(⌂)	tools to manage and edit document
(ctrl)(⌂)(1)(3) or (ctrl)(S)	to save a document

Grabbing a Point

Step 1   Use the NavPad to move the cursor to a point. The cursor becomes a hand (✍) and the point blinks.

Step 2   Press and hold $\textcircled{\tiny{\%}}$ to grab the point. The cursor becomes a closed hand.

Dragging a Point

Step 1   Use the NavPad to move the cursor to a point. The cursor becomes a hand (✍) and the point blinks.

Step 2   Press and hold $\textcircled{\tiny{\%}}$ to grab the point. The cursor becomes a closed hand.

Step 3   Use the NavPad to slowly move the point.

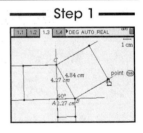

Clicking on Something

Step 1   Use the NavPad to move the cursor to a point. The cursor becomes a hand (✋) and the point blinks.

Step 2   Press $\textcircled{\tiny{\%}}$ or $\widetilde{\text{enter}}$.

Releasing a Tool

Step 1   Press (esc) to release a tool.

Manual Capture Data

Step 1   Use the NavPad to move the cursor to a point. The cursor becomes a hand (✋) and the point blinks.

Step 2   Press (ctrl)(.) to capture the data.

Step 1
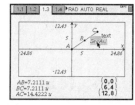

Step 2
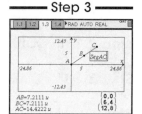

Editing Text

Step 1   Use the NavPad to move the cursor to the text to edit. The text will blink.

Step 2   Press (⊙) or (enter) once to highlight the text.

Step 3   Press (⊙) or (enter) a second time to make it editable. A cursor will be inserted in the text box.

Step 4   Edit the text. Use (clear) to backspace.

Step 5   Press (enter) to secure the change.

Step 6   Press (esc) to release the Editing tool.

Step 2

Step 3

Moving a Label or Text

Step 1   Use the NavPad to move the cursor to the label or text to be moved. Hover over the label or text until the cursor becomes an open hand (✋) and the word *label* or *text* appears.

Step 2   Press and hold (⊙) until the hand closes.

Step 3   Use the NavPad to move the label or text away from the point.

Step 4   Press (⊙) or (enter) to release the label or text in its new place.

Step 1

Step 3
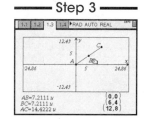

Sending Documents from One Handheld to Another

Step 1   Connect the handhelds using the link cord.

Step 2   Press .

Step 3   Use the NavPad to scroll to **My Documents** and press ⊙.

Step 4   Use the NavPad to scroll the cursor to the document to be sent.

Step 5   Press ⟨ctrl⟩ and then ⟨⌂⟩ to get the Tools menu.

Step 6   Press ⊙ to select **File**.

Step 7   Use the NavPad to scroll to **Send** and press ⊙. The file is automatically placed on the receiving handheld in a folder of the same name as the folder on the sending handheld.

Step 3

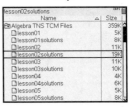

Step 7

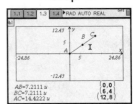

Using Text to Label Something

Step 1   Press ⟨menu⟩.

Step 2   Press ⊙ to select **Actions**.

Step 3   Use the NavPad to scroll to **Text** and press ⊙.

Step 4   Use the NavPad to move the text cursor (Ⅰ) to the location for the label.

Step 5   Press ⟨enter⟩ or ⊙. A text box appears.

Step 6   Enter the label in the text box. To enter a capital letter, press ⟨ctrl⟩ ⟨CAPS⟩, followed by the letter.

Step 7   Press ⟨enter⟩ to exit the text box.

Step 8   Press ⟨esc⟩ to release the Text tool.

Step 3

Step 4

Step 6

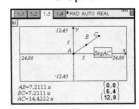

Labeling a Point

Step 1   Press (menu).

Step 2   Press (⚏) for **Actions**.

Step 3   Use the NavPad to scroll to **Text** and press (⚏).

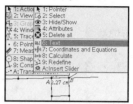

Step 4   Use the NavPad to move the cursor (⟑) over the point.

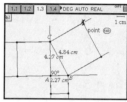

Step 5   Press (⚏) when the point blinks. A text box appears.

Step 6   Enter the label in the text box. To enter a capital letter, press (ctrl) (CAPS), followed by the letter.

Step 7   Press (enter) to exit the text box.

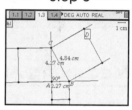

Step 8   Press (esc) to release the Text tool.

Measuring Length between Two Points

Step 1   Press (menu).

Step 2   Use the NavPad to scroll to **Measurement** and press (⚏).

Step 3   Press (⚏) to select **Length**.

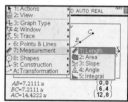

Step 4   Use the NavPad to move the cursor (⟑) to one of the points. Hover over the point until the cursor becomes a hand (☝).

Step 5   Press (⚏) or (enter) to select the point.

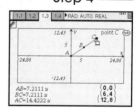

Step 6   Use the NavPad to move the cursor to the second point. Hover over the point until the cursor becomes a hand (☝).

Step 7   Press (⚏) or (enter) to select the second point. A "ghost" measurement will appear.

Step 8   Use the NavPad to move the measurement to a desired location.

Step 9   Press (esc) to release the measurement in that place.

Measuring Length of a Segment

Step 1   Press (menu).

Step 2   Use the NavPad to scroll to **Measurement** and press (⊛).

Step 3   Press (⊛) to select **Length**.

—— Step 3 ——

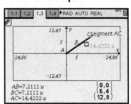

Step 4   Use the NavPad to move the cursor (↖) to the desired segment. Hover over the segment until the cursor becomes a hand (✋). A "ghost" measurement will appear.

—— Step 4 ——

Step 5   Press (⊛) or (enter) to select the segment.

Step 6   Use the NavPad to move the measurement to a desired location.

Step 7   Press (⊛) or (enter) to release the measurement in that place.

Measuring Angles

Step 1   Press (menu).

Step 2   Use the NavPad to scroll to **Measurement** and press (⊛).

Step 3   Use the NavPad to scroll to **Angle** and press (⊛).

—— Step 3 ——

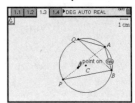

Step 4   Use the NavPad to move the pencil cursor (✎) to the first point in the angle. Hover over the point until the cursor becomes a hand (✋).

Step 5   Press (⊛) or (enter) to select the first point of the angle.

—— Step 5 ——

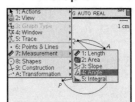

Step 6   Use the NavPad to move the pencil cursor (✎) to the second point in the angle. Hover over the point until the cursor becomes a hand (✋).

Step 7   Press (⊛) or (enter) to select the second point of the angle.

Step 8   Use the NavPad to move the pencil cursor (✎) to the third point in the angle. Hover over the point until the cursor becomes a hand (✋).

Measuring Area of a Shape

Step 1 Press (menu).

Step 2 Use the NavPad to scroll to **Measurement** and press ⊙.

Step 3 Use the NavPad to scroll to **Area** and press ⊙.

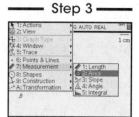

Step 4 Use the NavPad to move the cursor (↖) over the perimeter of the shape. Hover over the perimeter until the shape blinks and the cursor turns into a hand (✋). A "ghost" measurement will appear.

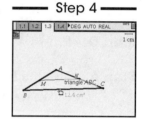

Step 5 Press (enter) or ⊙ to select the shape.

Step 6 Use the NavPad to move the measurement to a desired location.

Step 7 Press (enter) or ⊙ to release the measurement in that place.

Step 8 Press (esc) to release the Measurement tool.

Finding an Intersection Point

Step 1   Press ⓜ.

Step 2   Use the NavPad to scroll to **Points & Lines** and press ⓧ.

Step 3   Use the NavPad to scroll to **Intersection Point(s)** and press ⓧ.

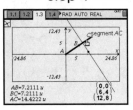
——— Step 3 ———

Step 4   Use the NavPad to move the cursor (↖) to a line. Hover over the line until the line blinks and the cursor turns into a hand (✋).

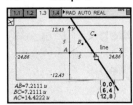
——— Step 4 ———

Step 5   Press ⏎ or ⓧ.

Step 6   Use the NavPad to move the cursor (↖) to a line that intersects the first line. Hover over the line until the line blinks and the cursor turns into a hand (✋).

Step 7   Press ⏎ or ⓧ. The intersection point will appear.

——— Step 6 ———

Step 8   Press ⓔ to release the Intersection point tool.

Constructing a Perpendicular Line

Step 1   Press ⓜ.

Step 2   Use the NavPad to scroll to **Construction** and press ⓧ.

Step 3   Press ⓧ to select **Perpendicular**.

——— Step 3 ———

Step 4   Use the NavPad to move the pencil cursor (✎) to a line. Hover over the line until the line blinks and the cursor turns into a hand (✋).

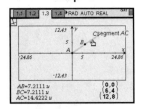
——— Step 4 ———

Step 5   Press ⏎ or ⓧ.

Step 6   Use the NavPad to move the pencil cursor (✎) to a point. Hover over the point until the point blinks and the cursor turns into a hand (✋).

Step 7   Press ⏎ or ⓧ. A perpendicular line will appear.

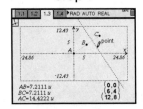
——— Step 7 ———

Step 8   Press ⓔ to release the Perpendicular line tool.

Constructing a Segment from a Point to a Line

Step 1   Press (menu).

Step 2   Use the NavPad to scroll to **Points & Lines** and press ⊙.

Step 3   Use the NavPad to scroll to **Segment** and press ⊙.

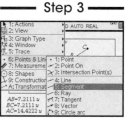

Step 4   Use the NavPad to move the pencil cursor (✎) to a point. Hover over the point until the point blinks and the cursor turns into a hand (☝).

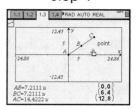

Step 5   Press (enter) or ⊙.

Step 6   Use the NavPad to move the pencil cursor (✎) to a line.

Step 7   Press (enter) or ⊙. A segment will appear.

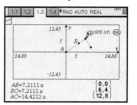

Step 8   Press (esc) to release the Segment tool.

Translating a Figure

Step 1   Press (menu).

Step 2   Use the NavPad to scroll to **Transformation** and press ⊙.

Step 3   Use the NavPad to scroll to **Translation** and press ⊙.

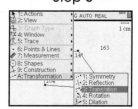

Step 4   Use the NavPad to move the pencil cursor (✎) to the outline of the polygon. Hover over the outline until the polygon blinks and the cursor turns into a hand (☝).

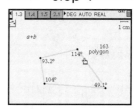

Step 5   Press ⊙ or (enter) to select the polygon for translation.

Step 6   Press ⊙ twice or press (enter) twice.

Step 7   Use the NavPad to move the polygon to a new location in the plane.

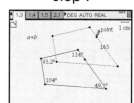

Step 8   Press ⊙ or (enter) to select the location.

Step 9   Press (esc) to release the Translation tool.

Rotating a Figure

Step 1   Press (menu).

Step 2   Use the NavPad to scroll to **Transformation** and press (⊙).

Step 3   Use the NavPad to scroll to **Rotation** and press (⊙).

— Step 3 —

Step 4   Use the NavPad to move the cursor (↻) to the outline of the polygon. Hover over the outline until the polygon blinks and the cursor turns into a hand (☝).

Step 5   Press (⊙) or (enter) to select the polygon for rotation.

Step 6   Use the NavPad to move the cursor (↻) to the point of rotation.

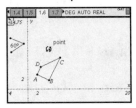
— Step 4 —

Step 7   Press (⊙) or (enter) to select the point of rotation.

Step 8   Use the NavPad to move the pencil cursor (✎) to the desired angle measure (on the left side of the screen).

Step 9   Press (⊙) or (enter) to select the degrees of rotation and to rotate the polygon.

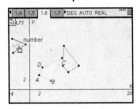
— Step 7 —

Step 10   Press (esc) to release the Rotation tool.

Reflecting a Figure

Step 1   Press (menu).

Step 2   Use the NavPad to scroll to **Transformation** and press (⊙).

Step 3   Use the NavPad to scroll to **Reflection** and press (⊙).

— Step 3 —

Step 4   Use the NavPad to move the pencil cursor (✎) to the outline of the polygon. Hover over the outline until the polygon blinks and the cursor turns into a hand (☝).

Step 5   Press (⊙) or (enter) to select the polygon for reflection.

Step 6   Use the NavPad to move the cursor to the location on the outline of the polygon for reflection.

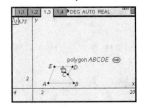
— Step 4 —

Step 7   Press (⊙) or (enter) to reflect the polygon.

Step 8   Press (esc) to release the Reflection tool.

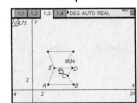
— Step 7 —

Using the Calculate Tool

Step 1   Press (menu).

Step 2   Press ⊛ to select **Actions**.

Step 3   Use the NavPad to scroll to **Calculate** and press ⊛.

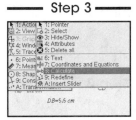
——— Step 3 ———

Step 4   Use the NavPad to move the cursor (↖) to the expression. Hover over the expression until the expression blinks and the cursor turns into a hand (✋).

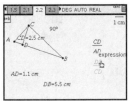
——— Step 4 ———

Step 5   Press (enter) or ⊛ to select the expression.

Step 6   Use the NavPad to move the cursor (🔍) to a measurement in the sketch.

Step 7   Press (enter) or ⊛ to select the measurement.

Step 8   Repeat steps 7 and 8 for each variable in the expression.

Typing a Formula into a Spreadsheet

Step 1   Use the NavPad to scroll into the diamond row cell of the column in which you would like to type the formula.

——— Step 1 ———

Step 2   Press (=), (enter), or ⊛ .

Step 3   Type the desired formula in the cell using number and letter keys.

——— Step 2 ———

Step 4   Press (enter).

Finding the Coordinates of a Point

Step 1 Press (menu).

Step 2 Press ⊛ to select **Actions**.

Step 3 Use the NavPad to scroll to **Coordinates and Equations** and press ⊛.

——— Step 3 ———

Step 4 Use the NavPad to move the cursor (↖) to a point. Hover over the point until the point blinks and the cursor turns into a hand (✋). A "ghost" coordinate will appear.

Step 5 Press (enter) or ⊛ to select the point.

Step 6 Use the NavPad to move the coordinate to a desired location.

——— Step 4 ———
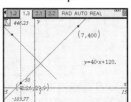

Step 7 Press (enter) or ⊛ to release the coordinate in that place.

Step 8 Press (esc) to release the Coordinate and Equation tool.

Using the Trace Tool

Step 1 Press (menu).

Step 2 Use the NavPad to scroll to **Trace** and press ⊛.

Step 3 Press ⊛ to select **Graph Trace**.

——— Step 3 ———

Step 4 Using the NavPad, press either ▶ or ◀ to trace along the function. When the coordinates are traced beyond the original window settings, the window will jump to show the new points. Tracing in the opposite direction will return to the window.

——— Step 4 ———
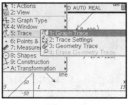

Step 5 Using the NavPad, press either ▲ or ▼ to trace on both functions simultaneously.

Step 6 Press (esc) to release the Tracing tool.

Moving Between Split Screens

Step 1   Press (ctrl) (tab).

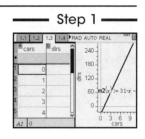
——— Step 1 ———

Moving an Equation

Step 1   Use the NavPad to move the cursor to the equation. Hover over the equation until the cursor changes to a hand (🖐).

Step 2   Press (ctrl) (🖐) to select the equation.

Step 3   Use the NavPad to drag the equation.

Step 4   Press (🖐) twice or press (esc) to release the equation.

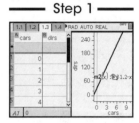
——— Step 1 ———

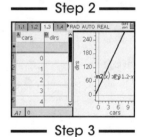
——— Step 2 ———

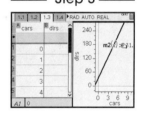
——— Step 3 ———

How-To Manual *(cont.)*

Adjusting Window Settings

Step 1   Press (menu).

Step 2   Use the NavPad to scroll to **Window** and press ⬡ .

Step 3   Select a window setting.

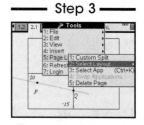

Splitting the Screen

Step 1   Press (ctrl) (⌂) to access the Tools menu.

Step 2   Use the NavPad to scroll to **Page Layout** and press ⬡ .

Step 3   Use the NavPad to scroll to **Select Layout** and press ⬡ .

Step 4   Select the layout you want.

Step 5   Press (ctrl) (tab) to switch windows.

Step 6   For new windows, press (menu) and select the type of page you wish to add.

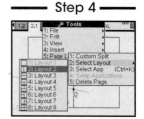

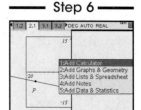

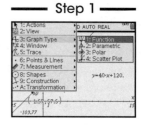

Selecting a Graph Type

Step 1   Press (menu).

Step 2   Use the NavPad to scroll to **Graph Type** and press ⬡ .

Step 3   Select the graph.

Using the Fill Down Tool

Step 1   Use the NavPad to move the cursor to the cell to copy.

Step 2   Press (menu).

Step 3   Use the NavPad to scroll to **Data** and press ⊛ .

Step 4   Use the NavPad to scroll to **Fill Down** and press ⊛ .

Step 5   Use the NavPad to move the cursor through the desired amount of cells to fill.

Step 6   Press ⊛ or (enter) to fill the cells.

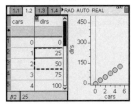
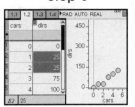

Inserting a Row in a Table

Step 1   Press (menu).

Step 2   Use the NavPad to scroll to **Insert** and press ⊛ .

Step 3   Use the NavPad to scroll to **Insert Row** and press ⊛ .

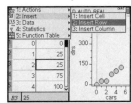

Entering Data in a Cell in List or Spreadsheet

Step 1   Use the NavPad to move to the cell.

Step 2   Press (enter) or ⊛ .

Step 3   Type in the data.

Step 4   Press (enter) or ⊛ .

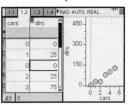
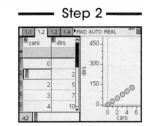

Hiding the Graph Equation Editor

Step 1   Press ⬭ctrl ⓖ.

——— Step 1 ———

Step 2   To bring back the equation editor, repeat steps 1–2.

——— Step 2 ———

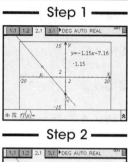

Hiding a Line or Graph

Step 1   Use the NavPad to move the cursor (↖) to a line. Hover over the line until the line blinks and the cursor turns into a hand (✋).

——— Step 1 ———

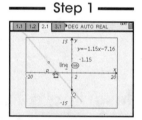

Step 2   Press ⬭ctrl ⬭menu.

Step 3   Use the NavPad to scroll to **Hide/Show** and press 🔘.

——— Step 3 ———

Step 3

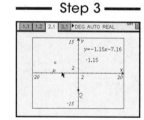

Adding a New Problem

Step 1 Press ⟨ctrl⟩ ⟨🏠⟩ to open the Tools menu.

Step 2 Use the NavPad to scroll to **Insert** and press ⟨🖉⟩ .

Step 3 Press ⟨🖉⟩ to select **Problem**.

Step 4 Use the NavPad to scroll to **Add Graphs and Geometry** and press ⟨🖉⟩ .

—— Step 3 ——

—— Step 4 ——

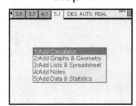

Opening a Document

Step 1 Press ⟨ctrl⟩ ⟨7⟩ to open the directory.

Step 2 Using the NavPad, press either ▲ or ▼ to highlight the folder containing the document.

Step 3 Using the NavPad, press ▶ to expand the folder.

Step 4 Using the NavPad, press either ▲ or ▼ to highlight the document to open.

Step 5 Press ⟨enter⟩ or ⟨🖉⟩ to open the document.

—— Step 1 ——

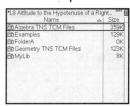

—— Step 4 ——

Saving a New Document in a New Folder

Step 1   Press .

Step 2   Use the NavPad to scroll to **My Documents** and press.

Step 3   Press (ctrl) (menu).

Step 4   Use the NavPad to scroll to **New Folder** and press.

Step 5   Type in the folder name.

Step 6   Press (enter) to create the folder.

Step 7   Use the NavPad to scroll to the *Unsaved Document* at the top of the screen.

Step 8   Press (menu).

Step 9   Use the NavPad to scroll to **Save As** and press.

Step 10   Press (tab) to move to the *Save In* drop-down menu.

Step 11   Use the NavPad to scroll to the folder name typed in Step 5.

Step 12   Press (enter) to select the folder.

Step 13   Press (tab) to move to the *File Name*.

Step 14   Type in the file name.

Step 15   Press (enter) to save the document to the file.

—— Step 2 ——

—— Step 5 ——

—— Step 11 ——

Moving a Line

Step 1 Use the NavPad to move the cursor to the line. Hover over the line until the cursor changes to arrows (✛).

Step 2 Press ⟨ctrl⟩ ⟨🖱⟩ to select the line.

Step 3 Use the NavPad to move the line.

Step 4 Press ⟨🖱⟩ twice or press ⟨esc⟩ to release the line.

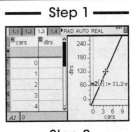

Step 1

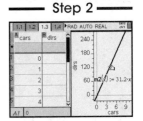

Step 2

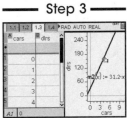

Step 3

Adding a Movable Line

Step 1 Press ⟨menu⟩.

Step 2 Use the NavPad to scroll to **Analyze** and press ⟨🖱⟩ .

Step 3 Use the NavPad to scroll to **Add Movable Line** and press ⟨🖱⟩ .

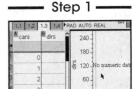

Step 1

Step 3

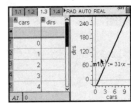

Step 3

Locking Intercept at Zero

Step 1 Press (menu).

Step 2 Use the NavPad to scroll to **Analyze** and press (⌘).

Step 3 Use the NavPad to scroll to **Lock Intercept At Zero** and press (⌘).

—— Step 1 ——

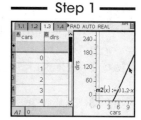

—— Step 3 ——

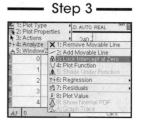

—— Step 3 ——

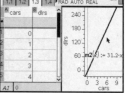

Redefining a Point

Step 1 Press (menu).

Step 2 Press (⌘) to select **Actions**.

Step 3 Use the NavPad to scroll to **Redefine** and press (⌘).

Step 4 Use the NavPad to move the cursor (↖) to the point. Hover over the point until the it blinks and the cursor turns into a hand (☝).

Step 5 Press (enter≈) or (⌘) to select the point.

Step 6 Use the NavPad to move the cursor (✎) to a new location (do not click on a tick mark on an axis).

Step 7 Press (enter≈) or (⌘) to select the new location.

Step 8 Press (esc) to release the Redefine tool.

—— Step 3 ——

—— Step 4 ——

—— Step 7 ——

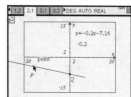

Using a Text Box to Graph an Equation

Step 1 Use the NavPad to move the cursor (↖) to a blank area on the graph.

Step 2 Press (menu).

Step 3 Use the NavPad to scroll to **Actions** and press ⊚ .

Step 4 Use the NavPad to scroll to **Insert Text** and press ⊚ . A text box will open.

Step 5 Enter the equation in the text box.

Step 6 Press (enter) to exit the text box.

────── Step 4 ──────
────── Step 5 ──────

To Edit an Equation

Step 7 Use the NavPad to move the cursor (↖) over the equation. Hover over the equation until the cursor turns into a hand (✋).

Step 8 Press ⊚ twice to select the equation. A text box will open.

────── Step 7 ──────
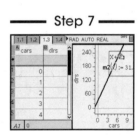

To Move an Equation

Step 9 Use the NavPad to move the cursor (↖) over the equation. Hover over the equation until the cursor turns into a hand (✋).

Step 10 Press (ctrl).

Step 11 Press ⊚ to grab the equation.

Step 12 Use the NavPad to drag the equation.

Step 13 Press ⊚ twice or press (esc) to release the equation.

Finding an Equation

Step 1   Press (menu).

Step 2   Press ⊙ to select **Actions**.

Step 3   Use the NavPad to scroll to **Coordinates and Equations** and press ⊙.

——— Step 3 ———

Step 4   Use the NavPad to move the cursor (↖) to the line. Hover over the line until the line blinks and the cursor turns into a hand (✍). A "ghost" equation for the line will appear.

Step 5   Press (enter) or ⊙ to select the equation.

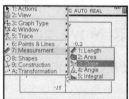
——— Step 4 ———

Step 6   Use the NavPad to move the equation to a desired location.

Step 7   Press (enter) or ⊙ to release the equation in that place.

Step 8   Press (esc) to release the Coordinate and Equation tool.

Finding the Slope

Step 1   Press (menu).

Step 2   Use the NavPad to scroll to **Measurement** and press ⊙.

Step 3   Use the NavPad to scroll to **Slope** and press ⊙.

——— Step 3 ———

Step 4   Use the NavPad to move the cursor (↖) to the line. Hover over the line until the line blinks and the cursor turns into a hand (✍). A "ghost" measure for the slope of the line will appear.

Step 5   Press (enter) or ⊙ to select the measure.

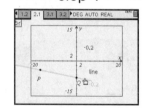
——— Step 4 ———

Step 6   Use the NavPad to move the measure to a desired location.

Step 7   Press (enter) or ⊙ to release the measure in that place.

Step 8   Press (esc) to release the Slope tool.

Adding a Function Table

Step 1 Press (menu).

Step 2 Use the NavPad to scroll to **View** and press (⌾).

Step 3 Use the NavPad to scroll to **Add Function Table** and press (⌾).

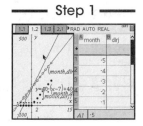
Step 1

Adding a Function Table *(Alternate Option)*

Step 1 Press (ctrl) (T).

Step 1

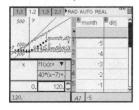
Step 1

Using the Coordinates and Equations Tool

Step 1 Press (menu).

Step 2 Press (⌾) to select **Actions**.

Step 3 Use the NavPad to scroll to **Coordinates and Equations** and press (⌾).

Step 3

Step 4 Use the NavPad to move the cursor (↖) to an intercept. Hover over the intercept until the intercept blinks and the cursor turns into a hand (☝). A "ghost" coordinate or equation will appear.

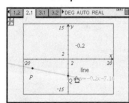
Step 4

Step 5 Press (enter) or (⌾) to select the coordinate or equation.

Step 6 Use the NavPad to move the coordinate or equation to a desired location.

Step 7 Press (enter) or (⌾) to release the coordinate or equation in that place.

Step 8 Press (esc) to release the Coordinates and Equations tool.

Creating a New Matrix

Step 1   Press .

Step 2   Use the NavPad to scroll to **Matrix & Vector** and press ⊙.

Step 3   Use the NavPad to scroll to **Create** and press ⊙.

Step 4   Use the NavPad to scroll to **New Matrix** and press ⊙.

Step 5   When *newMat(* appears on the screen, type in the number of rows.

Step 6   Press ⊙. If you do not use a comma between numbers, an error message will occur.

Step 7   Type in the number of columns.

Step 8   Press ⊙ and then ⊙.

—— Step 4 ——

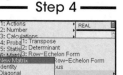

—— Step 6 ——

—— Step 8 ——

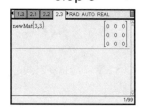

Lesson 1: One-Variable Statistics

Problem 1—Measuring Up
(page 37)

1a. htin:=12•ft+1•inch

2a. Answers will vary.

2b. Answers will vary.

3a. The shortest one fourth of the class. The tallest fourth of the class.

3b. The third fourth of the class. The second fourth of the class.

Problem 2—Gigantic!
(pages 38–39)

2. Answers will vary.

4. Most of the dots are bunched together and one dot is far to the right.

5. The mean should be larger than the median. The large value raises the mean.

6. Answers will vary.

7a. The giant; Answers will vary.

7b. The median may be the same, or will be close. The mean is different.

7c. The person in the middle was close to the middle before. Adding in the giant's height changed the mean.

7d. The median best describes the class as a whole.

Problem 3—That's Tall *(page 40)*

1.

	Mean	Median	Max.	Min.
cc	78.93	79.5	87	72
la	78.87	79	84	70

2. Answers will vary.

3. Answers will vary.

Lesson 2: Direct Variation

Problem 1—Julie's Car Wash
(pages 46–49)

1. Because they are going up by the same amount each time.

2a. dlrs=25•cars

2b. The 25 is how much it goes up for each car.

2c. The graph must go through (0, 0) because zero cars means zero money.

2d. The points would not lie on the line because the points would go up by different amounts.

3. The points went up by different amounts.

4a. suvtot=50•suv

4b. Answers will vary.

5a. mvtot=70•mv

5b. Answers will vary.

6a. total=25•cars

6b. variables: *Total, cars, suv, mv*; constants: 25, 50, 70

7a. $y = 70x$. It was the biggest change per car wash.

7b. Answers will vary. (*k* must be greater than 70.)

7c. Answers will vary. (*k* must be less than 10.)

7d. Answers will vary.

8a. 25, 50, 75

8b. Answers will vary.

8c. Larger slopes give steeper lines.

Problem 2—Don't Fence Me In
(page 50)

1. A=80•width

2.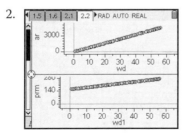

3. Area; It is in a line and goes through the origin.

4. $y = 80x$

Problem 3—Mr. Diaz Washes His Car *(pages 51–54)*

1a.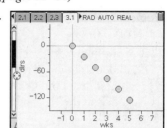

1b. It slants down from left to right.

1c. It is decreasing.

2a. $y = -7x$

2b. k is negative.

2c. Because the equation is in the form $y = kx$.

2d. −7

2e. y decreases

3a.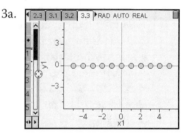

3b. $y = 0$, k = 0, slope = 0

4a.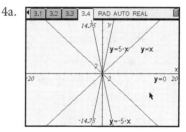

4b. k > 0, graph tilts up from left to right; k < 0, graph tilts down from left to right

4c. When k = 0, the graph is horizontal.

Lesson 3: Exploring Equations of Lines

Problem 1—Darting Around
(pages 62–63)

1a. Coordinates will vary, but students should place P in the 1st quadrant, Q in the 2nd, R in the 3rd, and S in the 4th.

1b. Answers will vary.

1c. 1st (+, +), 2nd (−, +), 3rd (−, −), 4th (+, −)

1d. Upper right-hand corner of 1st quadrant; 2nd and 3rd quadrant, near origin; 4th quadrant, near positive x-axis.

2b. The y-coordinate is zero.

2c. The x-coordinate is zero.

2d. Answers will vary. Either the 1st and 2nd quadrant, the 2nd quadrant near positive y-axis, or the 1st and 4th quadrant near the positive x-axis. On the x-axis, they should be to the far right or on the upper y-axis.

3a. distance from x- axis = y- coordinate and distance from y- axis = x coordinate

3b. They are equal.

3c. They are opposite.

3d. He could place them in any of the far corners.

Problem 2—Tilt! *(page 64)*

1b. If it tilts up from the left to the right, the slope is positive. If it tilts down from the left to the right, the slope is negative.

1c. It is the number in front of x.

1d. It is the number after x.

1e. Answers will vary.

Problem 3—On Target
(pages 65–68)

1b. They are parallel.

1c. They have the same slope.

1d. They are the same distance apart.

1e. If each equation has the same slope but different y-intercept, the lines are parallel.

2a. 90 degrees

2b. They are perpendicular.

2c. −1

2d. −1

2f. Answers will vary, but may include $\frac{2}{3}, -\frac{3}{2}$, or $-5, \frac{1}{5}$.

2g. They are opposite reciprocals.

2h. They intersect at 90 degree angles.

2i. Their slopes are opposite reciprocals, or the product of the slope is −1.

3b. y- is equal to y-intercept.

3c. The y-coordinates are all 4.

3d. $y = -3$

3e. $y = 0x-3$

3f. 0

3g. There is no x in the equation.

4. $y = 4$

4a. 0

4c. y = the y=intercept; x = x-coordinates of points

4d. They are all the same as the value in the equation.

4e. They are all $x =$.

4f. undefined

Problem 4—Lines, Man
(pages 69–70)

1. $y = -3x - 4$

2. $y = 3x - 4$

3. $-\frac{1}{3}$; $y = -\frac{1}{3}x + 5$

4. $\frac{1}{3}$; $y = \frac{1}{3}x + 2$

5. 3, −3; L_7 and L_8; L_6 and L_5

6. L_9, L_{10}, and L_{11}; $y = 3.5, y = 6$, $y = 10$

7. L_{12} and L_{13}; $x = 2$ and $x = -2$

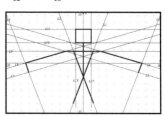

Lesson 4: Forms of Equations of Lines

Problem 1—Money in the Bank
(pages 79–81)

1a. $y = 25x$

1b.

1c. Answers will vary.

1d.

2a. −5, −4, −3, −2, −1. Jung had no money in his account.

2b. Answers will vary.

2c. Yes; (−5, 0)

3a.

Problem 1—Money in the Bank
(cont.)

3b. $(x - 3)$, $(3, 20)$

3c. $y = (x - 3) + 20$; $(3, 20)$

4a. $(7, 400)$

4b. $y = 40(x - 7) + 400$

4c. yes

4d. The equation should be the same.

4e. Answers will vary.

Problem 2—Walk a Mile?
(pages 82–84)

1a. Answers will vary.

1b. $3x + 8y = 19$

2a. 6 hours

2b. $(6, 0)$

2c. 2.25 hours

2d. $(0, 2.25)$

2e. $(2, 1.5)$

2f. $-\frac{3}{8}$; collnear (same slope)

3a. Answers will vary.

3c. $y = -\frac{3}{8} \times 2.25$

3d. x-intercept

3e. y-intercept

3f. Slope-intercept. Answers will vary.

3g. Answers will vary.

3h. Find the intercepts, graph them, and draw the line.

4a. $y = (-\frac{A}{B})x + (\frac{C}{B})$

4b. slope is $(-\frac{A}{B})$ and y-intercept is $(\frac{C}{B})$

5. -0.375, 2.25

6a. 6 and 2.5

6b. Answers will vary.

7a. Answers will vary.

7b. Answers will vary.

Problem 3—What's My Line?
(page 85)

1a. $y = -1,800(x - 5) + 5,000$

1b. $y = -1,800x - 4,000$

1c. $14,000

1d. Approximately 2.2 years

2a. $493b$, $563s$

2b. $493b + 563s = 1,500$

2c. About 2.66 hours

2d. About 3.04 hours

2e. $y = -\frac{493}{563}x + \frac{1500}{563}$

2f. Answers will vary.

Lesson 5: Systems of Linear Equations

Problem 1—How Old Are They?
(pages 92–93)

1a. $s = 2r + 20$

1b. $a = 10r - 4$

1c. $2r + 20 = 10r - 4$; Roberto is 3 years old.

1d. Angela and Sarita are 26 years old.

1e. $y = 2x + 20$

1f. $y = 10x - 4$

2a. $x = 3$, $y = 26$

2b. $x =$ Roberto's age; $y =$ the age of Angela and Sarita

2c. Answers will vary.

3a. $y = \frac{2}{3}x - 2$

3b. $y = \frac{5}{8}x - 1$

3c. $(24, 14)$

3d. $\frac{2}{3}x - 2 = \frac{5}{8}x - 1$; Leon is 24.

3e. Connor and Lavon are 14.

3f. $x =$ Leon's age; $y =$ the age of Lavon and Connor

3g. Answers will vary.

Problem 2—It's a Secret!
(pages 94–98)

1a. $y = x - 40$; $y = -3x + 88$

1b. Answers will vary.

1c. $x - 40 = -3x + 88$, $4x = 128$; $x = 32$; $y = 32 - 40$, $y = -8$

1d. $4x = 128$

1e. $x = 32$; Yes, it is the same.

1f. Yes, -8

1g. $x + 0y = 32$; $3x + y = 88$; -3

1h. $0x + y = -8$

1i. $y = -8$

2a. 14 is the LCM of 2 and 7. He used the negative so the y's would be eliminated.

2b. $21x + 14y = 70$ and $-4x - 14y = -2$; $17x = 68$; $x = 4$

2c. Multiply the first by -2 and add.

2d. $y = -1$

2e. $x = 4$, $y = -1$

3. $c = \begin{bmatrix} 3 & 2 & 10 \\ 2 & 7 & 1 \end{bmatrix}$

3a. 14

3b. $d = \begin{bmatrix} 21 & 14 & 20 \\ 2 & 7 & 1 \end{bmatrix}$

3c. $e = \begin{bmatrix} 17 & 0 & 68 \\ 2 & 7 & 1 \end{bmatrix}$

3d. $f = \begin{bmatrix} 1 & 0 & 4 \\ 2 & 7 & 1 \end{bmatrix}$

3e. $g = \begin{bmatrix} 1 & 0 & 4 \\ 0 & 7 & -7 \end{bmatrix}$

3f. $h = \begin{bmatrix} 1 & 0 & 4 \\ 0 & 1 & -1 \end{bmatrix}$

4a. Yes

4b. Yes

4c. $x = 32$; $y = -8$

5a. $x = -3$; $y = -1$

5b. $x = 24$; $y = 14$

6. 1 $(32, -8)$; 2 $(4, -1)$; 5a $(-3, -1)$; 5b $(24, 14)$; Answer: A Spare Rib

Problem 3—Kookie's Cookies
(pages 99–100)

1. $y = 2x + 1$, $y = 3x - 2$; Liza spent $3. Aaron and Jada each spent $7.

2. $2x + 3y = 2.95$; $5x + y = 4.45$; Brownies cost $0.80 each. Gingersnaps cost $0.45 each.

Problem 3—Kookie's Cookies *(cont.)*

3. $\begin{cases} 7x + 5y + 2z = 9.55; \\ 5x + 8y + z = 8.65; \\ 0x + 9y + 6z = 9.90 \end{cases}$ macaroons, $0.75; shortbread, $0.50; apricot bars, $0.90

4. Answers will vary.

Lesson 6: Coefficients and Exponents

Problem 1—Be Square *(pages 105–107)*

1a. $5l^2$; They are like terms.

1b.

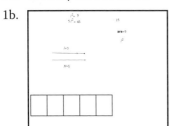

1c. $l^2 = 9$; $5l^2 = 45$

1d. It is the area of the square.

1e.

Length l	Area 1 l^2	N	Area N Nl^2	Ratio
1	1	1	1	1
1	1	2	2	2
1	1	3	3	3
1	1	4	4	4
1	1	5	5	5

2. Answers will vary. The ratio is equal to the number of squares.

3a. Answers will vary.

3b. The exponents stay the same because you are adding squares together and you come out with squares.

Length l	Area 1 l^2	N	Area N Nl^2
1	1	1	1
1	1	2	2
1	1	3	3
1	1	4	4
1	1	5	5
2	4	1	4
2	4	2	8
2	4	3	12
2	4	4	16
2	4	5	20
3	9	1	9
3	9	2	18
3	9	3	27
3	9	4	36
3	9	5	45
4	16	1	16
4	16	2	32
4	16	3	48
4	16	4	64
4	16	5	80
5	25	1	25
5	25	2	50
5	25	3	75
5	25	4	100
5	25	5	125

Problem 2—Combining Cubes *(pages 108–109)*

1. Yes, because they are like terms.

2a.

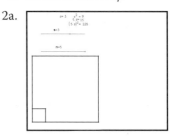

2b. Each is a cube.

2c. 27 and 135

3. Sample Answer:

Length l	Volume 1 l^3	N	Volume N Nl^3	Ratio
4	64	5	320	5
4	64	4	256	4
4	64	3	192	3
4	64	2	128	2
4	64	1	64	1

3a. Each l^3 term is represented with a cube.

3b. The ratio is the same.

3c. Answers will vary.

3d. They represent the same number of cubes. The cubes are the same size.

Problem 3—Isn't It All the Same? *(pages 110–111)*

1. Answers will vary.

2a.

2b. 9 and 225

3. Answers will vary.

3a. Each s^2 term is represented by the small square.

3b. It is the square of the number of sides.

3c. Answers will vary.

3d. It is the cube of n.

Lesson 7: Pythagorean Theorem

Problem 1—Right Away!
(pages 116–117)

1. $a^2 + b^2 = c^2$

2a. It equals $a^2 + b^2 = c^2$ when angle C is 90°.

2b. They are still equal to each other.

2c. The area of the square on the hypotenuse is equal to the sum of the other two squares.

2d. $c = \sqrt{a^2 + b^2}$

3a. Answers will vary.

3b. $a = \sqrt{c^2 - b^2}$

3c. Answers will vary.

3d. $b = \sqrt{c^2 - a^2}$

3e. Answers will vary.

Problem 2—Pick Two
(pages 118–119)

1. Answers will vary.

2a. Answers will vary.

2c. They are equal.

3a. Answers will vary.

3b. right triangle

3c. 90°

3d. right triangle

3e. They all work in the Pythagorean theorem.

3f. Answers will vary.

Problem 3—Pythagorean Trivia
(pages 120–121)

1a. Because 3, 4, and 5 are a Pythagorean Triple.

1b. $p = 16$, $q = 12$, $r = 20$

1c. 13.66 feet

1d. 6.32 feet

2. Answers will vary.

Lesson 8: Generating Parabolas

Problem 1—In the Area
(pages 126–128)

1a. length = absolute value of x

1b. length = width

1c. The farther from the origin, the larger the area.

1d. $A=x^2$. It does not matter if the x is negative or positive because it is a square.

2a. Answers will vary.

2b. x is the x-coordinate on the diagram. y is the area of the rectangle.

2c. Yes

2d. $y = x^2$

3a. The length is half the width.

3b. $A = 2x^2$

3c. Answers will vary.

3d. It is steeper.

3e. $y = 2x^2$

4a. Answers will vary.

4b. $A = nx^2$

4c. The larger the value of n, the steeper the graph.

4d. Answers will vary.

Problem 2—A Moving Experience
(pages 129–132)

1a. The length is the absolute value of x.

1b. The length and the width are equal.

1c. $|x - -4|$, -4

1d. $(x + 4)^2$

2a. $(-4, 0)$

2b. Yes

2c. $(x - R)^2$

3a. $h = 3$

3b. Answers will vary.

3c. The vertex is at $(h, 0)$.

4. They are four less.

5.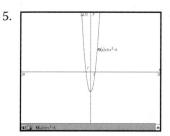

6.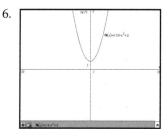

7.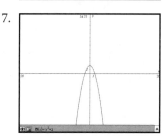

8. The vertex is at $(0, k)$.

9. The vertex is at $(4, -3)$

10.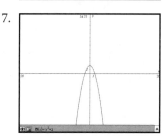

Problem 3—Where Are They Now? *(pages 133–134)*

1. $(0, 4)$; Opens down; same size as $y = x^2$; B

2. $(-2, 0)$; Opens up, narrower; A

3. $(0, 0)$; Opens up; E

4. $(-3, 0)$; Opens up, narrower; G

5. $(0, 0)$; Opens down, narrower; H

6. $(2, -3)$; Opens down, narrower; D

Problem 3—Where Are They Now? *(cont.)*

7. (2, 0); Opens up, wider; F
8. (0, –4); Opens up, same size as $y = x^2$; C

Lesson 9: One-Variable Inequalities

Problem 1—Glazed Over *(pages 141–143)*

1a. cost = 2.75 dozen salesd=:3 dozen; profit=:salesd–cost

1b. At $3.00 per dozen, the value in the *profit* column is always under $260. The price for a dozen donuts needs to be raised.

1c. Because the y-values are more than 260 in that region.

1d. In the shaded regions.

1e. (115.56, 260)

1f. Set 2.25 x = 260 and solve it. $x > 115.56$ or $x \geq 116$

1g. To the right

1h. $x > 115.56$

1i. Divide both sides by 2.25. There is no difference.

1j. They are solutions of the inequality.

1k. 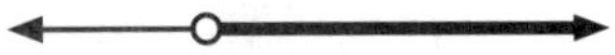

115.56

1l. True. 120 is a solution.

1m. It will be false.

Problem 3—Back and Forth *(pages 144–145)*

1a. $3 < 6$; A < B; A is on the left.

1b. $9 < 18$; A < B; A is on the left.

1c. $-9 > -18$; A > B; B is on the left.

1d. $1 < 2$; A < B; A is on the left. The inequality sign and the right and left were reversed.

2a. $-4 < 2$; A < B; A is on the left.

2b. $-8 < 4$; A < B; A is on the left.

2c. $8 > -4$; A > B; B is on the left.

3. An inequality sign is reversed when multiplying or dividing by a negative number.

Problem 4—Carnegie Hall (Practice, Practice, Practice) *(page 146)*

1. $2w + 4 \geq 9$

   $2w \geq 5$

   $w \geq 2.5$

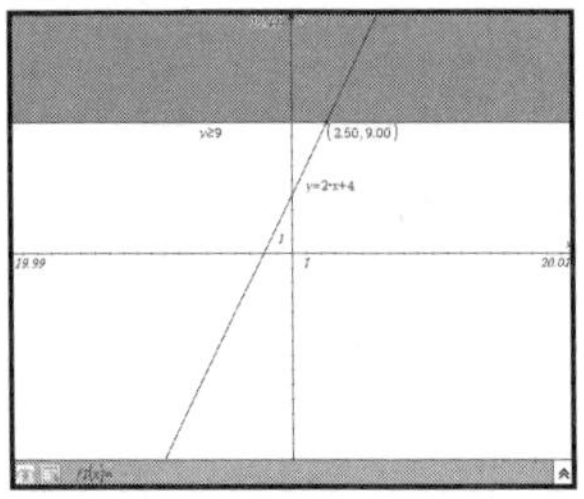

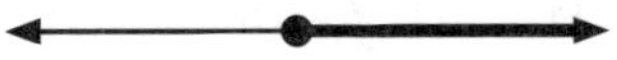

2.5

2. $7 - 3m > -28$

   $-3m > -35$

   $m < 11\frac{2}{3}$

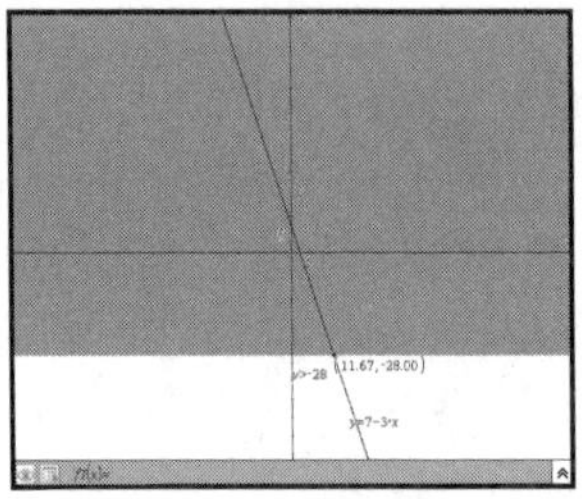

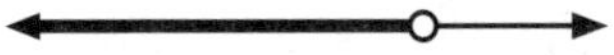

$11\frac{2}{3}$

3. $24 - k \leq -4k + 15$

   $3k \leq -9$

   $k \leq -3$

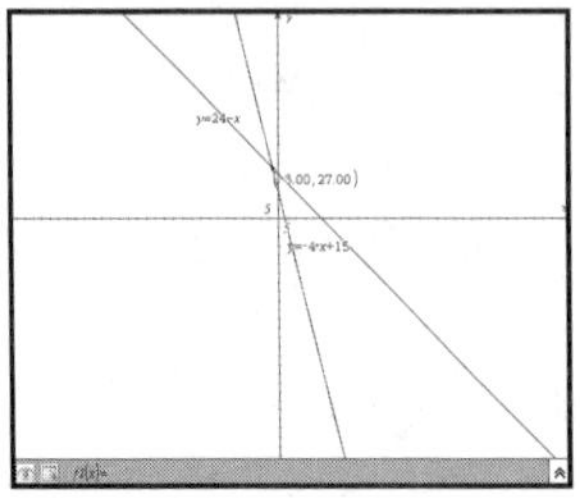

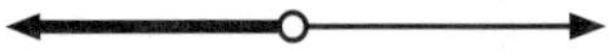

-3

4. $-3(2 - 2m) \leq 2(m + 4)$

   $-6 + 6m \leq 2m + 8$

   $4m \leq 14$

   $m \leq 3.5$

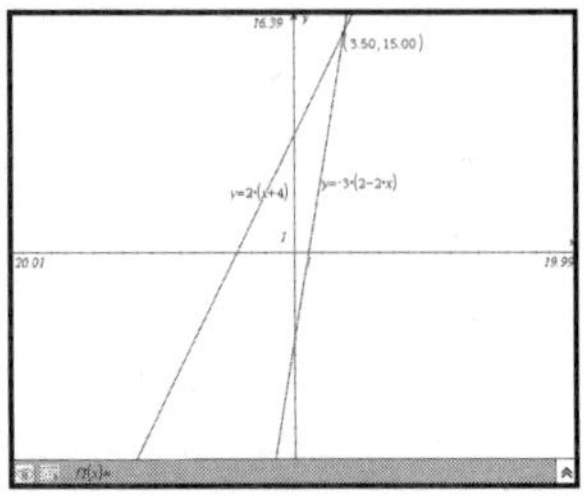

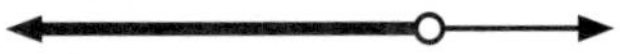

3.5

Lesson 10: Two-Variable Linear Inequalities

Problem 1—The Prize *(pages 153–155)*

1a. Jsales=4cc+3pb

1c. The dots to the right of 330.

1d. There is a lower limit.

1e. Yes

1f. Equations will vary. Above the line.

2a. $4x + 3y = 330$

2b. $y > -\frac{4}{3}x + 110$; Answers will vary.

2c. All the points are above the line.

2d. Yes, the points are still above the line.

2e. The line is dashed because it is >, not ≥.

2f. It is larger than the point on the line.

2g. They are in it.

3a. True

3b. True

3c. The point should be outside the shaded region.

Problem 2—The Cost
(pages 156–157)

1a. $3x + 4y$

1b. $3x + 4y \leq 54$

1c. Answers will vary.

1d. $y \leq 13.5 - \frac{3}{4}x$; below the line

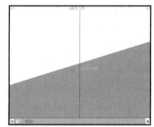

1e. The point should appear in the shaded region.

2a. $3x - 2y$

2b. $3x - 2y > 500$

2c. Answers will vary.

2d. $y \leq \frac{3}{2}x - 250$; below the line

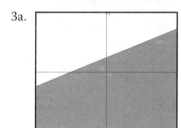

3a.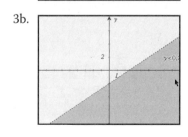

3b.

3c.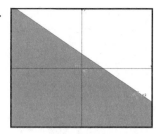

Problem 3—Cross Section
(pages 158–159)

1a. $x + y \geq 5$

1b. $12x + 6.5y \leq 50$

1c. $\begin{cases} x + y \geq 5 \\ 12x + 6.5y \leq 50 \end{cases}$

1d. $y \geq 5 - x$; $y \leq \frac{50}{6.5} - \frac{12}{6.5}x$

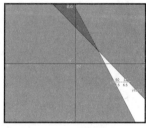

1e. Answers will vary.

1f. Answers will vary.

1g. Answers will vary.

2a. $x + y \leq 100$

2b. $5x + 8y \geq 300$

2c. $\begin{cases} x + y \leq 100 \\ 5x + 8y \geq 300 \end{cases}$

2d. $y \leq 300 - x$; $y \geq 37.5 - \frac{5}{8}x$

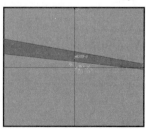

2e. Answers will vary. He could babysit 24 hours and work 68 hours.

2f. Answers will vary.

2g. Answers will vary.

Lesson 11: Absolute Value

Problem 1—Change of Direction
(pages 165–167)

1a. The car ended up two inches to the right of the center.

1b. It traveled 20 inches.

1c. One is position; the other is how far it traveled.

2a. The difference of the x-coordinates.

2b. The distance is never negative. It can be zero.

2c. They are either the same or opposite. They change at $x = 0$.

2d. They are the same when x is to the right of 0. On the left, they are opposites.

2e. They are the same.

2f. It equals x.

2g. It equals the opposite of x.

2h. 2, 0, 8, 1.2

2i. 3 or −3

2j. Is it to the right or left of 0?

2k. $x, -x$

3a. $y = x$ and $y = -x$

3b. The part where $x > 0$.

3c. The part where $x < 0$.

3d. The absolute value of x equals x if x is greater than or equal to zero, and equals $-x$ if x is less than 0.

3e.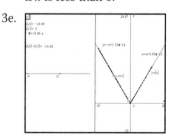

Problem 2—Above and Below
(pages 168–169)

1a. 4 and −4

1b. 4 and −4

Problem 2—Above and Below (cont.)

1c.
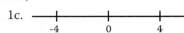

1d. It is below the line.

1e. The solution is inside the line segment; (−4, 4).

1f. The solution is outside the line segment.; (∞, − 4), (4, ∞).

1g. a and $-a$

1h.
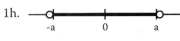

1i.

2a. (−3, 0) from the argument; Set it equal to zero.

2b. (−7 , 4) and (1, 4)

2d. 4 units

2e. Add and subtract four from −3.

2f.

2g.
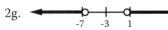

3. −3 and 7

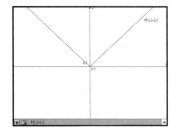

4. The entire graph is above $y = -4$.

Problem 3—Check Up (pages 170–171)

1. It can be zero, but answers may vary.

2. $b = 0$

3a. (0, 0)

3b. (−7, 0)

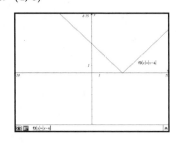

3c. (4, 0)

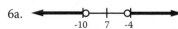

4a. 0

4b. −7

4c. −4

5a. −3 and 3

5b. −10 and −4

5c. 1 and 7

6a.
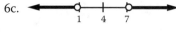

6b.
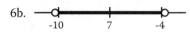

6c.

6d.

7. $|j - 8| \le 4$

Lesson 12: Factors, Zeros, and Roots

Problem 1—Zeros Are Something Else (page 178)

1. 1 and −1
2. 2 and −2
3. It easy to pair up the x– and y–coordinates.
4. 1 and −1; 2 and −2
5. The x-value that gives a y–value of 0.
6. 1 and −1; 2 and −2; 3 and −3
7. 3 and −3
8. They are the same numbers.

Problem 2—Take It Apart (page 179)

1. $f(x) = (x - 3)(x + 2)$
2. $f(x) = x^2 - x - 6$
3. yes
4. $2(f1(x))$ is steeper than $f1(x)$. They have the same x-intercepts.
5. $f(x) = (x - 2.5)(x + 1)$
6. $f(x) = (2x - 5)(x + 1)$
7. Answers will vary.
8. $(x - 5)(x - 6) = 0$
9. −0.5 and 4; $(2x + 1)(x - 4) = 0$

Problem 3—Too Square (pages 180–181)

1a. $x - 2$
1b. $x - 4$
1c. $(x - 4)(x - 2)$
1d. $x - 2$
1e. $x - 4$
1f. 1
1g. $(x - 4)(x - 2) + 2(x - 2) + 2(x - 4) + 4 = 80$
1h. $x^2 - 2x - 80 = 0$
1i. $(x - 8)(x - 10) = 0$; 8 and 10
1j. The solutions represent the length and width of the cardboard.

Problem 3—Too Square *(cont.)*

2a. 0 feet

2b. Because it is the value which makes the function value equal to 0.

2c. −0.1875 and 2; 2 would be the number of seconds

2d. $(16t + 3)(t − 2) = 0$

Lesson 13: Completing the Square/Quadratic Formula

Problem 1—Everywhere a Square
(pages 187–188)

1a. area of square is x^2; area of rectangle is bx

1b. $x = 10u$; $y = 4u$; area of a square = $100u$; area of a rectangle = $40u$; $x^2 + bx = 140u^2$

1c. $x\frac{b}{2} = 20u$

1f. 4 square units; $(\frac{b}{2})^2$

1g. $(x + \frac{b}{2})^2 = 144u^2$

1h. $4u^2$

1i. $140u^2$; Answers will vary.

Problem 2—Complete It
(pages 189–190)

1b. $f(x) = x^2 + 4x − 5$

1c. −5 and 1

1d. −5 and 1

2a. $a = 1, b = 4, c = −5$

2b. $x^2 + 4x = 5$; 2 and 4

2c. $x^2 + 4x + 4 − 4 = 5$
$(x + 2)^2 − 4 = 5$

2d. The difference of the big square and the shaded square.

2e. $(x + \frac{4}{2})^2 = 5 + \frac{16}{4}$; $(x + 2)^2 = 9$

2f. $x + 2 = ±3$; $x = 1$ and $x = −5$

3a. $a = 1, b = 3, c = −8$

3b. −4.7 and 1.7

3c. $x^2 + 3x − 8 = 0$
$(x + \frac{3}{2})^2 − \frac{3}{4}^2 = 8$
$(x + \frac{3}{2})^2 = 8 + \frac{3}{4}^2$
$x + \frac{3}{2} = ±\sqrt{(8 + \frac{3}{4}^2)}$
$x = −\frac{3}{2} ±\sqrt{(8 + \frac{3}{4}^2)}$

3d. The values of a, b, and c from the graph. −4.07 and 1.70

3f. They are the same.

3g. The calculations are undefined.

Problem 3—Formalize It
(pages 191–192)

1a. $a = 2, b = 1, c = −6$

1b. $x^2 + \frac{1}{2}x −3 = 0$

1c. $x = −\frac{1}{2} •2 ± \sqrt{3 + \frac{1}{2} •2^2}$

1d. $x = −2$; $(−2, 0)$

1e. yes; 1.5

2a. $a = 3, b = 4, c = −5$

2b. .79 and −2.12

3a. $a = 1, b = 4, c = 0$

3b. 0 and −4

4a. one

4b. Answers will vary.

5a. The values are undefined.

5b. It is negative. You cannot take the square root of a negative number.

Lesson 14: Exponential Growth

Problem 1—Uncle Buck$
(pages 198–200)

1d. 1

1e. 2

1f. C1•B1

1g. C1•B2

1h. multiply by 2

1i. Day 10

1j. $1,024

2.

Day	Dollars	Factors of 2	Power of 2
0	1	0	2^0
1	2	1	2^1
2	4	2	2^2
3	8	3	2^3
4	16	4	2^4
5	32	5	2^5
6	64	6	2^6
7	128	7	2^7
8	256	8	2^8
9	512	9	2^9
10	1024	10	2^{10}

2a. 2^{20}

2b. $y = 2^x$

2d. 1; It is the amount on day 0.

3a. It is tripled.

3b. $y = 3^x$

3c. 1

3d. The graph is steeper.

3e. $y = 5^x$

3f. 1

4a. $3

4b. They are 3 times as much. $y = 3(2^x)$

4c. 3; The original amount was $3.

4d. $y = 10(2^x)$

4e. a is the initial amount; b is the factor

Problem 2—More Buck$
(pages 201–202)

2a. 3

2b. d1+c1•d1

2c. d2+c1•d2

2d. Previous day's total plus 2 times previous day's total.

Problem 2—More Buck$ *(cont.)*

3.

Day	Dollar1	Sum	Combine	Power of 3
4	81	$2 \cdot 3^3 + 1 \cdot 3^3$	$3 \cdot 3^3$	3^4
5	243	$2 \cdot 3^4 + 1 \cdot 3^4$	$3 \cdot 3^4$	3^5
6	729	$2 \cdot 3^5 + 1 \cdot 3^5$	$3 \cdot 3^5$	3^6
7	2,187	$2 \cdot 3^6 + 1 \cdot 3^6$	$3 \cdot 3^6$	3^7
8	6,567	$2 \cdot 3^7 + 1 \cdot 3^7$	$3 \cdot 3^7$	3^8
9	19,683	$2 \cdot 3^8 + 1 \cdot 3^8$	$3 \cdot 3^8$	3^9
10	59,049	$2 \cdot 3^9 + 1 \cdot 3^9$	$3 \cdot 3^9$	3^{10}

3a. $y = 3^x$

4a. D1

4b. $y = 5(3^x)$

5a. D1 and C1

5b. No

5c. $y = 4(3^x)$

Problem 3—Compound Buck$
(pages 203–205)

1b. B1+C1•B1

1c. cell above + C1 times cell above

1d. exponential

2.

Year	Total	Sum	Combine	Simplify
3	112.49	$.04(1.04)^2(100)+(1.04)^2(100)$	$(1+.04)(1.04)^2(100)$	$(1.04)^3(100)$
4	116.99	$.04(1.04)^3(100)+(1.04)^3(100)$	$(1+.04)(1.04)^3(100)$	$(1.04)^4(100)$
5	121.67	$.04(1.04)^4(100)+(1.04)^4(100)$	$(1+.04)(1.04)^4(100)$	$(1.04)^5(100)$
6	126.53	$.04(1.04)^5(100)+(1.04)^5(100)$	$(1+.04)(1.04)^5(100)$	$(1.04)^6(100)$

2a. $y = 100(1.04)^x$

2b. $y = 1,000\,(1.025)^x$

2c. 2a $P = 100, r = 4\%, t = x$
    2b $P = 1000, r = 2.5\%, t = x$

3a. 2%

3b. 10

3d. $y = 100\left(1 + \frac{.04}{2}\right)^{2x}$

3e. It would exceed $500 after about 41 years.

Lesson 15: Exponential Decay

Problem 1—Heads or Tails?
(pages 210–214)

1a. Answers may vary. (250 is the expected answer.)

1b. Answers may vary. (125 is the expected answer.)

1c. Answers will vary.

2a. 500

2b. Answers will vary. (250 is the expected answer.)

2c. Answers will vary. (250 is the expected answer.)

2d. Answers will vary. (250 is the expected answer.)

2e. Create random 0s and 1s. The number will equal the number of heads from flip 0.

2f. Find the number of heads from flip 1.

2g. Each flip creates heads and tails. The number of entries is determined by the sum of the previous flip, which is in column B.

3a. Answers will vary.

3b. Answers will vary.

3c. The number of coins reached zero before getting to the end of the simulation.

3d. Yes

3e. Answers will vary. The graph should look like an exponential decoy graph.

4a. $\frac{1}{2}$

4b.

Set (x)	Coins	Product	Exponential Expression
3	62.5	$500\left(\frac{1}{2}\right)\left(\frac{1}{2}\right)\left(\frac{1}{2}\right)$	$500\left(\frac{1}{2}\right)^3$
4	31.25	$500\left(\frac{1}{2}\right)\left(\frac{1}{2}\right)\left(\frac{1}{2}\right)\left(\frac{1}{2}\right)$	$500\left(\frac{1}{2}\right)^4$
5	15.625	$500\left(\frac{1}{2}\right)\left(\frac{1}{2}\right)\left(\frac{1}{2}\right)\left(\frac{1}{2}\right)\left(\frac{1}{2}\right)$	$500\left(\frac{1}{2}\right)^5$
6	7.8125	$500\left(\frac{1}{2}\right)\left(\frac{1}{2}\right)\left(\frac{1}{2}\right)\left(\frac{1}{2}\right)\left(\frac{1}{2}\right)\left(\frac{1}{2}\right)$	$500\left(\frac{1}{2}\right)^6$

4c. no

4d. $y = 500\left(\frac{1}{2}\right)^x$